The Art of Survival

Books by Cord Christian Troebst:

CONQUEST OF THE SEA
GRASPING FOR THE MOON
THE ART OF SURVIVAL

The Art of Survival

Cord Christian Troebst

Translated from the German
by Oliver Coburn

Dolphin Books
Doubleday & Company, Inc.
Garden City, New York   1975

Originally published in English by
Doubleday & Company, Inc., 1965

Dolphin Books edition, revised: 1975

AUF WUNDER IST KEIN VERLASS © Econ-Verlag GMBH, 1963

Grateful acknowledgment is made for permission to reprint the following
material:

J. & A. CHURCHILL LTD. From SHIPWRECK SURVIVORS by Dr. Mac-
Donald Critchley. Reprinted by permission of J. & A. Churchill Ltd., Pub-
lishers.
ECON-VERLAG GMBH. From DER HIMMEL HAD KEINE GRENZEN by Rolf
Strahl. Reprinted by permission of Econ-Verlag GMBH.
HUTCHINSON AND CO., LTD. From DOCTOR IN STALINGRAD by Dr.
Dibold, translated by H. C. Stevens. Reprinted by permission of Hutchinson
and Co. Ltd.
G. P. PUTNAM'S SONS. From THE WIND CANNOT READ by Richard Mason.
Copyright © 1947 by Richard Mason. Reprinted by permission of G. P.
Putnam's Sons.
CHARLES SCRIBNER'S SONS. From WHERE WINTER NEVER COMES by
Marston Bates. Reprinted by permission of Charles Scribner's Sons, Pub-
lishers.
SIMON AND SCHUSTER, INC. From THE VOYAGE OF THE HERETIQUE by
Dr. Alain Bombard. Reprinted by permission of Simon and Schuster, Inc.;
Odette Arnaud and Andre Deutch Ltd., publishers of the book in England
under the title, THE BOMBARD STORY, 1953.
JOHN WILEY & SONS, INC. From PHYSIOLOGY OF MAN IN THE DESERT by
Edward Frederick Adolph. Reprinted by permission of John Wiley & Sons,
Inc.

Grateful acknowledgment is made to Agence DALMAS and WIDE
WORLD PHOTOS INC. for permission to use photographs.

ISBN: 0-385-01129-6
Library of Congress Catalog Card Number 74–10030
Copyright © 1965, 1975 by Doubleday & Company, Inc.
All Rights Reserved
Printed in the United States of America

Contents

Contents

Prologue

The idea for this book came up during a cold New England winter under somewhat unusual circumstances. My wife and I had asked several friends to spend the weekend with us in our house on Cape Cod. For several hours we had been talking, eating, and drinking when suddenly a fierce blizzard hit the Cape. With it, the electric power failed and did not return for the next forty-eight hours.

For an American country home such an event resembles a minor disaster, especially in winter. With no electricity, the pump for our domestic water supply stopped running. So did the fuel pump for the heating system. Well, once we ran out of water we could always melt down some snow. But how were we to heat it? With no electricity, our kitchen range was useless, despite its twenty-four push buttons. So were the washing machine, the electric can opener, the lights, and, worst of all, our electric blankets.

Fortunately, we had some candles to light the living room and, since some of us were smokers, we even had a couple of lighters. But what about wood for the fireplace? I had been too lazy to chop some during the summer, and the logs were somewhere in the garden under a heap of snow, too wet to be of any use. As cold started to creep into the house, we broke up some old book crates to use for fuel. Finally, we and our guests could all settle in front of the open fire, with our ten-day-old daughter in the middle where it was warmest.

As we sat there, wrapped in blankets, the conversation naturally enough turned to the helplessness of modern man when exposed to the elements. The comforts provided by industry have spoiled him and made him soft. In most cases he has forgotten how to help himself in emergencies, how to improvise and meet sudden dangers. We even wondered which one of us would be able to survive the blizzard out in the open, without the protection of a home or car.

As we all considered this point, everybody began recalling dramatic cases of people who had succumbed to the elements in unusual circumstances. There were the people who died during the California floods and snowstorms in the winter of 1964–65. There was the couple who was caught in a blizzard a few years earlier on a highway in the Midwest and rescued three days later suffering from severe frostbite. There were the ten schoolboys and their three teachers who, in 1954, perished in the Austrian Alps because they went off on a climbing expedition without proper equipment and were caught in a snowstorm—of which they had actually been warned beforehand.

The stories of ordeals by snow and of mountain climbing accidents led on to great natural disasters, to tragedies at sea like the sinking in the Atlantic of the German training ship *Pamir,* and the party of Frenchmen who in 1959 died horribly in the Nubian Desert, their bodies burned black by the blazing sun. We talked of Polar explorers who starved to death, of cannibalism and unbearable thirst, of castaways who went mad from drinking salt water, and travelers in the desert who drank gasoline or even their companions' blood. These grim accounts were confined to more or less vague recollections, since none of us knew any exact details of the various episodes. What, for instance, did the survivors of a shipwreck think, feel, and do before death overtook them? How did they manage to survive the original disaster, and for how long? Had they simply resigned themselves to their fate—or had they made efforts to save themselves? Had they had any chance at all of survival?

A few days after we had "survived" the blizzard, freezing but safe, protected by the house walls, I began looking for answers to these questions. The material I managed to unearth in the next weeks and months, showed that carelessness, faulty and inadequate equipment, panic and completely wrong behavior are the main causes for the death of many castaways, mountain climbers, and pilots who have made emergency landings. While I was going through the reports of such tragedies, I also came across a number of fantastic survival stories and cases of extraordinary human endurance. In apparently hopeless situations people had indeed saved themselves by correct assessment of the danger, a clear head, and resourcefulness.

I discovered, too, that there are so-called Survival Schools in which athletes and scouts, but more especially men in the armed forces, are taught "how to survive" in the desert, in jungle and Polar regions or at sea. Their training is based on research by biologists and doctors as to how long a human being can survive without water or without food; how much heat or cold he can stand; how much noise, how many hours of solitude or complete silence.

Recent discoveries in this field have also shown that many traditional first-aid measures do not have the beneficial effects attributed to them, and so have added to the suffering of accident victims. We know today, for instance, that iced water (not oil) is good for blisters from burning, and that a hot bath is the best thing for frostbite (instead of rubbing the body down with snow).

Almost every year, new aids to survival are also being developed. A whole industry, I found, had grown up after World War II, concerned with developing rescue equipment, some of it quite amazing: iron rations in self-heating cans, inflatable small aircraft, hooks to pick up castaways in the water from a flying airplane, floating hospitals that can be dropped by parachute over disaster areas.

All these devices, of course, had been mainly designed for military pilots, sailors, and members of expeditions. I wondered whether they would be of any use to the ordinary city dweller. But just then the news came that a tremendous flood had hit the West German city of Hamburg, something never heard of since the Middle Ages. On the night of February 17–18, 1962, about four hundred people lost their lives and thousands were rendered homeless. The main reason for the high number of casualties was

that the rescue warning system had been inadequate, the rescue
equipment had proved insufficient and faulty, and the victims
hadn't considered doing anything for themselves—until it was too
late.

While I was already at work on this book, it was only natural
that I followed every bit of news about a disaster or an individual
survival drama with special interest. I was not surprised any more
that almost every week added new material: in the summer of
1962 alone there were hundreds of climbing accidents in the Alps,
most of them a result of carelessness; twenty-six people drowned
the same year, mostly from panic, when their plane came down in
the Atlantic; there were floods and earthquakes, in which many
people perished because they did not know what to do.

Since this book was first published, many new tragedies of
human beings in distress have occurred throughout the world. In
some, victims were claimed by natural disasters, with little chance
for survival. The hurricane that hit the state of Honduras in September 1974, for instance, claimed the lives of about 10,000 people. Most of them drowned, some suffocated in the mud, but a
great many became victims of the hurricane's aftermath: diseases,
hunger, thirst. In other tragedies, accidents were the main cause of
death: fires aboard cruise ships or crashes of airplanes, with cases
of panic, thirst, hunger, even mass cannibalism. And then there
were the victims of political circumstances—refugees trying to escape a totalitarian regime: The young man from East Germany
who paddled on a rubber mattress across the Baltic by night was
only one of many thousands trying to escape to freedom—or
whose escape failed through (under the circumstances) inadequate preparations. According to Danish estimates, several
hundred people drowned within the first three years after the
Berlin Wall was built in 1961, trying to escape to Denmark across
the Baltic in makeshift, ill-equipped rafts—or even swimming.
Since Fidel Castro took power in Cuba in 1959, many Cubans
have tried to leave their homeland in all kinds of vessels. In
December 1964 a spokesman of the State Department in Washington said that the U. S. Navy has picked up an annual average of a
thousand refugees in the Caribbean. There are no figures available, of course, on how many may have drowned. It is known,
however, that a good number of refugees had to go through great

hardships before being rescued. In other parts of the world the picture is the same: thousands of people surviving, or failing to survive, some perilous flight from the troubled areas of Africa and Asia.

More recently, perhaps in the course of a nostalgic desire for adventure, a new craze has hit the affluent Western World: individuals, couples, even whole families with baby and all feel the need to "leave the rat race" by sailing in a wall-to-wall carpeted yacht across an ocean or even around the world. Others try to brave a desert in an air-conditioned automobile or even walk across on foot. Some have the experience to succeed—others don't.

The question, therefore, whether the material contained in this book will be of any use to the average person is easy to answer: terrible cold, the heat of the desert, ferocious storms at sea are events that in today's travel-happy and once again (fortunately) adventuresome world can hit almost anyone. And natural disasters like earthquakes, floods, and blizzards have never sought out their victims merely among sailors and explorers, but also among "the fellow next door." Afterward, one fact almost certainly emerged: only he can survive who has prepared himself best.

Hamburg, West Germany, Spring 1975   C.C.T.

The Art of Survival

Chapter 1
Why Train for an Emergency?

Every year 50,000 castaways die in the lifeboats.
Dr. Alain Bombard

On July 2, 1816, the French bark *Medusa* sank a hundred miles off the African coast. One hundred and fifty of her passengers managed to get safely onto a makeshift raft. Soon enough, the raft was discovered by another ship and taken into tow. But during the night the rope broke. Thus, the survivors, who had thought themselves already saved, drifted off into the open sea.

Even though there was enough wine and water on the raft, panic broke out after only a few hours. Some of the survivors killed themselves, others jumped overboard and tried to swim to shore, although they had no idea of its direction. After three days, there was wholesale murder and cannibalism; and those repelled by the flesh of their slaughtered companions ate their own excrement.

On the twelfth day, when the raft was finally picked up by another vessel, only fifteen of the original survivors were still alive. Of these fifteen, ten more died soon after being taken aboard the rescue ship.

Since that incident the world has been through two great wars and countless "little" ones. Most people, therefore, should know what to do in an emergency. At least, one would suppose so. The reverse is true.

Failure to cope starts with the inability of modern man to "scent" approaching danger. He has lost that sixth sense which often protects members of primitive tribes and all those who have remained close to nature by giving them a premonition when threatened by some natural disaster.

In today's modern world, premonitions have been replaced mostly by scientific data. But what good are any amount of temperature and pressure readings indicating a severe storm, if meteorologists are unable to translate these signs of warning into simple, everyday language? Example: When a giant spring tide was about to hit the city of Hamburg on February 17, 1962, the weathermen on radio and TV merely repeated what they had been told by the weather bureau, "a very high tide" was to be expected after midnight. Instead, they should have interrupted the program, telling their listeners: "Look, folks, you better pack up and leave such and such a danger area by such and such a time." Similarly, when Hurricane Audrey was approaching the coast of Louisiana in 1957, weather reports were only referring to "gale warnings." Admittedly, in one town a loudspeaker truck drove through the danger zones calling on people to leave their houses; but it was also advertising "a gay evening at the theater." The evening turned out to be not a gay one, but the beginning of a night in which Audrey killed 373 people.

Man very often survives an actual disaster, but not the hours or days after it, simply because he was not prepared for such an "emergency" situation. It is taken for granted that every soldier has learned to handle a rifle, so that he can use it in an emergency. Yet very few civilians think of preparing themselves with the same thoroughness if, for instance, they want to go off mountain climbing. There are still sailors who can't swim. And before the Hamburg floods only 5 percent of the town's householders had taken part in Operation Squirrel, i.e. laid in a store of basic foods. Dr. Barton of New York University commented in 1962: "The broad mass of people, one may deduce from experience to date, will scarcely devote some of their free time to train for emergencies or other safety measures. Even though such a training might save their own and their families' lives, most people believe they will never need it."

This attitude costs hundreds of thousands of lives every year. It is a significant fact that so many people die in lifeboats. According to the French doctor Alain Bombard, who voluntarily drifted alone in a dinghy across the Atlantic, of the 200,000 or so people who perish at sea every year, 50,000 die from lack of survival training in the very boats provided to save their lives.

Many recent examples bear out the helplessness and feckless behavior of most "accident victims." When the Italian luxury liner *Andrea Doria* went down in 1957, there were "only" fifty-one deaths, but that was simply due to the calm weather and the fact that the ship sank comparatively slowly. Yet some of the crew actually thrust their way into the boats before the passengers—and half the boats were unserviceable at that. Had it been cold, foggy, or a rough sea, the number of deaths would have risen enormously. Only a few years later panic, confusion of the crew, and partially outdated survival equipment claimed further victims, when two cruise ships caught fire on the open sea: 128 people died aboard the *Lakonia,* when she became a flaming inferno not far from the island of Madeira on December 23, 1963. The ship had carried a total of 1,036 persons. In November 1965 a similar fate caught up with the *Yarmouth Castle* on her way from Miami to Nassau with 370 passengers and a crew of 175 on board. That time, eighty-three persons lost their lives. The notorious *Titanic* disaster would have claimed far more lives had the sea not been smooth as a mirror.

In this connection, data relating to the Korean War published by the American defense authorities are of special interest. The GIs taken prisoner by the North Koreans had survived the dangers of the battlefield. Yet about 2,700 men, i.e. 38 percent, died in the North Korean prison camps—a higher percentage than for all the American soldiers who died in captivity from the time of the Civil War up to 1952. The main reason for the high mortality was not, as one would assume, that they were badly treated. They died rather because they had been softened up by too comfortable a civilian life, and too slack a training. It had prepared them only for a possible military conflict, but not for an existence in captivity with the privations this involved. It also involved despair, resignation, fear of an uncertain fate, and of an enemy with a reputation for inhumanity.

During World War II there were countless reports about castaways and air force personnel who died, after forced landings, simply because they didn't know how to use their survival equipment. It is true that two thirds of all American and British airmen adrift in warmer waters were eventually saved, and one third of those in colder waters; yet most of them complained: "We were taught to fly, but not how to survive."

By the time of the Vietnam War things—at least in the military field—had changed. So much emphasis had been put on survival training and rescue operations, that the number of casualties among bailed-out pilots (and POWs) was relatively small in comparison to the Korean War or World War II.

On the civilian sector, matters still have not changed. When mentally and physically unprepared people are forced into desperate situations, they very often die because of their own inexperience and helplessness, plus the fear and despair to which these give rise. Leave your ordinary city dweller on a deserted island, in the tundra, or merely on the edge of a glacier or a desert, and it is most improbable that he will still be alive after a few weeks. He wouldn't know how to set about finding food or water, and so would come to a miserable end. He might even commit suicide for fear of a slow, painful death. At least that is what the Japanese fisherman Inichi Kimura, forty-three, did in October 1974, after his boat had drifted out into the Pacific with a damaged engine. After four days Kimura had lost his bearings—and his head. He scribbled a note, explaining that "there is no hope, this is my farewell to life." He marked time and day on it—and then hanged himself. Only twenty minutes later, Kimura was found by the crew of another fishing vessel that had been looking for him.

A recent test given in a German vocational training school showed that sixty out of a hundred pupils thought cheese was a synthetic product. This may illustrate the extent to which most of us are alienated from nature—so much that we are unable to subsist alone in natural surroundings without the aids and appurtenances we are used to from our mechanized everyday life. As soon as we miss some amenity which we have learned to take for granted, many of us, like Kimura, find the bottom has fallen out of our world.

In the winter of 1956–57, for example, a New Yorker and his wife driving along a highway got stuck in a snowstorm. They found shelter in an icy-cold disused builders' shed on the side of the road. The man tried to light a fire in the stove with his sodden matches, but did not succeed. When all his matches were spent, he and his wife wrapped themselves in their coats and some old rags they found there, and lay down to die. They were rescued, with severe frostbite after their car had been discovered. Somehow, it had never occured to the man to use the gasoline, battery, and cigarette lighter from the car to get a fire going. Equally helpless were two young men caught in their car when, in January 1970, the West German state of Schleswig-Holstein was struck by a snowstorm, cutting off more than one hundred villages and hundreds of motorists. Among the latter were a butcher by the name of Manfred Koscholles, twenty-four, and his twenty-five-year old partner, Helmut Hinrichsen. To keep themselves warm, they kept the engine of their car running—quite successfully at first. However, it got so warm inside the driver's compartment that the two men had to take off their jackets. They should have opened the window instead to get some fresh air. For when they were found the next morning, both had died of carbon-monoxide poisoning: the fumes from the snow-plugged exhaust pipe of their car had seeped inside, slowly killing the two men.

These two episodes clearly prove that anyone may find himself facing a situation that requires some sort of training for an emergency. American statistics, in fact, show that every resident of the United States in the course of his lifetime will be at least once a victim of or a witness to a natural disaster. That means he will have to help either himself or someone else.

For particular regions of the United States where such disasters are common, the statistics look even worse: according to the American Disaster Research Group, one inhabitant in a hundred in Mississsippi, for example, must expect to be injured by a tornado during his lifetime. In Kansas, every single inhabitant will be within the danger area of a tornado at least once a year. Ten million Americans and forty million Europeans live in coastal zones which are constantly endangered by floods.

No other event in the recent past, however, has convinced so many people at one and the same moment how dependent modern man has become from the push-button facilities of our mechanized society. It was not a natural but a technical disaster, by millions still remembered as "the Great Blackout." It hit the northeastern United States and parts of Canada in November 1966: a single, burned-out relay in a Niagara power station had caused a chain reaction of power failures, stopping everything that was operated by electricity. For thirteen hours an area as big as the federal republic of West Germany was practically paralyzed, including such major cities as New York and Boston. Thirty million people suddenly were facing the question of how to get along without the conveniences they all were used to: elevators did not run, refrigerators stopped, lights did not work, faucets and toilets ran dry, traffic came to a standstill. In New York City alone damage was estimated to have reached one hundred million dollars. If the power failure had lasted only two days longer, the gigantic short circuit would probably have cost several billion dollars—and the lives of many citizens.

No one, therefore, should be surprised at the high casualty figures accompanying major disasters. According to the International Union of Geodesy and Geophysics, they amount to about 100,000 every year all over the world. But what is amazing is that quite a large proportion of the victims (about 20 percent) ran blindly to their doom or perished owing to the negligence of others. The reason: lack of training to meet disasters.

For example, when the town of Beecher, Michigan, was ravaged by a tornado some years ago, the same residential districts were searched for survivors several times by different rescue groups, while in the confusion other districts were left out of the search altogether. Ambulances raced past first-aid stations because the drivers did not know of their existence; and meanwhile casualties were bleeding to death.

The same confusion is a major factor for many needless deaths during earthquakes (such as 1968 on Sicily, 1970 in Peru and 1972 in Nicaragua), during shipwrecks and aircraft emergency landings. Here is an eyewitness report of the Val d'Isère disaster in southern France, where in February 1970 an avalanche struck a mountain lodge, killing thirty-nine people: "The rescue operations were orderless. There was no coordination. Nobody knew where to dig first. Nobody gave any instructions. When we suddenly spotted a half-buried car with two passengers calling for help, everybody ran toward them to get them out. Meanwhile dozens of youths in the breakfast room of the lodge were suffocating under masses of snow."

The effects of a large-scale disaster are made even worse by the crowds of people who rush up from all directions, some with a creditable desire to help, but most out of sheer curiosity. There have been plenty of instances when traffic casualties died because too many people crowded around the accident spot for the ambulances to reach it in time. When Judsonia, Arkansas, lay in shambles after a tornado, both of the major roads leading into the little town were blocked by the cars of curious spectators—and the Red Cross vehicles couldn't get through. As a result, many of the injured died.

Not even danger to life and limb can keep away some of these spectators. In 1947, the freighter *Grandcamp* exploded in a dry dock in Texas City. Soon afterward a second freighter, *High Flyer*, was in danger of blowing up. The rescue teams who, as one report put it, "waded up to their ankles in blood," tried to thrust back thousands of sightseers without success. The crowd's curiosity was fatally satisfied: the freighter did explode, and a rain of fire descended on everyone in the vicinity.

Fate and chance, too, are often held responsible where people meet their death mainly through their own fault: they carelessly expose themselves to dangers in which they ultimately perish. In the Alps, for instance, mountain-climbing accidents are rising from year to year. In 1973, according to the five Alpine countries —Austria, Switzerland, Italy, France, and West Germany—760 people were killed in the mountains, most of them because of negligence. The Mountain Watch of Bavaria rescued two thousand people who had gotten into difficulties during the same year.

Negligence, in fact, is the major reason for most accidental deaths—be it in the mountains, at the beaches, on highways, in factories, or in the private home. In 1961, for instance, a record number of about one thousand persons a month were burned to death in the United States, many of them because they had smoked in bed. Each year, an average of 800,000 Americans poison themselves through negligence, and about 1,500 a year die from the effect of these poisonings. In West Germany, the number of fatal labor accidents in 1973 amounted to 4,011, or 10.9 workers killed every single day of the year. Three quarters of these deaths, experts agree, could have been avoided, if the victims would have taken better precautions, like wearing the recommended safety equipment. Traffic experts all over the world will tell you, too, about the high number of needless fatalities on the highways. Safety belts, for instance, save at least seven thousand lives each year in the United States alone. If the more practical air cushions were used in all cars registered in the United States, the number of lives saved could be doubled, according to a 1974 estimate of the U. S. Traffic Department. The number of injuries, the same study shows, could be reduced by more than one million per year. But, as an American psychologist, Donald Michael, once said: "Most people will never think of taking proper precautions until it is too late. And they will disregard all warnings until they more or less have dug their own graves."

There are many examples to prove Michael's statement. Here are just two of them. In the first months of World War II, many pilots who had been shot down might have survived if they had not been too proud to radio an SOS to base when a crash was imminent. After the crash, when they tried to walk out unaided, most of them had paid for their false pride either by death or at least by great ordeals.

In March 1970, the authorities of Pozzuoli, a suburb of Naples, Italy, decided to evacuate several hundred people from their homes since volcanic activity had elevated the ground in the area by as much as twenty inches within only a few months. Many houses showed dangerous cracks in their walls, and steam and sulphur fumes were rising from fissures in the ground. Still, only a few people were willing to leave their homes. Most had to be evacuated by "forceful persuasion."

The analysis of any disaster will show time and again that the number of casualties rises in proportion to their inadequate mental and physical preparedness. In moments of extremity and panic these are the very people among whom one will see unselfishness replaced by the brute urge for self-preservation.

The facts prove this time and again. In his book *A Night to Remember,* an account of the *Titanic* disaster, Walter Lord writes: "Hundreds of swimmers thrashed the water, clinging to the wreckage and each other. Steward Edward Brown, gasping for breath, dimly noticed a man tearing at his clothes. Third-class-passenger Olaus Abelseth felt a man's arm clamp around his neck. Somehow he wriggled loose, spluttering, 'Let go!' But the man grabbed him again, and it took a vigorous kick to free himself for good."

Some of the survivors had swum up to a collapsible raft that was already fully occupied. But nobody offered them a helping hand. After three or four men had managed to scramble onto it, the raft wallowed under the weight of thirty men. "Steward Thomas Whiteley . . . tried to climb aboard, someone swatted him with an oar, but he made it anyhow. Fireman Harry Senior was beaten off by an oar, but he swam around to the other side and finally persuaded them to let him on too. All the time men straddling the stern and the bow flayed the water with loose boards, paddling to get away from the scene and steer clear of the swimmers." And after being rescued from the burning *Lakonia* a German lady passenger recalled: "I was in the water, everybody was clinging to somebody else. Two or three people had taken hold of my legs. I started to kick like a mule, trying to get rid of them, and finally succeeded. If not, they would have pulled me under the water."

It was much the same with the passengers of the American Superconstellation forced down over the Atlantic some 500 miles off the Irish coast on the night of September 22–23, 1962. In the first minutes after the crash they were all very calm. They counted on there being enough room for all in the rescue dinghies. But in the dark, stormy night all but one of the dinghies were lost.

A gruesome struggle began for this one dinghy. It was less than ten feet in diameter and designed for twenty-five people at most, but soon fifty people were crowding it. One of the passengers, a twenty-one-year-old paratrooper, Frederick Caruso, recalled after his rescue: "When I had reached the dinghy, they all just looked at me dumbly. Someone said: 'Don't let anyone else on, we're overloaded already.' Then I yelled, I yelled and raged, till I was pulled onto the dinghy."

Another paratrooper, eighteen-year-old Fred Gazelle, said: "I was sitting on the rim of the dinghy when a woman swam up and kept on shouting: 'Please let me on, please let me on!" I caught hold of her arm, but several soldiers clambered right over us onto the dinghy. No one took any notice of the woman. She went under." Of the seventy-four passengers of the Superconstellation, only forty-eight people were saved.

Lack of mental and physical preparedness for a disaster could, in the event of a third World War, lead to Americans firing on their fellow citizens. This view, at least, was expressed in the sixties in the editorial columns of American magazines: shelters would be so short, it was suggested, that long-established friendships would collapse and all neighborly feelings vanish in a matter of seconds. Father McHugh, an American Jesuit priest, was quoted by newspapers as defending the use of force in such an eventuality in order to save one's own family: "If you are in your shelter and others try to break in, they may be regarded as unjust aggressors, and driven out with all available means."

American investigations show that a lack of training to meet disasters not only snuffs out nearly everyone's "love of their neighbor" but is often a cause of active greed and selfishness. When people involved in accidents—through apathy or lack of discipline—lose the sense of being "members of one another," they will act on the principle, "every man for himself": it will be a heyday for looters and corpse-strippers.

In his book *Doctor at Stalingrad,* the German surgeon Hans Dibold writes of the days in Russian captivity: "The deepest misery was caused by man himself: by the thieves who stripped the corpses. They were the incarnation of the scum that rises wherever the noble are destroyed. Even while the dying still lay in their last agony they lost their footwear, their coats and their rings. One man sold sips of water for money. When he himself died, he had eight thousand marks in his pocket . . . A waiter from Rumania robbed, stole and traded incessantly . . . When he expired like a beast (from typhus) a sack full of gold rings was found at his side."

In complete contrast to this description many accounts show an exemplary discipline and unselfishness if those concerned have been prepared for an emergency. A panic among miners, for example, is extremely rare. Police and firemen are always risking their lives to help others. Doctors and priests, who are used to seeing people in great need and distress, are the first to intervene helpfully in disasters. Again and again castaways have declared after rescue that they owed their lives to a mental preparedness: they had remembered some exercise from their scouting days or had read a particular pamphlet on survival techniques.

Beyond any doubt, therefore, it is desirable that everybody should train for emergencies and "be prepared." Nobody should expect to be saved by a miracle: you just can't rely on them.

Chapter 2
Learning to Survive

The art of survival can be learned. Many have had to learn it the hard way after shipwrecks or air crashes; others have undergone systematic training so as to be masters of the art in an emergency. Some of these have even gone off into "the wilds" of their own accord to test their survival technique.

One of the first "castaway volunteers" was the French doctor Alain Bombard. In 1951 he was working as a surgeon in the hospital at Boulogne, a port which loses from a hundred to a hundred and fifty fishermen at sea every year. Bombard had already been occupied for some time with experiments on the human body's powers of resistance to all kinds of privation. His investigations soon convinced him that men can endure far more than is generally supposed, provided that they know what to do; and he concluded that most deaths among castaways could have been avoided. But how was he to prove himself right, and so help shipwrecked sailors? He decided on a dramatic experiment to demonstrate that anybody in distress at sea has a real chance of survival: he would cross the Atlantic by drifting in a dinghy.

He made extensive preparations and selected a companion, Jack Palmer, from among a stream of volunteers. The two men set out from Monte Carlo on May 25, 1952, with Tangier as their first objective, a "dress rehearsal" for the real crossing. Bombard later described their craft as "a sort of horseshoe-shaped inflatable sausage, some fifteen feet long and six feet wide," which "seemed the perfect piece of equipment for such an expedition as ours."

Many people believed they were crazy. When they boarded their tiny craft, one of the onlookers on the quay said to Bombard's young wife: "You will never see your husband again. The preparations are quite inadequate. These two expect to be at sea for six weeks, and they haven't even got a chamber pot with them."

Another man came up out of the crowd, and gave Bombard a piece of advice: "Young man, I know something about this business . . . There is no point in being squeamish. If your companion dies on the way, don't throw him overboard. Eat him. Anything serves as food; I have even eaten shark."

Bombard thanked the man politely, but in fact the temptation to eat his companion never came up. For after they had crossed the Mediterranean with some adventures and reached Tangier, Palmer had lost enthusiasm and hoped to dissuade Bombard from continuing. Deciding to "go it alone," Bombard left a note for Palmer; then, with the help of a customs officer "put out to sea, borne along by a combination of anger, ambition, and confidence." It was August 13.

He put in at Casablanca, and eleven days later near Las Palmas in the Canaries. From there to the other side of the Atlantic the distance was 3,750 miles, a forbidding expanse of water for one man in a small dinghy.

Bombard waited till October 19, then struck out from Las Palmas on that very long "last lap." He had taken a sealed crate of food, which he meant to touch only in an emergency. The sea alone was to feed him.

With a sponge he mopped up the salt-free condensation from the deck of his boat and found the moisture as delicious as spring water. He caught dolphins and birds, and ate them raw. He collected flying fish which dropped on his tiny deck at night, pressing every ounce of liquid out of them. He drank a pint of salt water a day, for he considered it one of the most important features of his experiment to demonstrate the value of sea water as a thirst-quencher and provider of vitamins.

On November 11, when the first rain fell, he wrote in his log: "I had proved conclusively that a castaway could live for three weeks (and even longer, because I could have continued perfectly well) without fresh water. It is true that Providence was to spare me the ordeal of having to rely again on the flat, insipid fish-juice. From that day on I always had enough rainwater to slake my thirst. It sometimes seemed as if my stock was about to run out, but a shower always came in time."

On November 27 he caught a fly in the boat: "This must be a good sign. Land cannot be far away." It was his forty-first day in the Atlantic. Even then, his mental state varied between optimism and despair; there were hours when he was sorry he had ever set out on the expedition. He developed a rash all over his body, and suffered from terrible itching. Owing to constant contact with the salt water, small pockets of pus formed under his finger nails. But he stayed alive, and nearly always had some food. The conviction that he was right in his survival theory gave him the courage, after fifty-two days at sea, to decline the offer of a passing steamer, SS *Arakaka,* to take him on board. Feeling he had practically completed the experiment, Bombard only accepted a hot shower and a hot meal. Then he sailed on.

He had been sixty-five days out from the Canaries when he finally landed at Saint Lucia on the island of Barbados. Here, with the help of a few spectators, he pulled out the still sealed crate of food, and later "had the presence of mind to take immediate steps to prove that my food reserve was intact. One or two of the more intelligent spectators agreed to serve as witness . . ."

In the summing up at the end of his book, *The Voyage of the Hérétique*, which describes his expedition, Bombard writes: "Any survivor of a disaster at sea should be able to reach land in as good a physical condition as I did. Mine was a perfectly normal case and my health was that of the average man. I have had three attacks of jaundice in my life and several more or less serious ailments due to the effects of wartime undernourishment. I therefore made the crossing with no particular physical advantages . . . It was not a question of living well but of surviving long enough to reach land or meet a ship. I claim to have proved that the sea itself provides sufficient food and drink to enable the battle for survival to be fought with perfect confidence.

". . . I lost fifty-five pounds in weight and suffered various minor ills. I became seriously anemic (my red corpuscle count was five million at the start and two and a half million on arrival) and my hemoglobin level had reached the safety limit. The period following the light meal I had on board the *Arakaka* was very nearly fatal.

"My blood pressure varied greatly with my state of mind. It remained more or less normal until the beginning of December and became dangerously low as my despair increased after that date. My meeting with the *Arakaka* sent it up to normal again, after which it slowly declined again with my growing fatigue. It showed clearly the effect on the system of extraneous events and their capacity to cause psychological disturbances and fluctuations in the state of health.

"I was racked with diarrhea for fourteen days . . . with sizable hemorrhages. I nearly lost consciousness on two occasions. . . . My skin became dehydrated and I had a rash covering my whole body. I lost the nails from my toes. I developed serious defects of vision, suffered a marked loss in muscular tone, and was hungry. But I got there." (In due course these symptoms disappeared.)

His impressive proof of the powers of resistance which the human mind and body possess created a brief sensation. It was even proposed to provide every ship's library with a copy of his book. This plan, which would doubtless have benefited some castaways if they had read his work, was unfortunately not carried out. By an irony of fate, having survived the physical and mental hardships of his voluntary shipwreck on the high seas, Bombard later broke down in the long years of struggle on land, when he was attempting in vain to convince the skeptics. At the end of 1962, reduced to poverty, and almost forgotten, he tried to commit suicide in a cheap Paris hotel.

Nevertheless, he had a whole succession of imitators. Some were merely sensation-hunters who, under the mantle of science, proposed to undertake so-called "survival experiments." For several weeks in 1958 Parisians could watch a man practicing the crawl stroke in the Seine while pushing a rowboat ahead of himself; he was supposed to be training for an attempt to swim the Atlantic. Another man said he planned to cross the Atlantic on a raft made of Ping-Pong balls.

Many of Bombard's emulators, however, were making serious efforts to collect practical experience in the art of survival for the benefit of others. The German doctor, Hans Lindemann, successfully crossed the Atlantic singlehanded in a canoe, getting his sustenance, as Bombard had done, from what the sea offered. An American, William Willis, drifted on a raft from South America to Samoa. He too lived mainly on fish.

Others undertook survival expeditions on land. In July 1956 a group of nine young Frenchmen went into the caves in the valley of the Dordogne, where they lived for several weeks like Cro-Magnon Stone Age men thousands of years ago. At the beginning of their "holiday" they had neither food, matches, nor modern weapons; all the equipment they took along for their venture were some sheepskins, bows and arrows, and a few earthenware pots and plates. They spent four hours trying to light a fire by rubbing together two dry sticks of wood (which an "uncivilized" African can do in two minutes). Then they ate their first meal: roast snails, grass soup, stewed nettles, and wild cherries.

After two weeks they had managed to construct their first fish trap; now they had fresh fish every day. With less time then to be spent hunting, they had enough leisure to shape suitable stones into knives and axes, and make their abode more habitable. When the adventurous young men concluded their experiment, most of them had lost several pounds in weight, and some suffered from rather low blood pressure; but otherwise there was no obvious change in them except for their wild man's beards.

The same sort of experiment was carried out in July 1960 by nine men and five women who started to climb the French Alps from Saint-Jean-de-Maurienne in their ordinary clothes. Stopping just after dark at a height of 9,000 feet, they built a snow hut with their bare hands, and crawled into it. Some equipment and food were dropped for them by parachute, but not until forty-eight hours later. After six days they climbed down into the valley again, unscathed. The group consisted of Frenchmen, Germans,

Italians, Swedes, and Swiss; the whole venture was sponsored by the French Ministry of Tourism and Transport. Like Bombard's and Lindemann's experiments, it showed that survival in adverse conditions is quite possible if you only know what to do.

After the construction of the first atomic shelter in America a new kind of survival test came into being. Instead of having to subsist in the open for a certain time on the fruits of nature, the volunteers for these experiments had to stand days or even weeks of confinement in an underground home, living on tinned food and with "modern conveniences." Some of the tests were carried out in groups, others by individuals.

At the end of 1962 an Australian, Bill Penman, equipped himself with a generous amount of food and reading matter, and spent about two months in a deep cave. He distinguished between day and night by the temperature and the behavior of the bats. On the sixty-fourth day he had to leave his shelter because he had gone almost completely blind from the glare of his acetylene lamp. But he claimed to have proved that in case of a nuclear war one could find protection if food stores were sufficient.

In France, also in 1962, twenty-three-year-old Michael Siffre lowered himself by a rope three hundred feet down into a glacial cave. Equipped with tinned food and a supply of books, he "survived" the planned period of sixty-two days—although he entirely lost his sense of time. In fact, when the test time was over, he had a nervous breakdown after being brought to the surface.

Survival tests, of course, do not always end as successfully as Bombard's or Penman's. Some fail because the participants have not prepared themselves sufficiently, or else make mistakes which go against the basic rules of survival technique. One such case was that of Harvey R. Boyd, a forty-one-year-old American who called himself "the last man on earth." He was a reporter on the staff of a big San Francisco daily paper, and hoped to show in a series of articles how, as an average city dweller, he could survive after a nuclear war "without the aid of anything but his head and hands." It was, naturally, also intended as a publicity stunt for his paper.

He carried out his experiment in the summer of 1961, having chosen a place on the Lower Lipstick Lake, about 250 miles north of San Francisco. His wife, two daughters (aged fifteen and twelve), and eight-year-old son were to keep him company. For equipment he took only some salt, an ax, five knives, fifty feet of nylon rope, toothbrushes, a first-aid kit, and a gun. The gun was kept under seal, to be used only in an emergency.

Right from the start, the problem of finding sustenance proved almost insoluble for this "average city dweller." Every evening the children crawled hungry into their sleeping bags, growing visibly weaker. Boyd's wife became irritable and finally broke down. All five were soon suffering from dysentery. After twelve days Boyd gave up, and returned to the amenities of life. Nothing came of the great series of articles announced. He admitted ruefully: "I used to call myself proudly a child of nature. I thought I was tough—but I was a failure."

At least he came off better than some members of a group of Frenchmen who in 1960 undertook a survival experiment in the Sahara. Foolishly they allowed themselves to lose track of the main group and were only rescued days later, almost dead of thirst. Clearly such tests are hazardous, and should not be undertaken without due preparations.

The difficulties of both experimental and real survival episodes have led to "survival" being practiced today as a regular science. In America, as well as in a number of European countries, there are now several groups and organizations whose members constantly carry out such exercises. They spend nights in the forests, living off plants and grasses and quenching their thirst with dew or natural spring water. Some schools, by encouraging their students to spend a good deal of time in the outdoors, help these youngsters to learn and respect the perils (and the beauty) of nature. These boys and girls will never again be helpless like many city teenagers, should they ever be caught in a blizzard or in some type of disaster. The Dartmouth Outing Club for instance, part of Dartmouth College in New Hampshire, already numbered 1,200 undergraduate students in February 1965. "One of the results of our efforts," declared John Rand, founder and director of the club, "is to give each of us the best possible chance of survival in an emergency. Quite frequently our students have been called out for search and rescue missions in our area during real emergencies."

At Eglin Air Force Base in Florida, parachutists have for several years been trained for certain rescue missions. Called "the Jumping Angels" of the U. S. Air Force, they can, in an emergency, parachute down over disaster areas, inaccessible aircraft wrecks, or shipwrecks.

Part of these parachutists' training consists in dropping into the vast Everglades marshes in southern Florida. Equipped only with hunting knives, small arms, map and compass, they must get through to an assembly point within two weeks—in an area which is not only boggy but swarming with snakes and alligators. From there they are taken to an uninhabited island off the shores of the Gulf of Mexico, where they must subsist for a fortnight, in tropical heat, on what they find on the island's beaches and in its cypress woods. Their motto is: "You can eat anything that doesn't eat you." After undergoing this test, they are next sent into the Mohave Desert between Nevada and California. With rucksack, compass, and details about the position of some water holes, they must reach a destination sixty miles away in three days. The training ends with a drop into the ravines of the Rockies, in an icy wind and at many degrees below freezing point.

Volunteers, trained in mountaineering, parachute jumping, first aid, and all survival techniques also form the core of the Mountain Watch in the Bavarian, Austrian, and Swiss Alps.

The most thorough survival drill, however, is given to the armed forces of many countries. After the tragic experiences of World War II and the Korean War, the American defense authorities have decided to make survival technique an important part of basic training. The actual idea of founding "survival schools" was born by accident one evening in 1949, in an American Officers' Wardroom, the Rod and Gun Club in Wiesbaden (Germany), where three senior officers of the U. S. Air Force were discussing the possibilities of saving the lives of pilots after crash landings. The officers were Major General Curtis E. LeMay, then Commander-in-Chief of the Strategic Air Command, Colonel Demetrious G. Stampados, and Major Burton T. Miller.

Looking through the records of plane crashes in war- and peacetime, LeMay had found that men very often survived the actual crash but not the hardships that followed. Thousands of pilots had frozen to death in Polar zones, or died of thirst in deserts, or drowned at sea. To prevent this in the future, the three officers decided that every aircraft crew of the Strategic Air Command must be "taught" how to stay alive after a crash, whatever the conditions, until help came. They must learn that they cannot conquer hunger, thirst, and cold by passively waiting to be rescued; the success of the search operation which starts immediately an SOS message is received from a ship or aircraft, depends largely on the missing men themselves. If they are freezing, they should know how to get warm; if tormented by hunger, how and where to obtain food; if parched with thirst, where to quench it. Finally, they must know how to attract the attention of an approaching search party; and even if they are not discovered, their courage must never sink so low that they give themselves up for lost.

A few weeks after the preliminary talks, Training Section 3094 of Strategic Air Command was established in Carson Air Base, Colorado. It formed a foundation for the first survival school, under the command of Colonel Stampados; with Major Burton T. Miller, his right-hand man, in charge of developing a program. Apart from these two men, no one in the new department had any experience in the art of survival, nor was there a single trainer.

But somewhere in America, land of cowboys, scouts, and pioneers, you could surely find men with the basic skills needed for a survival school. Colonel Stampados decided to comb the Air Force and Reserve for explorers, skiers, mountain climbers, rangers, forestry men, and other specialists.

After several weeks of intensive examination of indexes, of interviews and meetings with countless servicemen, Stampados and Miller had eventually collected a group to form the nucleus of the school's staff. The group included Lieutenant Colonel Charles Innes-Taylor, who in 1934 had acted as supply officer on Admiral Byrd's Antarctic Expedition; Captain Willy Knudsen (of Norwegian origin), an expert on Arctic conditions; Per Stoen, from the Arctic training school at Nome, Alaska; a fur hunter from Greenland; a sledge-dog trainer from Canada; an American sergeant major who had three times broken out of German prisoner-of-war camps; and finally a great many skiers, paratroopers, mountain climbers, and marine sportsmen.

The first results achieved in Carson were considered so important by trainers and trainees alike that LeMay soon decided to expand the scheme; moreover, the training was no longer to be confined to members of the Strategic Air Command, but to include pilots in the Far Eastern Air Command, Tactical Air Force, Military Transport Command, and also the Canadian Air Force.

So, in 1952, the same year as Dr. Bombard made his Atlantic crossing, which was to provide such vital material for later courses in the survival schools, the school moved from Camp Carson to the large new camp at Stead Air Force Base, Nevada.

Although only ten miles north of Reno, famous for its speedy and comfortable divorces, Stead has been called Nevada's Hell, and certainly it must be one of the grimmest, wildest landscapes in the whole of the United States. The ground is covered with red dust and rubble, which all summer, from May to September, radiate the terrible heat of the sun the whole day long. There are no trees to give shade, and there isn't a breath of wind. Temperatures of 122° F. are quite common, and in the summer only a few drops of rain will fall every few months. In winter, when snowstorms are roaring down from the Sierra Nevada, your tongue might freeze. In short, this is the ideal climate in which to practice the art of survival.

Here is a description that some of the men who, at one time or another, had the "pleasure" to be guests of Stead AFB, gave of those days. Every course at Stead lasts about two weeks, with between three and four hundred men taking part, divided into several smaller groups. As soon as they arrive in the camp, their minds are completely geared to the overriding idea of survival. They talk of nothing else, and probably dream of nothing else. Their heads reel with all the safety rules, instructions, commands, and prohibitions their trainers are drumming into them amidst the sweltering heat. Much of it they will remember all their lives, while some of it will sink into their unconscious, perhaps to come to the surface again in some emergency. Instead of the dangerous attitude of "Of course it won't happen to me," they acquire the attitude of "If 'it' happens to me, I shall at least be prepared for it."

The theoretical part of the course lasts about ten days. Then the trainees are sent into the wilds to show what they have learned: they are "shipwrecked by order," as it were. Each of them is given a pocket first-aid kit, a parachute panel, ten cubes of dried meat, three pounds of fresh meat, some root vegetables, a few tools, and some small arms—more or less the emergency equipment of all American aircraft crews. Then, in groups of six, they are taken in trucks for a two-hour ride over a dusty paved road into the mountains north of Reno. At the altitude of the Honey Lake the trucks turn off into a track, and, engines roaring, climb a steep pass with hairpin bends. To the right and left of the track is "survival country," an area of stunted pines and granite boulders, the air flickering with the glaring heat of the day.

Every quarter of a mile one group jumps off its truck and disappears into the undergrowth. Destination X, the assembly point for all groups, is several days' march away, with no-man's land in between: there is not a town or village, not even a single house.

Each group is accompanied by a trainer. Although he knows the dismal country inside out, he just brings up the rear of his group, apparently taking very little notice of how his charges are getting on. He only helps, advises, or occasionally gives orders, if the men make too many or too dangerous mistakes. By the time the groups meet at Destination X, every man will have a fair idea of his capabilities: either he will realize he has a lot to learn before he could survive such a period in a real emergency, or he will feel confident of being able to keep alive in the most adverse conditions.

Survival training as described above was conducted at Stead AFB regularly until 1969, when the base was finally closed—in order to be replaced by Fairchild AFB in the state of Washington. Also, since then training has become even more realistic and more specialized because certain survival courses were moved to certain climatic areas. Thus, the U. S. Air Force is now teaching "survival in Arctic and Antarctic regions" in remote areas of Alaska. Survival in the tropics is taught in the Philippines and in the Panama Canal Zone, while desert training is conducted at Nellis AFB, Nevada.

Those who attend these schools have not finished their training when the course is over. After returning to their units, they will be recalled for further exercises at regular intervals so that they don't forget the lessons learned.

Other countries' armed forces are by now also convinced of the utility of these schools. It is known that the Russians train their men for the hardest climatic conditions. The British too have established camps on the pattern of Stead, such as the Royal Air Force Winter Survival School at Bad Kohlgrub, near Oberammergau in West Germany, where British officers and men are trained to face hunger, cold, ice, and snow.

In all these schools, and in some institutes concerned with the subject, information of potential use for future training is being collected all the time. Thus, when a missing airman is rescued, the U. S. Air Force, instead of regarding the incident as closed, starts gathering all details of his ordeal for possibly new survival data. Experts from various branches of survival technique interrogate the pilot on how he kept alive after a crash landing, whether he built himself a shelter, whether his lifesaving equipment stood up to the test, and so on. Where there are no survivors, the logbooks are studied or any other leads on the dead men's last hours, and the circumstances of death, are reconstructed.

Both the British and American navies have a similar research program. In 1960, when the participants in the Transatlantic Regatta, having sailed from Plymouth by yacht, arrived in New York, experts from both navies pounced on their logbooks. Psychologists wanted to find out how some of the contestants (particularly those who had been alone in their boats) had faced the solitude of the long voyage, and how they had occupied themselves all the time. Nutrition specialists were interested in what they had lived on, if they had lost any weight, and how much.

The London doctor, David W. Lewis, who interviewed some of the participants, compiled a questionnaire with such questions as:

Were you bored on your voyage? Not bored, because there was too much to do?

Did you enjoy cooking? Or had you no time for it?

Did you think of women a lot, or didn't this worry you?

The results of this and similar questionnaires have since proved very valuable to survival experts. Industrial companies which manufacture lifesaving equipment naturally have also taken a great interest in such interviews.

In this way material has been collected over the years, which includes not only many highly dramatic shipwreck episodes, but a mass of information on the best ways of survival in the desert, the tropics, the mountains, at sea, in Polar regions, or in any other circumstances where people must face the dangers of both nature and their own frailties.

A further substantial contribution to the above material are the ship logs, reports, and diaries of countless mariners who, since the end of the sixties, have sailed in tiny crafts around the world, either competing for money or for the sheer fun of it.

Chapter 3
Survival in the Desert

Live with the desert, don't fight it.
Survival School slogan

In June 1959 a party of four young men, two French and two American, set out in two old 2 hp Citroëns from Paris to Johannesburg. They expected to reach South Africa early in September, having covered a distance of about 8,400 miles. They arrived at the Egyptian town of Aswan on July 15, intending to make their next stop Wadi Halfa, the famous oasis town on the borders of the Sudan. Between Aswan and Wadi Halfa lies the Nubian Desert, a dismal expanse of sand and rock with a pall of heat above it. There was no road or railway leading through it, and even the Bedouins avoided it. When the party told some Egyptians that they were proposing to cross this desert, the Egyptians were horrified, saying you could only get to Wadi Halfa by going up the Nile: anything else was suicide.

But the young men persisted: they would cross the desert by car. They hoped by fast driving to cover the two hundred miles to Wadi Halfa in two days: so if they had water, food, and gasoline for four days, that should be ample. But as an extra precaution they decided to look for a guide who would see them safely to Wadi Halfa. There was a plentiful supply of guides, and the man they eventually engaged was cheap enough. But he had never crossed the Nubian Desert before.

They left Aswan on July 16, and none of the five ever reached Wadi Halfa. Three months later an Egyptian search party found their bodies, and a daily log kept by Yves Thomy-Martin, the leader of the party. From the evidence it was possible to reconstruct more or less what had happened.

Difficulties arose almost from the moment the two Citroëns began grinding their way through the dry, stony soil. The men could scarcely think straight for the heat, which was made even more unbearable by the metal of the car bodies and the steaming engines. Jagged stones cut into the tires, and whenever there was a gradient of any steepness, the overloaded cars would flounder in the sand.

After a few hours one car broke down, and the party stopped. The sun beat down on the two canvas roofs, and there was no longer even the relief of the slight breeze while the cars had been in motion: none of the men could bear to stay inside. Thomy-Martin and the two Americans, John Armstrong and Donald Shannon, started on repairs under the glaring sun, while the other two men lay down in the small strip of shadow cast by the other car. Any physical activity in that heat was a tremendous exertion. Shannon also made the mistake of taking off his shirt. The sun roasted his bare back till it was like raw flesh.

Nevertheless the car was repaired within two hours, and they drove on. The next day Thomy-Martin ordered more and more frequent stops, so that they could rest for a few minutes in the shadow of the cars. They kept on asking the Egyptian guide about the direction, and he eventually admitted he wasn't sure—he thought they were lost. The party suddenly realized in horror that they might die of thirst, for they might even be driving in a circle. Thomy-Martin decided to ration the water. The few mouthfuls he now allowed were not nearly enough to appease their raging thirst. The five men grew visibly weaker. They had long ceased to sweat. Their mouths were dry, their tongues swelled, they found it an effort to speak. Only the cool night brought some relief.

"As soon as the sun appears on the horizon, the desert is a hell," Thomy-Martin wrote in his log on the third day. That day one of the engines broke down. They could not get the car to go, and decided to abandon it. In the full glare of the midday sun Thomy-Martin had the most important belongings loaded into the other car, a job so exhausting in the blazing heat that they all collapsed in turn. Rallying his last powers, Armstrong just managed to drag his camp bed into the shade of a hill, then stretched himself out on it, probably knowing he would never get up again. The other four crept into the shadow of the roadworthy car.

That evening Shannon and the guide set off on foot to fetch help or find water. In fact the party had gone far off course, and they were about 275 miles south of Aswan, a long way east of the Nile. So the nearest human settlement was not Wadi Halfa but Al Allaqui, ninety miles away. With his stick the Egyptian hobbled on into the wilderness, Shannon stumbling after him.

When the sun came out next morning, the young American lost heart: he turned round and went back to his friends. But the guide plodded on for another day and night, to collapse some twenty miles from the cars. His drinking water was used up, and he was probably the first to die, before Shannon and the others. A last entry in Thomy-Martin's log said: "Death is approaching us. It is 2 P.M. Our water is finished. We tried to find a well, but in vain. All four of us have given up hope!"

In due course the families of the missing men became anxious, but it was not till October that the Egyptian authorities sent out the search party which found the wrecks of the cars, the four men's bodies, and a little later the Egyptian guide's body. Colonel Fuad, the Aswan chief of police, told reporters: "Probably they were all dead by the middle of August, for after their water ran out, none of them could have lived much longer in the heat of the desert."

For centuries this heat has stopped people from crossing the world's deserts. The Bedouins are an exception, but they too avoid the desert in mid-summer. Up to the Middle Ages, Mediterranean sailors refused to go south of the equator, afraid they would be burned up by the blazing sun. But with the discoveries of modern technology man has lost his healthy respect for the dangers of great heat and drought. Attempts to cross the seventy minor and major deserts of our earth have ceased to be anything out of the ordinary; distances which it once took weeks to cover on a camel, can now be managed by car in a few days. Today the Land-Rovers of American oil-drilling teams roar through the Rhub-al

Khali Desert in Arabia. In the deserts of Persia, Iraq, and the northern Sahara, oil derricks, pumping stations, and settlements are sprouting up. The deserts of Jordan and Arabia are served by passenger buses.

But wherever such ventures succeed or turn into routine services, the special arrangements made are extremely thorough and some of them very expensive. The vehicles used have ample reserves of water and fuel, and are sometimes air-conditioned. Their large tires are better adapted than those of private cars to stony or sandy terrain. Lacking signposts, the drivers find their way by compass like sailors. Many of them, too, have radio transmitters so that they can call for help in an emergency. Then again, it is known at their destination exactly when to expect them, and should they not arrive on time, a search party is sent off at once.

It might almost seem as if, with the aid of modern equipment and science, man had overcome natural hazards. But this is an illusion, the very illusion by which most amateur adventure-seekers are deceived. A powerful car or their own plane is enough to make many desert travelers feel like another Livingstone or a Bedouin sheik—until some little piece of machinery goes wrong, when the desert exacts a grim revenge. Take the fairly typical case of the English party in 1955 who tried to cross the Sahara in a small car, starting from Kenya. There were four of them, Alan Cooper, a forty-eight-year-old farmer; a boy of eighteen, Peter Barnes; Reda Taylor, a teacher (aged thirty-eight); and Barbara Duthy, a zoologist (aged forty).

The car soon got stuck in the sand. None of them thought of jacking it up at once and pushing stones under the tires. Instead, Cooper, who was driving, tried to get through onto firm ground by stepping on the accelerator. The result was that the car went in still deeper, and finally had both its axles buried. After that there was no chance of digging it out.

Cooper at once set off to fetch help. He marched the amazing distance of fifty miles. Then he collapsed from thirst and exhaustion. A little later a convoy of trucks passed him, and one of the drivers noticed the apparently lifeless figure. A few gulps of water brought Cooper round enough for him to show his rescuers the way to where the car was stuck.

The three others were still alive. Barbara Duthy was carried to one of the trucks and put down in the back. The rescue party succeeded in pulling the car onto firm ground, after which Cooper, Barnes, and Reda Taylor got back in. They drove off again in their original direction with the first truck behind, but a broken axle brought the truck to a halt. The driver blew his horn madly to get the car to stop, but its three occupants did not hear him and drove on into the desert.

When they eventually looked around for the truck, there was nothing to be seen of it. For fear of getting lost, they dared not turn back. But they didn't want to drive on, for this time they hadn't a single drop of fresh water with them. Sure that the truck would be following them, they hadn't refilled their containers. That was a fatal mistake.

At first the three of them waited in the shadow of the car for the missing truck to appear. Hours passed. Their thirst was so great that in the end they drank the rusty water from the radiator. It didn't help much. Reda Taylor was the first to die. Cooper in his utter desperation eventually resorted to the gas tank, swallowing down several mouthfuls of gasoline. The following morning he too was dead. The truck arrived at last, in time to rescue young Barnes.

Death came even more cruelly to five of seven German youths who during Whitsun of 1965 started out from Cairo for a weekend trip through the Libyan Desert. Their destination, which some of them never reached alive, was the oasis Siwa, 440 miles away. The road to Siwa is not too easy, but quite safe provided one stays on it. Instead, the young party boldly decided to cross the notorious Qattara Basin, a valley with searing temperatures whose floor lies almost 400 feet below sea level.

On June 3 the group started out in three cars: Reinhold Rimm, Günther Wanderscheck, and Hans Hauser shared the first vehicle. In the second car were Gudrun and Klaus Böhme, a married couple. The last car was occupied by Günter Steding and Dieter Benzinger.

Following a telegraph line of World War II, the party traveled along the rim of the basin, when it suddenly met an Egyptian military patrol. The Egyptians, reporting the meeting to their commanding post by radio transmitter, received strict orders to stop the Germans from proceeding and instead lead them back to El

Alamein and to safety. But where even a Field Marshal Rommel had lost a battle his fellow countrymen were not willing to give up: Böhme argued for so long with the military patrol that the Egyptians eventually gave up and allowed the Germans to continue. All warnings by the soldiers that the cars of the Germans would get stuck in the sand were laughingly turned down.

After a few miles Rimm's car, a German type of station wagon, got stuck in the sand up to its axle. Suddenly, out of nowhere, the Egyptian patrol reappeared and got the car moving again. It was as though death had knocked at the door—and nobody was willing to listen. The Germans kept moving on.

After another couple of miles Steding suddenly felt sick, probably because of the heat. He had to throw up repeatedly. Red-faced, he managed to persuade Benzinger to turn back with him and head for El Alamein. That decision saved both their lives. For when they saw their friends again twelve days later, it was only to identify the blistered, heat-blackened bodies. They had been found and picked up in the desert by an Egyptian helicopter crew, 125 miles from the spot where Benzinger and Steding had turned back.

A reconstruction of the events that had happened since the split-up of the party was immediately performed by the authorities. It proved beyond doubt: Hauser's and Rimm's car was the first one to get stuck again. Both men remained in it, while Wanderscheck and the Böhmes drove on to get help. After about eight miles, their car too got stuck.

On foot the three of them started out in the blistering heat of the day to reach the oasis Kara. For thirty-five miles they kept walking, and finally crawling. When their bodies were found, there were no signs of emptied water canteens or traces of food. All survivors—before dying—had literally buried themselves alive up to their necks in the sand in order to escape the heat. Rimm and Hauser too had tried to get help, but they only got five miles farther before they died.

In the United States a lot of people find crossing a desert almost unavoidable. Anyone who wants to get from Las Vegas to Los Angeles must cross the Mohave Desert. Anyone who wants to get from Salt Lake City to Reno must cross the Great Salt Lake Desert and a record 605,000 tourists crossed the once dreaded Death Valley in 1973—most of them in the comfort of their air-conditioned cars. There are several highways leading right through it, and so long as you do not leave them, nothing much can really happen to you; regular patrols will bring first aid where needed or get broken-down cars towed away. So many vehicles use the highways through other deserts too, that you would rarely have to wait more than an hour for help.

The tragedies occur only when inexperienced desert travelers leave the paved road despite the many warning notices, and in irresponsible quest of "adventure" try a small detour along gravel roads without signposts.

An American couple, Frederick and Catherine Viehe, left the Los Angeles-Las Vegas highway and drove into the Mohave Desert, without telling anyone anything about it: that was their first mistake. They wanted to look for semiprecious stones, which are often found in that region. After about an hour's driving their car got stuck in the sand.

Now Viehe made his second mistake: instead of setting out on foot directly after sunset to fetch help, he waited till dawn the next morning. Then, a third mistake: instead of going back the way he had come, he continued in his original direction. He did not know how many miles it was before the graveled road led back to the paved road, but he knew it did so eventually. He was a man of over fifty, and by ten o'clock the heat was so great that he found it a terrific effort to keep going. In the evening, after covering ten miles, he collapsed. From where he lay, the lights of cars could be seen, as they drove along the highway only five miles off. He died, presumably the same night.

A group of telephone workers looking for a cable break discovered his wife a few days later, near death. Soon afterward they found Viehe too. By then his body was completely dehydrated. His weight had dropped from 197 pounds to 155 pounds.

As far as is known to date, only one person in this century has managed to cross California's Death Valley on foot, in summer, and in daytime. His name is Jean-Pierre Marquant, a French ex-paratrooper, and when he started out on his dangerous trip in 1966 he was twenty-eight years old. However, for safety's sake Marquant had decided to do it "the easy way"—during the seven days he needed to cover his one hundred miles across the valley, he was watched by rangers, followed by press-photographers in air-conditioned cars, and supported by a number of friends who regularly supplied him with fresh clothing, food, and particularly water. Despite all this Marquant confessed at the end of his experiment: "Already on the first day I felt the impact of the 132-degree heat around 2 or 3 P.M., when the sand had been heated up fully by the sun. But you have to tread on. To stop would mean certain death. You must not think of the heat, not of your thirst, not of the dryness in your throat, because then you would stop. Therefore, I tried to recall things of the past. I tried to recall my life, my entire life, and what had become of me. I thought of my friends and how I would like to see them again, and I thought of the girls whom I had known, and with whom I had been happy. . . . Anyone who is not trained for it could die in the desert within two hours." This was Marquant's warning to all those who felt any ambitions to copy his walk through the desert —especially without assisting escorts.

These few examples make one thing clear: for anyone who has to survive in the desert, the heat of the day, both cause and effect of the lack of water, is the chief danger. Temperatures reach an amazing height. In Baghdad the thermometer in the hot summer months often climbs to 150° F., occasionally even to 180° and over (in the sun). In the Sahara near Azizia (Libya) temperatures of 134° in the shade have been recorded, and in July 1913 that was also the temperature in the Great Salt Lake Desert (also in the shade). But if the thermometer is put in the sand there at noon during the summer, the mercury goes up to 176°. On the side of Highway 91, which goes through the Mohave Desert, it has sometimes been 140° in the shade at noon; in the evenings the thermometer sinks to a "low" temperature of 90°. In Libya, Montgomery's and Rommel's soldiers sometimes fried eggs on the armor plate of their tanks.

So it is no tall story if pilots who have come down in the desert often report after their rescue that they burned their hands on the hot metal of their aircraft. Some had the idea of putting their hands under their armpits from time to time to prevent blisters, and others found that blisters were caused by heat penetrating the leather of their boots.

Everyone knows that people sweat in heat, but fewer people know the reason for this. It is because human skin works like an air-conditioning system, which should keep the body temperature at about 98.6° F. This happens at normal external temperatures, by means of the skin's cooling system, consisting of an extensive network of fine blood vessels. Blood, which draws off the super-fluous heat from the internal organs and the muscles, flows through these vessels and gives off heat.

But if the external temperature is extremely high, as in the desert, the body cannot balance its temperature merely by giving off heat like this; so the sweat mechanism is switched on. The skin's two and a half million sweat glands secrete tiny drops of water which they take from the body cells and tissues. These drops evaporate, thereby using up the natural heat; so this leads to the body cooling off. The fluid sweated out may amount to over two and a half pints per hour, often for five or six hours on end, provided that it is constantly being replaced. If that does not hap-pen, and the body goes on sweating, a man will suffer one of the most agonizing forms of natural death.

An American airman rescued from the Sahara in 1941, described afterward how his companion had died of thirst: "At first we felt uncomfortable. We had enough solid food with us, but no appetite. We had become distinctly lazy, real sluggish. We didn't sweat as much as we had done at first—and Bill got the first cramps. I told him to lie down, and gave him our last sip of water to drink, having mixed some salt with it. That seemed to help for a time. Bill couldn't take heat as well as I could, because I had grown up on the edge of the Arizona Desert.

" 'I feel giddy,' he said suddenly, and then complained of head-aches, which grew worse and worse. His skin all of a sudden became moist and cool. He lay there, his breath rattling, and his mouth completely dried up. Sometimes he tried to scratch his arms and legs. 'It's itching so,' he said. His body eventually went bluish, and I could hardly understand the words he whispered to me in a thick voice. Once he tried to get up, but immediately collapsed.

"Then he fell into delirium. He imagined he was lying by a lake, and was greedily trying to lap up the water, but didn't seem to be succeeding. The arm he tried to reach the water with suddenly seemed paralyzed. He couldn't swallow either, his throat had swollen so much.

"He kept on jerking about, and by kicking furiously at the slashed wing of our aircraft he gave himself a deep flesh wound. But the dehydration of his body had thickened his blood so much that instead of bleeding the wound closed at once.

"In the few lucid moments he had, he was deaf and could hardly see me. His eyes were glassy. His skin began to shrivel. When he had to pass water, he could only manage this with great pain. His skin, however, seemed completely numb. Half an hour later he was dead."

When, in the summer of 1974, sixteen-year-old Donnie Warrington was rescued from the Gila Desert in southern Arizona, he described the final agony of one of his five companions, who died in the 158° heat: "Dave [Capistran] was the first one to go. He suddenly began to laugh, then to sing. His eyes were bloodshot, with a mad look. Suddenly he jumped up and ran towards a huge organpipe-cactus, embracing it with both arms. The thorns penetrated his face, his throat, and went deep into his chest—blood was squirting out of all those wounds. He roared like a mutilated animal and then took off into the desert. We never saw him again." Capistran was later found, dead, lying on his back with his legs bent under the body, and bloody wounds all over.

Everyone who suffers from lack of water shows the same symptoms in a definite and invariable order: lassitude, loss of appetite, sleepiness, are the first signs that blood, tissues, and organs are not getting enough fluid. Liver and brain are least tolerant of lack of water. In hot climates (but rarely in temperate latitudes) these organs give people immediate warning by making them feel very thirsty. In stages of acute thirst, people have often tried to dull this feeling—by smoking, chewing gum, or pure will power. An American airman even sucked pebbles. According to the report, he swallowed some, and this worried him so much that he tied the next stone to a piece of thread, one end of which he kept hanging out of his mouth. The idea, purportedly, was that if he swallowed the stone, he could pull it out again by the thread.

Such measures may stop one feeling thirsty, but they do not bring the body the water it needs so urgently. So it is thrown back further onto its reserves, and this starts the dreaded dehydration process which finally leads to dying of thirst. While the body is using up its own stocks of water, it also loses weight; an adult's body is 50–60 percent water, a child's 70–80 percent; and according to an investigation by a Minnesota hospital, even a 2½ percent loss of water by the body "must be considered critical." But those in acute stages of thirst lose far more.

The next symptom of continuous lack of water is a rise in body temperature. Nausea occurs as soon as the body has lost 5 percent of its weight in water. When it has lost 6–10 percent, feelings of giddiness occur, with headaches and itching of the limbs. The mouth dries up. If the dryness increases, the lips get sore and begin to ache. The skin on the tongue and mucous membranes start peeling. A man rescued from dying of thirst said: "I felt as if my tongue had swollen so much that I couldn't keep it in my mouth." The corners of the eyes also dry up; and every grain of sand that gets into their parched folds, burns like fire and is extremely hard to remove. (Curiously enough, people saved from ordeals in the desert can still weep tears of thankfulness. It has not yet been explained where the body in such cases obtains the moisture needed to form tears.) The great secretion of sweat also causes a dangerous lack of salt in the body, which changes the consistency of the blood, and leads to acute cramps in abdomen and limbs.

However, anyone suffering from even 10 percent dehydration can quickly recover without any subsequent ill effects, if he gets enough water to drink. His intestines absorb it at once and send it straight to the blood, which immediately renews the supply in all the cells. But if this water is not forthcoming, the feeling of thirst is so overwhelming that the sufferer will gulp down any fluid he can find, however nauseating.

In 1932, for instance, the German airman, Hans Bertram, went off with his friend Klausmann on an exploring flight over the wild, dry North West coast of Australia without water or adequate food supplies on board. He had to make a forced landing, and the next day was already trying to drink the plane's radiator water. "A cup was filled with the oily, dirty water from the radiator. After the first mouthful we spat the muck out. We just weren't thirsty enough." But a day later the two men drank it as if it were delicious spring water, and they were soon craving for kangaroo's blood to quench their thirst. Thirst sufferers at the 10 percent dehydration stage have also drunk urine, gasoline, oil, and salt water. But none of these, of course, can be a substitute for drinking water.

The dehydration proceeds, and soon the sufferer begins to imagine things. Usually he sees mirages involving water. If he is not alone, the others may well see the same mirage. In August 1941 two farmers and their families got stranded in a truck in the Sonora Desert in Mexico. There were nine of them, and their only can of water was empty, having accidentally been kicked over. On the second day without water they all believed they could see a lake ahead of them. "Look! Look!—all that *water!*" they shouted, and avidly stuffed the hot sand into their mouths.

After such hallucinations most thirst-sufferers lose consciousness, and then death comes quickly. With an air temperature of 90° F. even a 15 percent dehydration can lead to death. But if it exceeds 25 percent, people die from it even in cool or cold weather.

In the case of the farmers stranded in the Sonora Desert, within five days all but one of the men, and a four-year-old child, were dead. A young man of twenty-three and a girl of nineteen were the only survivors, found on the sixth day by a passing car.

Naturally, various physiologists have tried for years to establish the minimum amount of water a man needs to stay alive (without any harmful aftereffects). The best-known work in this field was carried out by the American scientist, Dr. E. F. Adolph, based on experiments with volunteers, and careful analyses of survivors' reports.

A man's capacity for survival, Dr. Adolph found, depends on three mutually related factors: the temperature of his surroundings, his physical activity during the survival period, and the amount of water he can get. This means that the more physical work a man does, the more water he needs, to make up for the dehydration of his body from loss of sweat. His need for water increases with the temperature of his surroundings, and is, of course, especially great if he is physically active in hot weather, as can be seen from countless examples. In the Sahara, road workers and the teams in the French oil fields receive thirteen pints of water a day merely for drinking and cooking. Soldiers in Rommel's desert army, when fighting conditions were especially hard, drank more than two and a quarter gallons a day. At the building of the Hoover Dam on the frontier between Nevada and Arizona there were workers who drank up to six and a half gallons a day.

On the basis of his findings Dr. Adolph drew up the following table, showing how long a man can live with various amounts of water in various temperatures (in the shade), assuming that he is not physically active:

HOW LONG CAN A MAN SURVIVE IN THE SHADE?

Max. Daily Temp. Shade Degrees Fahrenheit:	with no water	1 qt.	2 qt.	4 qt.	10 qt.	20 qt.
			EXPECTED DAYS OF SURVIVAL			
120	2	2	2	2.5	3	4.5
110	3	3	3.5	4	5	7
100	5	5.5	6	7	9.5	13.5
90	7	8	9	10.5	15	23
80	9	10	11	13	19	29
70	10	11	12	14	20.5	32
65	10	11	12	14	21	32
50	10	11	12	14.5	21	32

Source: E. F. Adolph's *Physiology of Man in the Desert* quoted by William Allen in his article "Thirst," published in *Natural History,* December 1956

This table is more interesting than it looks at first sight; for it refutes the widespread idea, often applied, that people stranded in the desert can increase their survival chances by dividing up their water supplies. There are hundreds of accounts of how time and again sufferers from thirst have strictly rationed their last water supplies—one cup, or even a spoonful, of water a day per person. Experts know today that such rationing is not only futile but positively harmful. It may merely have a psychological effect: there is hope as long as there is some water left.

The top line of the table shows that a man without water can survive for two days at a temperature of 120° F.; and if he has one and three-quarter pints of water, this will not enable him to keep alive any longer. Even with double the amount he would still die of thirst after two days; and seven pints would increase his expectation of life by only half a day.

At that temperature, in fact, the human body uses up more water by secretion of sweat than it can make up by an intake of even four pints; while even thirty-five pints would not be enough to allow survival for more than four and a half days. So, against the common idea, it does not help the thirst-sufferer at all if he divides his water supply of, say, eighteen pints into fifty cups, so as to stretch his supply over a longer period of time. Irrespective of how much or how little he drinks per day of his eighteen pints, he will have died of thirst after three days.

Dr. Adolph's researches led him to the conclusion that it was best "to renew the store of body fluid every hour." Survival instructors make the same recommendation: "Drink in the desert whenever you are thirsty, no matter how large or small your water supply is."

A number of pilots in the war saved their lives by working this out for themselves. Before every operation which was taking them over a desert, they drank as much water as they possibly could. Two of them reported later: "We were shot down over the Sahara and ordinarily would have died of thirst. But we were literally saturated with water, which our bodies could subsist on till a search party found us the third day after our forced landing." And the U. S. Army has a saying: "It's the water in your belly, not your canteen, that keeps you alive."

Survival instructors give the following explanation to reassure those who are afraid to "overdrink," and so waste water that would be precious in an emergency: "A man can drink about three and a half pints of water at a time. At desert temperatures of over 110° F. this water simply can't be superfluous, for the body sweats as much as that in less than two hours to maintain a normal body temperature of 98.6°. Besides, the body needs extra quantities of water to excrete products of the metabolism like urine and feces (human urine is at least 92 percent water). Of course a man can force himself to drink more water than his body needs (in this sense he would be squandering it), but this is in it-

Many pilots who made crash landings in the desert soon found that the metallic fuselage of their planes turned into a sort of furnace. With blankets or parachute panels spread over it they got shade and a cooling breeze.

People stranded in the desert protected themselves from the scorching heat by such shelters of stone and tarpaulin.

self a symptom of disease." There are people, in fact, who in normal temperatures drink up to four gallons of water a day.

"The great danger," survival experts argue, "is that the average man does not drink enough water. His thirst is often slaked before the water 'budget' is balanced again." This observation was made by American doctors in the last few years at various bases in the Arctic and Antarctic. The soldiers stationed there had no thirst because of the cold climate, and therefore drank little; as a result, their bodies suffered from progressive dehydration. The fact was discovered because many of them complained of continual tiredness. Since then they have been urged to drink a certain amount of water after every meal.

Clearly, a man's need for water will rise sharply (and his expectation of life will drop as rapidly) if he is physically active in great heat. Yet this is just the mistake people often make when unexpectedly stranded in the desert: as Viehe did by setting off to fetch help in the glaring sun, thereby greatly reducing his chances of survival.

Similarly, on July 31, 1953, two American boys in the Great Salt Lake Desert, Charles Ludlow (aged twenty) and his seven-year-old brother, left the solid track and soon got their car stuck in the sand. Also, in the glaring sun, they tried to walk back to the highway. It was not long before they completely stopped sweating, a sign that their bodies had already lost 5 percent of the normal water content. They threw their shirts away and walked on bare-chested! After two hours the small boy collapsed. His brother tried to carry him, but after about a third of a mile gave up. The next day, a search party found the two bodies: literally burned black, the backs covered with large, dried-up blisters.

The report of a British bomber crew, which had to make a forced landing in Ethiopia during World War II, shows even more impressively how a man's walking capacity decreases in great heat. Six men set off from the wreck of their plane with a few cans of food and two gallons of water. They walked till evening, had a brief rest, and then went on till daybreak.

The next day they were so weak they could only keep going for a quarter of an hour at a time. That day they covered ten miles. Eventually they rested in the shade of a tree quite exhausted. At sunset they set off again, but walking in the glaring sun had weakened them so much that they had to give up after an hour and a half. Instead of giving themselves the whole of the next day to recover, they started again at sunrise. At nine in the morning the sun was already so hot that one of them couldn't go on.

They now had only four and a half pints of water left, and decided to divide up into two parties of three men each. The first party was to go ahead with half the water ration, despite the heat, to find a well or get help; while the second waited for the sixth man to recover before following. The first party disappeared and was never seen again. The three men in the second party crept forward at a snail's pace in the blazing sun. They did a few yards an hour, too weak to walk for more than five minutes, after which they needed the remaining fifty-five for rest. For four days they moved on like this, and then had to rest for two whole days. Finally, on the ninth day of their ordeal, they tried to go on, but after only ten minutes collapsed for good. They were near death when a rescue plane spotted them that afternoon.

The figures given by Dr. Adolph and other scientists show that anyone standing in the hot sun (even if not physically active) needs three times as much water as those in the shade. But by sensible behavior he can reduce his need for water to a minimum and thereby increase his chances of survival. This is the meaning of the slogan from Stead AFB quoted at the head of this chapter: "Live with the desert, don't fight it."

Those who live in the desert do this by instinct. Like the camel, they move slowly, almost lazily (which has nothing to do with the often-quoted "Southern indolence"). Just as the camel has a thick coat of hair, they wear tightly woven clothes so that their sweat should not evaporate too quickly, since it is the evaporation which uses up the body's heat. Like desert rats, they keep in the shade whenever they can. And while in the world of Noël Coward's song, "mad dogs and Englishmen go out in the midday sun," the natives of these parts refrain from all strenuous physical activity during the hottest hours of the day. Finally, like all wild life in the desert, people who live there drink and drink whenever they get the chance.

Anyone who keeps to these few basic rules can greatly increase his chance of survival in the desert, as many examples would show. A British captain shot down over the western Sahara covered 140 miles in eleven days, walking only at night. The water he had with him would not have been enough had he done his walking during the day.

In all deserts it is cool at night, and often cold. In the western Sahara, the thermometer drops from 131° F. to 59°. In the Gobi Desert the difference is about 54°, and in the winter months the temperature drops at night to well below freezing point. Obviously far greater exertions are possible at night in these temperatures, even without much water, than by day. There are reports of survivors from the Sahara who covered 350 miles in twenty, ten, or even five days—but only because they walked by night.

One of the best illustrations of the advantages of walking by night in hot regions is the story of an American called Roger

Jones. In August 1953 he was stranded on a road in the Great Salt Lake Desert, when an axle of his car broke. As a former Marine, he had taken a short survival course, and now—unlike Viehe and the Ludlow brothers—did just the right thing; he lay down in the shadow of his car, and slept through the hottest part of the day.

At about four o'clock, when the sun had lost its full impact—though the temperature was still 95° around six—he set off along the road. He knew there were steel water tanks for tourists at regular intervals. Twice that evening he came to one of these tanks, painted bright red, and drank as much as he could, also filling up his water bottle. Wherever he found any shade, he stopped for a rest. Every so often he collected large stones and laid them out on the road to spell the word HELP, with an arrow showing the direction he was walking in. The next day a car driver saw one of these signs, at once followed the arrow, and caught up with Jones after a four hours' drive. He was resting in the shade of a rock. His condition was excellent despite a midday heat of 110° F.

Sometimes when people have got themselves into desperate situations by carelessness or irresponsibility, they do the right thing by instinct. In 1959 Viryl and Laura Scott with their six children were on an excursion into the Grand Canyon. Instead of staying on the much-used main road, they went off on to a side track which came to a dead end about half a mile farther on. Trying to turn the car back, Scott hit his radiator against a jagged boulder, which pierced the thin pipes inside, so that the water began to leak out. He drove on, hoping the road would soon lead out of the Canyon, but after ten miles or so, the engine overheated. The temperature was 124° F. The Scotts had neither drinking water nor food with them, though there was a little water mixed with antifreeze at the bottom of the radiator—this they soon finished up. It was fifty miles to the nearest town, which they had left that morning. They had been staying with friends, but hadn't told anyone exactly where they were going.

They all got out of the car, and lay down in the shade of a rock. When evening came, Scott looked through the car for equipment that might come in handy, but didn't find anything very useful. There were two blankets, which he cut up by the light of the moon, to make a big SOS sign with the pieces. He dipped the spare tire in engine oil, so that he could quickly light a fire with it

as a signal. Then he dismounted the mirror, to flash a distress signal with that if a plane passed overhead. He put out the four hub-
caps to catch the morning dew.

The next day the first search plane appeared in the sky. Scott's
fire didn't smoke enough, the pilot failed to spot it, and a few
moments later the plane had gone again. There were, in fact, several search parties looking for them by then with all urgency, for
there was little hope of finding them alive after the second day.

As the sun climbed higher, Laura Scott got out her vanity case,
applied lipstick to the blisters and swollen lips of her husband and
children and covered everyone's cheeks and arms with rouge. Discovering that the ground was cooler a few inches below the surface, she and her husband buried the children up to the neck in
sand, and applied sand to the children's faces; then they did the
same for themselves. (In most deserts the temperature a foot
below the surface is less than 72° F., and on a hot summer day it
may be 18° cooler than at the surface directly above.)

But Scott had spotted a cedar quite near, so he got up out of the
sand, walked very slowly over to it, and returned to his family
with a branch: they tore off the bark, and tried to suck moisture
out of the wood. At midday the heat was so intense that the skin
on the children's faces began to shrivel. Earlier in the day the
parents had collected everyone's urine in a can. They now dipped
some bits of clothing in the can, and pressed them on the
children's faces: the smell was unpleasant, but the evaporating
moisture was refreshingly cool.

In the afternoon Laura discovered a box of crayons in a small
suitcase. They were made of wax, and contained harmless plant
dyes. She fed her children with them. After that they ate the contents of a glue pot. According to the label the glue was made from
milk products, so it too was harmless.

Scott was very weak by now, but in the evening Laura and the
eldest daughter set off in the hope of finding water. They were unsuccessful, and returned at dawn exhausted. They began to cut
some cactuses into strips and roast these over a fire, hoping it
might slightly quench their raging thirst. But the pieces tasted dry
and bitter, so their last hope was gone: they gave themselves up
for dead. Two hours later a rescue party arrived.

The doctor who treated them in the hospital said: "The Scotts

have survived all their ordeals far better than we could have expected, but only because in the great heat they instinctively did the
right thing."

Nevertheless, they would clearly have died of thirst, had the rescue party arrived twelve hours later. This was the fate suffered by
hundreds of pilots after emergency landings in various deserts during the last war, although they observed all the rules for survival in
the desert. So today's survival schools teach their trainees how to
look for water even in places which are apparently without a drop
of it.

Not that you find streams, pools, or even puddles in such places;
but there is often hidden water, discovered sometimes by accident,
and sometimes by systematic search. People rescued from the
desert have often found that certain kinds of cactus are "natural
water-storers." An American airman who crashed in the Arizona
Desert said: "I experimented with various species, till I found a
small bottle-like cactus, which seemed most suitable for my purpose. I knocked the top off with an empty food can I had found.
The flesh contained a whole lot of moisture. When I had pressed it
out and quenched my thirst, I filled the inner pocket of my flying
suit with juicy cactus pulp. That was my lucky break, for I
shouldn't have found the same kind again in a hurry."

Another airman after a crash landing, also in the Arizona
Desert, quenched his thirst for several days with the juicy pulp of
the same kind of cactus. He also rubbed his skin with the chewed
pieces, to keep himself cool.

It is amazing, in fact, how much moisture can be stored in certain desert plants, particularly species of cactus. About seven pints
can be pressed from a "bottle cactus" (though this species is only
to be found in the Arizona Desert). Of course the leather-hard,
prickly skin must first be cut through, which takes forty minutes
even with a good knife. Some of those who have drunk the juice
say that it tastes bitter at first, "like an aspirin," but add that they
soon got used to it, especially if there was nothing else to drink.

Other species of cactus store a great deal of water in their juicy
stems and can thus survive droughts lasting for several years. The
stem of the Central American bisnaga quickly fills up with water
if you cut off its top and scoop it out. A lot of people have died
of thirst in its meager shade because they did not know this secret;

and you sometimes hear of people digging round desert plants in the hope of finding underground water reserves. But most of these plants get their moisture from millions of drops of dew, and take even the slightest moisture out of the ground. Usually, therefore, it is completely futile to look for water near them. Tamarisks, for example, plunge their roots as much as a hundred feet deep, and those of the Mexican giant cactus spread out like a fine spider's web just below the surface in a circle two hundred feet in diameter. All the water is in the plants, not the ground.

Some survivors report after their rescue that they first tried all the soft parts of a desert plant. Then they dug up the roots and peeled them, then ate the pulp, which sometimes even had water dripping from it. In desperation people have even eaten all sorts of flowers, fruits, and seed pods, also the bark of trees and skins of cactuses, to quench their thirst from the moisture these contained. But such attempts are the exception; and many survivors, asked why they never tried to get moisture from desert plants, said the plants looked so "dry and leathery, and they might be dangerous too." But the only desert plants which are really dangerous are those with milky sap, like the cactuses in African deserts. Three American airmen who were not sure about the harmlessness of desert plants, said after being rescued that they had all three chewed sappy cactus flesh simultaneously, "so as to die together," in case it should be poisonous.

Thirst sufferers in the desert have gone about satisfying their need for moisture in even stranger ways. During the war, for instance, an American flight lieutenant bartered a female camel from a Bedouin tribe in the Sahara. The sheik showed him how to milk it, then indicated the direction of the Allied lines, and the flight lieutenant rode and milked till he got back to his unit.

Many kinds of fauna can be useful as water suppliers. A pilot who had made a forced landing in the Australian desert copied the aborigines: to quench his thirst he hunted for a particular kind of frog. During the rainy season these frogs store so much water in a cavity in their hind-quarters that they grow to the shape and size of a Rugby football. Just before the beginning of the dry season they bury themselves about a foot deep in the mud, and so survive the greatest heat by subsisting on their store of water until the next rainy season starts. The aborigines literally sniff out these frogs on all fours, dig them out of the sand and suck them dry.

Again, thirsty Bedouins often hunt for a species of worker ant, which in wet months stores water in its stomach. Their fellow ants "milk" them during the dry season. Medical officers of the U. S. Air Force have been investigating how many such ants a man must eat to satisfy his requirements of water. Their British colleagues have made similar investigations on snails following the experiences of an R.A.F. bomber crew during the war who had to make a forced landing in the Libyan Desert.

While these airmen were walking over some rocky plateaus, they saw that the ground was covered with a lot of big white snails; when trodden on, fluid spurted out of them. The men immediately began to gather in the snails and suck them dry. Many had already been "drained" by birds, but they managed to collect enough "full" specimens to be able to quench their thirst. On hearing reports of this, the R.A.F. sent a commission into the Libyan Desert to collect several hundred snails, which were taken to their Medical Institute at Farnborough, near London. There it was established that this species of snail, the Ehrenbergi Roth (also found in Israel in the Negev), can stay alive for four years at temperatures where a man without water would die of thirst after four days.

Each of the snails taken to Farnborough contained about a teaspoonful of watery fluid. First this was fed to rats. They not only survived, but even put on weight, since the fluid contained valuable proteins. Then there was a test with volunteers who were put in a heat chamber and given only "snail water" to drink at a temperature of 122° F.; half a gallon of snail water per day, it was found, was all the liquid a man required.

In Egypt's Qattara Depression, two American airmen who had to make a forced landing discovered hundreds of small shells in a wadi (dried-up river bed). They bit them open and sucked out the fluid, which stank so much, however, that at first they vomited. But gradually they got used to it, and then quenched their thirst every hour with the fluid from thirty shells each. Walking by night, they eventually reached a desert airfield. (A third man, the navigation officer, died of thirst, because after the landing he went off on his own and walked during the heat of the day.)

Dew, which settles after cold nights in many stretches of desert, has also been a lifesaver. Survivors have mopped it up from the metal of their wrecked planes, or collected it in tarpaulins. Thirsty Bedouins sometimes dig up cool stones just before sunrise and wait till the dew settles on them, then lick it up. In many desert regions, according to the Israeli scientist Shmuel Duvdevani, dew falls in a quantity which would amount to twenty-five inches in a year.

During the war one of the strangest sources of water were the wrecks of burned-out or shot-up jeeps, tanks, and trucks. Airmen, after forced landings, walked twenty miles a day, filling up their water bottles regularly from the radiators of such vehicles. The record is held by a British paratrooper in the Special Air Service, who covered a distance of two hundred miles, quenching his thirst exclusively from radiators.

Survival experts have recently been taking an increased interest in the methods of the Bedouins, with their amazing sixth sense, which again and again leads them to sources of water. Mornings and evenings, for instance, they listen to the twittering of birds, to locate where the birds collect their drink. They also find water holes by watching the direction in which birds are flying, or by following animals' trails. Flocks of birds circling over one spot (unless they are vultures) usually indicate a drinking place in the desert.

Of course the water there is not always pure! A British airman who found such a water hole said there was such a stench of excreta that he was almost sick, but his thirst was much greater than his disgust. He had no iodine with him to disinfect the water, nor anything to make a fire with and boil it. But he drank it and was none the worse.

Dense clouds of flies swarming over a place in the desert show the Bedouins where there was water only a short while before; and they almost always find it worth digging there. With unerring instinct they also discover fairly large supplies of water either on the edge of a desert very near salt lakes or in the middle of deep dune valleys. The rain water collects there, seeps into the ground and settles between different layers of soil. If while digging they hit upon wet sand with a dry layer underneath it, that is a sign the water here has already drained off farther downhill or evaporated; in which case they start digging again in a lower-lying spot.

Almost every desert has wadis, where sometimes water is still found only a few feet under a surface which is apparently bone-dry. Of course there is often no more than a layer of mud left, but thirsty people have pressed it into a cloth and drunk the water unharmed. Africa's bushmen, however, dig a small hollow in the mud, stick a suction pipe into it, then suck the moisture out of the ground drop by drop; a grass-filter stops any sand getting into the bottom of the pipe. Water not needed at once is stored in blown-out ostrich eggs—in which quite a large amount of liquid can be carried.

If water tastes very "soapy" or salty, it may be poisonous. In the Gobi Desert, for instance, there are springs which contain alkali. In Arizona several springs containing arsenic are a special tourist attraction: no plants grow near them, and the skeletons of animals can be seen bleaching in the sun. In the pioneering days of the Wild West, Nevada's one waterplace had to be fenced off because it gave only hot water; the first settlers' thirsty oxen and horses drank there and burned their mouths. A spring in the Sahara contains so much chlorine that it corrodes clothes. The smell alone is enough to scare you off, as is the smell of a nearby sulphur spring.

But these poisonous springs are not nearly so common as the safe wells and cisterns to be found in most of the great deserts which nomads have always frequented. During the war the water from these saved the lives of many men in the Sahara, Libya, and Mesopotamia. In the Sahara there are hand-dug wells in deep valleys, at the foot of big dunes and in dry river beds; their water level is often as much as fifty or sixty feet below the ground. But in seasons of great drought these wells usually dry up altogether, so then the Bedouins depend chiefly on the cisterns, a remarkable system of trenches and tunnels dug by desert inhabitants in the course of many centuries. The water which oozes into the desert during occasional showers collects in these cisterns, and as they are underground, it does not evaporate easily; the system of trenches and tunnels often stretches for some miles through the desert, so a considerable amount of water will collect in it.

The building of a cistern usually started with a trench being dug leading from the bank of an old river bed or a depression into the open desert. This cut deeper and deeper into the sand, so that in the end it could no longer continue as an open trench but took the shape of a tunnel. When the light got too bad to go on with the tunnel, a new trench was started, and so on, until all the trenches were finally connected up by tunnels. The actual "catchment" is at their deepest places, often hewn into the rock, sometimes lined with boulders joined by mortar or the roots of desert plants. Occasionally steps lead down to the water, but as a rule there is only a rope ladder to climb down or a hauling rope with a leather bucket.

These remarkable reservoirs are to be found also in the deserts of Iraq and Iran, in Saudi Arabia and Morocco. In the Negev Desert a similar irrigation system was discovered only a few years ago, and is now to be put back in use again, like the aqueducts of ancient Mesopotamia, which once supplied forty million people (there are only five million living in the same area today). In Libya, too, reconditioned cisterns are once more in use, as they were two thousand years ago.

Most desert paths eventually lead to a cistern, and the cistern usually leads to an oasis. Where two paths meet, they form a sharp angle, which always points to the watering place. In the Sahara, however, even during the war, the exact position of most of the cisterns was a secret known only to the Bedouin tribes who used them. Since the campaigns in Africa, many of them have been marked by heaps of stones and entered on maps of the desert.

The cisterns hold thousands of gallons of water. It doesn't always taste very good, of course, being sometimes brackish or infused with minerals contained in the soil below. In South Arabia, for instance, it is mostly rust-brown and tastes of iron; in Ethiopia of magnesium; and in Syria there are some sulphurous cisterns. The look and taste of cistern water, however, have not worried the thirsty very much. A group of American airmen crossing the Sahara during the war, having discovered three pools at the base of such a cistern, even made their home in it and stayed the night there. They camped by the first pool, used the second for drinking water, the third for bathing. At night it became so cold in the cistern that they had to wrap up in their blankets. The next day, much refreshed, they laid out SOS signals on the surface—which were soon spotted by a search plane.

In the Australian bush (where conditions during the dry season are like those in the desert), the German airmen Bertram and Klausmann came upon a big pool with a rocky base. "We squatted in the water, and only had to bend a little and open our mouths. I had never imagined a man's body could take in such quantities of water. For hours we lay laughing and crying for joy, and drinking. . . ."

Whereas water is essential, we do not need solid food to anything like the same extent. People who have been stranded in the desert and suffered from terrible thirst, were often little affected by hunger. This is not surprising, since we know today that you can go for up to sixty days without solid food; but of course you *will* be tormented by hunger, accompanied by dizziness and fainting spells.

By the fourth day after their crash landing. Bertram and Klausmann were so weakened by heat and hunger that their hunt for a passing kangaroo was a pathetic failure. As Bertram wrote afterward: "The pistol was loaded, and rested on my left arm at the ready. I fired, the creature bounded off unscathed—and I sat dazed, inwardly crying with pain and dismay. I was too weak to stem the recoil. The pistol made a deep wound directly under my left eye . . ."

In twenty days they only caught a small fish and two lizards of finger length. "We are so weak it's an effort to stand up. You have to pull yourself up inch by inch on a piece of rock or a tree. Everything is black, and dances in front of the eyes. The stomach hurts, for some days it's been contracting in cramps . . ." After twenty-eight days they were "growing weaker every hour. If we want to get up, we have to prop each other. Everything is going round and round . . ."

Most people stranded in the desert try to assuage their hunger as soon as the problem of water supplies seems even partly solved. By so doing, they unwittingly break one of the basic rules laid down by survival experts: "If a survivor can get only a pint of water a day, he shouldn't eat anything at all. If the ration is up to seven pints a day, he can eat all food containing carbohydrates and fats (i.e. fruit, sweets, biscuits), but should not eat fish, meat, beans, cheese, etc. These contain proteins, and proteins require water for digestion; if there is none available, the water gets drawn from the tissues.

If there are ample supplies of water, you can eat as much as you like of any food. But in the true desert where nothing grows, it is just as hard to find solid food as a drop of water; much easier, on the other hand, is the finding of food on the edge of the desert, or where there is some vegetation. Airmen who had to come down on the desert in Tunisia, lived for days on alfalfa grass roots. An air crew who crashed in Ethiopia ate grass for days: raw, boiled, and roasted. Bertram and Klausmann tried leaves. "We only had to reach up and pull off the leaves of the tree in whose shade we were lying. Our cheek muscles were quite unused to chewing after twenty days' rest! Were these sun-roasted leaves good, did they taste nice? We didn't know, the sense of taste had gone. For hours we chewed . . ."

Many starving desert travelers have waited for game at a water hole, killed it, and often swallowed the meat raw. One party of American airmen lived for six days on raw gazelle meat. You might think that the meat of any dead animal would go bad at once; but the desert's great dryness stops the process of decomposition. The Bedouins exploit this fact by cutting game up into strips, wiping the meat dry, then burying it six to eight inches in the sand. There it shrinks to a sort of cured meat, which keeps up to three years. To make it edible, you simply soak it in water.

Starving men in the desert have also eaten birds. Two American airmen in Somaliland discovered an owl's nest, in which there were some nearly hatched eggs. Without hesitation they swallowed the eggs, embryos and all. Anyone disgusted by this had better not go to Thailand, where embryo chickens are a great delicacy, often offered to honored guests.

To lure birds, Bedouins kiss the backs of their hands with a light noise, which sounds like an animal lapping water. A party of American airmen who had come down in the desert made some bird-lime out of the sticky sap of a desert plant, and smeared it over a rock to catch birds. No birds were caught, but it shows the ingenious methods for getting food people will resort to.

It is extremely hard to catch birds without weapons, so that survivors often have to look for other, less appetizing forms of food. Another party of American airmen lived for days on overripe dates which had dropped off the trees and were crawling with maggots. The maggots were big, white, and juicy, but they tasted exactly like the dates. The airmen said afterward: "If you weren't directly looking out for them, you just didn't notice you were eating them."

There are lizards in most deserts, and they too can serve as food. A pilot who made a crash landing in Arizona killed some by throwing stones at them, then skinned them with a belt buckle, which he had sharpened on a rock; he ate them raw. Many survivors have eaten turtles, after first drinking their blood; others have eaten desert mice and rats. But trainees at survival schools are told to avoid rats' heads, since the masticators may be infected.

Other survivors have hunted insects. A young airman found dozens of dung beetles in the dung of other desert creatures; he pulled off the hard wings, and swallowed the soft, still writhing bodies. It is well known, of course, that for many Africans locusts are a delicacy. The Japanese have lately been canning locusts and exporting them to Western supermarkets, where they are in great demand.

The great dryness, heat, and barrenness are by no means the only dangers which people stranded in deserts have to face. The intense, blinding sunlight can lead to a sort of snow-blindness, produced by the sandy ground reflecting the short-wave ultraviolet rays. Slitted discs of cardboard have often served as an effective substitute for sunglasses.

Even the sand itself can be dangerous. Often it "gives" so much that walking in it becomes an immense labor. Trainees at survival schools are advised to pay special attention to the color of the sand: in Syria, for instance, it is the red sand which is soft, in southern Libya the black. It is this soft, fine sand which the desert wind blows into noses, ears, mouth, and eyes. One rescued pilot said that to anyone already suffering from dehydration each single grain will feel as big as a stone.

In a sandstorm, which may last several days, this is particularly troublesome; and the tongue and jaws will be completely parched by the hot air. The best protection against it, rescued pilots have found, is to dig a hole in the ground, cover it with a tarpaulin firmly fastened down at the sides, and crawl underneath. Bedouins squat down with their backs to the wind in the shelter of their recumbent camels, and try to sleep, waiting patiently till the storm is over.

Stories of people being buried alive by the *gibli* (sandstorm) are pure legend, however; for the wind blows the sand away as well as onto you. In the Sahara, the wrecks of aircraft from the war are still lying there just as if their crews had abandoned them only a few days before. In February 1962 a French patrol in the Sahara found near Reggane a big plane wrecked as long ago as 1933, with the pilot a few yards away in an old-fashioned-looking flying suit. The logbook was also found intact, showing that he was called William Newton, had been in the R.A.F., and was flying from Algiers to Gao on the Niger. The engine had failed over the desert, and he had made a crash landing with only slight injuries, and tried in vain to repair the wreck. After four days his water and food supplies were used up. He must have died about three days later, but the sand had buried neither him nor his aircraft; it was a ghostly picture indeed which faced the French patrol.

A sandstorm, of course, will often completely alter the outlines of the landscape, leaving valleys where there were dunes, and vice versa. So if before the storm you have given yourself an objective to make for, you may be lost without a compass, unless you have marked your direction with an arrow of stones, as instructors recommend; this will give you your bearings again.

Worse than the sandstorms are the insects. Although as a rule bleeding soon stops in the dry air, every scratch will at once attract big black flies. "No beast of prey," Bertram commented, "can be as dangerous as the flies and mosquitoes on Australia's northwest coast. . . . If you speak a few words, you get these pests in your mouth. They settle in the nose, the ears, and particularly in the corners of the eyes . . . It's torture for the nerves."

When he and Klausmann lost all their clothes escaping from crocodiles, the flies settled in hundreds on the festering wounds caused by stones and bushes. The two naked men buried themselves in the sand for protection against the night's cold and the mosquitoes. "But when we had heaped sand over our legs and the rest of our body with the right hand, it was impossible to get the right arm itself under the sand, and the mosquitoes sat in their

thousands on this unprotected arm. . . . For hours we endured
the torment. . . . Then we lost our nerve, threw off the sand,
jumped up and ran around yelling, thrashing about us to drive
away the swarms of mosquitoes. But that was impossible: they
settled on our bodies and in the festering wounds. Impossible to
escape from the danger. We had to go back into our 'graves.' "

In many deserts swarms of mosquitoes are driven far into the
waterless interior. In 1942 soldiers in the Libyan Desert sighted a
swarm of gnats "as dense as a sandstorm." The sandflies are even
worse: tiny but vicious, they get through the finest mosquito nets
and give their victims painful bites, which cause itching and even
fever. A party of survivors discovered that rubbing themselves
with chewed tobacco drove off the flies.

"These pests are at least real, and you can try to drive them
off," said a pilot after his rescue from the Sahara. "But twice I saw
mirages which almost sent me crazy. They kept moving farther
and farther on the horizon, the longer I was heading for them."

Such mirages occur through an optical illusion, caused by the
break in the light passing from a layer of thick cold air to one of
thin hot air. When the light reaches the latter, the sky is reflected,
so that it appears below the horizon like a lake with clear blue
water. What the thirsty traveler sees as ripples on the surface is really the flickering movement of the hot air over the desert sand.
Rocks appear in the reflection as towns, scrub as palm groves.
Less common are mirages which make objects up to sixty miles
off, such as an oasis, look as if they were quite near. For the
thirsty who hurry toward it, such a mirage literally vanishes in the
sand.

In view of all these hazards, it is not surprising that people
stranded in the desert have found that merely to keep going on
foot was the hardest part of their efforts to survive, next to the
water problem; and this even when they walked only at night.
Alfons Gabriel gives this account in his book *Die Wüsten der Erde*
(*The World's Deserts*):

"The desert can weigh on the lonely traveler like a nightmare.
In the *seghir* (flat but with undulations) small stones neatly distributed seem to extend to the end of the world. In the *hamada,* a
particularly unpleasant kind of desert, trying to make any head-

way is infinitely wearisome. No one who has encountered such a
Hell will ever forget it. Between the jagged (volcanic) black rock
fragments, it is impossible to keep to a definite direction. You
wander hither and thither according to how the fragments are
lying, wherever it looks as if there's a way through. Massive seas
of dune can also offer terrors enough . . . what a penance it is to
keep going! After panting up each dune, you see fresh 'waves'
from morning to evening. . . . The salt desert is worst of all. In
the Persian *kawir* a caravan exposed to sudden rain is lost, unless
it manages to reach firm ground very quickly. In other deserts
showers are the greatest boon, but there they are the worst enemy,
for in a few moments the ground is transformed into a ghastly
swamp. . . . Cases have been known where beasts and their bur-
dens had to be abandoned, while the men fought on alone through
the bog to escape with their bare lives."

After a crash landing during the war, some airmen made the
mistake of walking across crusted-over salt lakes. "After the first
hour," one of them reported afterward, "our boots fell off, cut to
shreds by the ground, corroded by the salt crystals. Our feet
became sore and burnt like fire. In the end we wrapped our shirts
around them, and hobbled on over the sandy ground." Another
pilot who ventured on to an apparently dried-up salt lake said: "I
went through the salt crust like thin ice. I had great difficulty in
saving myself from the whitish caustic mud."

"The surface of such salt deserts or salt lakes," says Gabriel, "is
full of humps and bulges riddled with tunnels and holes. The top
caves in under you, and you step into hollows the size of a big
fox's lair. . . . With incredible patience the camels of a caravan
make their way, although the ground is always caving in, causing
them to stumble. They keep their balance as best they can, their
feet bleed, and the caravan's trail is sprinkled with red."

Walking in dried-up river beds has proved equally dangerous
for desert travelers. These beds are usually stony, and during sudden showers at the edge of the desert, the rain water, instead of
sinking in, fast becomes a raging torrent, washing away everything
it meets. An eyewitness of this in the Mohave Desert said: "The
water rose furiously, carrying loose stones and rocks with it, and a
torrential river of mud was soon pouring towards the railroad. The
engine was overturned and washed away like a piece of wood. It

was found afterwards over a mile away, buried under rubble and stones."

Many survivors have made the mistake of taking off their boots when walking; then they couldn't put them on again after a rest, because their feet were so swollen. Others have cut holes into them to relieve their aching feet, but that only allowed sand and stones to get between soles and leather tops, causing them agonies of pain. Sweat sores shredded the skin down to the raw flesh, and complete rest was the only thing which would help them.

Another way in which people have very often gone wrong, is to abandon a wrecked plane or vehicle without leaving a note of the date and the direction they are taking, or signs en route to show their direction. Often they have not even had a compass, but simply walked off at random. If they didn't know how to get their bearings by the stars, this rash procedure usually proved downright suicidal. The desert as a rule looks monotonous in color and shape, with no landmarks to keep the eye on. In the great sand-flats of North Africa survivors have fought on through the sand for days, only to find in the end they had been going round in a large circle. Others again, in the clear desert air, have underrated by many miles the distance to an objective they had set themselves, such as the top of a hill: although it constantly looked within easy reach, it was really more than a day's walk away. So they would keep walking to a point of complete exhaustion, always hoping to be "there in a few minutes," instead of taking a regular rest every hour.

For all these reasons the experts at all the various survival schools repeatedly tell their trainees that in the desert you must never set off on foot from the scene of a crash, while any hope remains of a search party coming to look for you. If there *is* such hope, it is always better to stay by a wrecked vehicle, or make an emergency landing with your plane rather than bail out by parachute.

This advice is confirmed by both logic and experience. In the war some pilots landed in the Sahara behind the enemy lines as often as seven times during one flight, to repair damage to their planes, and "leapfrogged" back to their units. Others who fought in Africa say that only the wreck of their plane or vehicle saved them from certain death: during the day its shade gave them protection from the sun, and at night the bodywork gave protection against the raw cold. As a rule it contained more supplies of food and water than the crews could have carried along into the desert on foot. Again, a search party can more easily spot the wreck of a vehicle (including aircraft) than it can a single man or even a group, especially if the group is already some distance from the presumed scene of the crash. There have been cases where people spotted by search parties were so revived by supplies from the air that they left their wreck trying to walk out of the desert; they were never seen alive again.

Above all, survival experts say, distress signals can be given better, and at the crucial moment, if this is done from a permanent camp; and distress signals are as important as water supplies. If you can't attract the attention of search parties, you may just as much consider yourself dead as if you haven't any drinking water.

Very few servicemen stranded in the desert during the war were fortunate enough to be able to call for help by radio because their radios had usually been shot to pieces. Many pilots successfully used the landing searchlights or flares, to send out signals at night: in the dark desert nights these flashes could be seen more than eighty miles away. (Viryl Scott, for instance, whose story was given earlier in this chapter, could have dismounted his headlights and tried sending out distress signals with them during the night.)

After emergency landings pilots have soaked rubber tires, rubber boots, and flying suits in engine oil, so that they could light smoldering fires which would give off smoke visible from a long distance away. Those who bailed out, however, or left their aircraft after landing, had to be content with less effective aids. A German pilot arranged stones in the shape of an arrow, taking care that they would cast the maximum shadow, which could thus be seen from the air. A British pilot, with nothing but sand around him, used parachute panels to lay out big SOS signs. Both men were saved, although their chances of being rescued were smaller than if they had stayed by their aircraft.

One of the many incidents to prove this point is the story of the American bomber *Lady Be Good,* which in April 1943 disappeared without trace after a raid on Naples. The U. S. Air Force recorded crew and aircraft as missing. Sixteen years later, in May 1959, a party of British geologists discovered the wreck of a B-24 in the Libyan Desert, about four hundred miles south of Bengasi. It was the *Lady Be Good*.

It was almost undamaged, showing not a single bullet mark from machine gun or antiaircraft. The only things wrong were a busted cockpit, broken wings, and the landing gear still inside the fuselage. A crash landing? It really looked as if the pilot (Flying Officer William J. Hatton) had come down in a smooth belly landing only the week before. Certainly the fuel tanks were empty, but the radio compass was still working perfectly, and in the dry desert air even the sensitive wireless apparatus had remained intact. Several cans of drinking water were still on board; and some of the geologists drank black coffee from a water bottle, unspoiled, as if it had been made only a few days before. The flares too were intact. Medicine chests and their contents and oxygen tubes for high flying were also still serviceable. The crew's fur-lined flying suits hung in the fuselage in good condition. But there was no trace of the men who had once worn them.

A few days later a U. S. Air Force Investigation Committee landed with helicopters near the place of the accident. For weeks its members searched all round the *Lady Be Good* in a wide radius, without any success. Months passed. Then, early in 1960, they discovered strips of parachute some thirty miles from the plane. Following the direction in which these pointed, they discovered further strips marking a trail that was fifty miles long altogether. At the end of the trail lay the mummified bodies of five men in American flying suits. A few days later the remains of four other members of the crew were found. By the side of one of them (the co-pilot) there was a logbook, from which I quote some extracts (my comments in parentheses):

Sunday, April 4. (the day *Lady Be Good* took off for Italy from Soluch in Libya) Naples—28 planes—quite a party. Bearings lost on the return flight, no fuel left, bailed out, came down in the desert. (So the plane flew on unpiloted and made a smooth landing of its own accord.) 2 A.M. Nobody seriously hurt. We can't find John (Worovka, the gunner), but everyone else here. (The wind had carried the gunner so far with his parachute that he never found the others. His body, too, was discovered by the search party in 1960.)

Monday, April 5. Began walking, still no John, some of our rations eaten. (They were making for a chain of hills in the North, which they wrongly took for the Mediterranean coast.) Only half a flask of water, one screw-top full a day. Sun pretty hot. Cool breeze from the north-west. Very cold at night.

Tuesday, April 6. Rested at 11:30. Sun very hot, no breeze. Afternoon was Hell, no planes. Rested till 5. Walk and rest all night —15 minutes walk, 5 minutes rest.

Wednesday, April 7. Same as before. All of us much weaker, can't get very far. Pray all the time, hot as Hell again in the afternoon. Nobody can sleep, pains like gout (heat cramp).

Thursday, April 8. Hit on sand-dunes, feeling terrible, cool wind, but blows sand in our faces. All very weak now, think Sam and Moore have had it. Lamette can't see any more. The rest of us in bad shape too.

Friday, April 9. Shally, Rip and Moore split off from us and hope to find help. The rest very weak, eyes inflamed, couldn't go on walking. Still very little water . . .

Saturday, April 10. Still praying for help, nothing to be seen, only a few birds. (If they had walked only by night, they could have saved their strength and might now perhaps have followed the direction in which the birds were flying.) All very weak by now, and can't walk any more . . . (In a week they had covered seventy miles in difficult terrain. But the Mediterranean was still four hundred miles away.)

Sunday, April 11. Still waiting for help and praying. All very emaciated (through the dehydration), pain all over the body, could get on if we had water . . . Hope for help soon. No rest, still in the same place.

(Then the last entry, in shaky hand)

Monday, April 12. No more hope.

The Investigation Committee, which included survival experts, found unanimously that the crew of the *Lady Be Good* would probably have been rescued if they had made a crash landing, instead of bailing out: they could have radioed for help, and their water supply would have lasted till the rescue party arrived.

Chapter 4
Survival at Sea

To starve to death was impossible.
Thor Heyerdahl—the Kon Tiki *expedition*

"Although we were hungry, the possibility of our starving just didn't occur to us. The thing that finished us was the idea that we should soon die of thirst in the watery wastes of the Atlantic." These words are those of a naval cadet, Folkert Anders, one of the twelve rescued from the German windjammer *Pamir,* a naval training ship which sank on September 21, 1957, during Hurricane Carrie.

Like survivors in the desert, castaways at sea are tormented by the fear of dying of thirst. But for them the psychological burden involved is far greater, for instead of having dry sand all round, they have only "water, water everywhere, nor any drop to drink." They know that to drink this water might endanger their lives; so they have a double fight on their hands, against the elements and against the temptation to drink the salty water. Unless they can get some drinkable fluid, they usually succumb to this temptation. But before reaching that point, they will try all other possible ways of quenching their thirst.

In his book *Down in the Drink* Ralph Barker tells the story of five British airmen who came down in the Mediterranean during World War II, and drifted in a dinghy. For solid food they had some chocolate in tablet form; but there was nothing to drink. In his despair and raging thirst, one of the five (Irving) urinated in an empty chocolate tin and kept it by him, "sipping at it whenever he could bring himself to do it." The time on the dinghy had brought his bowel activity to a complete standstill, and he had no bowel movements for five days. (This is "normal" for a castaway, and a condition giving no cause for anxiety. There are attested cases in which castaways had had no bowel movements for up to thirty-nine days.) His urine had turned into a thick yellow liquid. It looked repulsive in the extreme, and tasted equally disgusting; but he mixed it with pieces of chocolate, and tried desperately to go on swallowing it. The others followed suit, but two of them, Bancroft and Bell, "were so revolted that they were unable to swallow anything and afterwards felt sick and disgusted." On the eighth day of their ordeal these two held a whispered conversation about one of their companions who seemed to be dying: "Do you think his blood would be any use to us?" Bancroft asked. "If he dies, we'll cut a vein in his leg at once."

Attempts to drink their own urine, or even a dead man's blood, are generally the last desperate measures castaways take before they start giving in to the temptation to drink salt water—like the first relapse of an alcoholic struggling to reform. The idea, which had perhaps occurred to them before, that sea water "may not be so dangerous after all," suddenly becomes overwhelming as was the case with an American pilot rescued three weeks after his crash into the sea:

"Before my water supply came to an end, I was already thinking of ways and means which would allow me to drink sea water. I tried to rig up a distilling apparatus out of two empty food cans, but without success. Then I tried to 'filter' some mouthfuls of salt water with disinfectant tablets, although I knew from the outset that it wouldn't be possible. But somehow I hoped for a miracle, which naturally did not take place. Then I mixed some iodine from my first-aid kit with some mouthfuls of water. It tasted horrible. I had very little idea of chemistry, but somehow hoped the iodine would separate the salt from the water. In the end I cut a small slit in the rubber stopper of my water bottle, and lowered it into the sea on a long fishing line. I imagined that the deeper water would contain less salt than on the surface because of the high pressure—it was much colder down there, I believed. I hoped

it would steam like a champagne bucket if I put a can of it out in
the sun. Then the steam would condense on the sides of the can,
as salt-free moisture." The report ends: "When they found me, I
was on the point of drinking salt water."

That man had indeed reached the stage when most castaways
begin to swallow the first drops of salt water. At first they only
rinse the mouth with it, but soon they are surreptitiously drinking
small quantities, to some extent "by accident."

To return to the five airmen mentioned above, Barker writes:
"All day they were tormented by raging thirst, which they tried to
relieve from time to time by gargling and dousing their heads in
sea water. They did not try too hard not to swallow just a little
water. They found it refreshing. Irving had at last given up trying
to swallow his own urine, and he followed their example, but
Robinson resolutely refused to take sea water and persisted in
drinking his urine. During the day they discovered small jelly sea
horses about the size of a dime resting on the sea foam, and they
put them on their tongues until they melted. They were fishy and
salty to the taste, seemed less salty than sea water, and the
cool moisture brought fleeting relief."

The result of such self-delusion is nearly always the same: with
every mouthful of salt water the thirst grows. The castaway then
tries to quench it by new mouth-rinsing. But once he has lost his
self-control, nothing in the world can stop him drinking himself to
death on salt water, and "salt-water death" is almost as frightful as
dying of thirst. The English doctor MacDonald Critchley in his
medical study, *Shipwreck Suvivors,* describes its different stages in
the sober language of a clinical report:

"When a thirst-crazed castaway drinks salt water, although he
quenches his thirst at that moment, it will return quite soon in
even more acute form, so that he is forced to drink again and
drink a lot. Then the victim becomes quiet and apathetic, with a
strange fixed and glassy expression in his eyes. The condition of
lips, mouth, and tongue deteriorates, and according to most
accounts the breath begins to stink. Within an hour or two delirium sets in, at first quiet and slight, then violent and uninhibited.
Slowly consciousness disappears: the colour of the face changes,
and froth appears at the corners of the mouth. Death comes

quietly—but the actual moment of death is often loud. Frequently the sufferer jumps overboard in his delirium and is lost."

Castaways' accounts of their shipmates' death from thirst are certainly horrifying, as in the *Pamir* tragedy quoted at the beginning of the chapter. In one of the lifeboats the cadets had a water barrel of wood, and the storm had knocked a leak in it. They couldn't dilute their sweetened condensed milk, but some of them drank it all the same, which of course only made their thirst worse. By tacit consent the cadets had recognized Martin Dummer, the cook, as their leader, and he warned them repeatedly, "Don't drink salt water." But two boys could not resist the temptation: these two were delirious by dawn the next day.

As Folkert Anders describes it: "Meine suddenly stood up. He thought he was on board the *Pamir*. 'Hey, where's the ship's doctor?' he asked all the boys. 'I looked for him in his cabin, but he wasn't there. I'm chilled to the bone. I shall complain. When you're sick like I am, you really ought to get a bed.'

"The other boys grabbed him, but Meine thrashed about with terrific strength, yelling: 'I'll make a complaint about you. You won't let me go to the doctor.' He called desperately for the first mate.

"After a while he seemed to calm down. But suddenly when no one was watching him, he jumped up shouting triumphantly, 'Now I'm going to the Captain,' laughed loudly, and jumped overboard, to disappear under the water. No one saw him again.

"Soon afterward it struck Peter Frederichs too. 'I'm just going below deck to see the steward,' he said, and stood up. 'I must get myself something to drink.' He bent down and started looking for the plugs. He thought he was in the *Pamir*'s washroom. He shouted desperately: 'Look, everything's under water here, we must take the plugs out so that it can drain off.' A few seconds later he jumped overboard."

Hans Georg Wirth, one of the boys sitting close to the edge of the lifeboat, grabbed for Frederichs' arm, but missed it. "At that moment I felt the touch of death," Wirth said afterward. Then Frederichs too disappeared—and there were only six of them left in the boat.

Suddenly one of them yelled "Land! Land!" and they all shouted the same. They even pointed out the cliffs on the shore and thought they could distinctly see a mountain and a town. Dummer was the only one who kept a clear head: he saw nothing. Racked with thirst, the rest had all fallen a victim to one boy's wish-fulfillment mirage.

Alcohol is sometimes mentioned as having saved castaways' lives, and in this case Dummer had taken a bottle of gin into the lifeboat with him, the contents of which he distributed equally. "Everyone got a mouthful," one of the rescued boys related. "But from fear the sea might tear the bottle away, Dummer took a mouthful himself, then pressed his lips over the lips of each of us in turn and poured the gin into our mouths. Just as he was going to take the last mouthful for himself, a wave tore the bottle out of his hand. He almost wept in frustration and despair." (According to American survival experts, however, alcohol has no place in a lifeboat: it can only lead to ill-considered actions and increase the danger.)

Some people have maintained in recent years that a castaway can satisfy his body's need for fluid by drinking a pint of salt water a day. One of the first to make this claim was the American Flight Lieutenant John Smith, who in July 1943 was shot down over the Pacific. In his tiny dinghy he drifted between Munda and Guadalcanal. It was almost unbearably hot. He hoped for a ship or a rescue plane, but no one seemed to have missed him. His mouth parched with thirst, he stared at the waves, and could hardly believe his eyes: a sea bird was bobbing on them—and drinking!

"It almost sent me crazy," he commented after his rescue. "It was just beyond me how this bird, a creature of flesh and blood like me, could drink sea water, and I couldn't." Unfortunately he did not say what sort of bird it was, but we know that albatrosses, for instance, except for occasional drops of dew, drink nothing but salt water; they reject the salt by a kind of filter arrangement in their nostrils. Smith reached for his pistol, took aim, and shot the bird. He fished it out of the water and began to dissect it like a zoologist. "I tried to follow the course the water must take from the beak through the alimentary tract. Eventually I discovered that a handful of fat was packed round the bird's intestine. Was that the 'filter' which allowed it to tolerate salt water? Perhaps I could make sea water drinkable by adding some of this fat?"

He experimented for a while in vain, and then made a discovery: whenever he drank a few mouthfuls of sea water, he felt sick. But the nausea disappeared if he afterward swallowed some of the bird fat. Finally he ate all he had left of the fat, "lining" his throat and stomach with it. "For five days afterwards, I drank two pints of salt water a day."

Twenty days after his crash he was picked up by a passing troopcarrier. He was in fairly good physical condition, and when he told his story, the doctors thought they were on to something sensational. But soon they came unanimously to a sobering conclusion: Smith had been saved not by the bird fat and salt water, but by two other factors. One was that before his crash he had drunk a great deal of water, saturating his cellular tissue, so that his water content stood at "normal" to "full." The other thing was that, on the fifth day of the "salt-water cure," there was a shower of rain. He drank as much fresh water as he could, thereby replenishing the amounts in the cellular tissue, which was beginning to dry up. But for that, he would have lasted out only a few days drinking salt water, with or without bird fat, and would have died in agony with all the symptoms of "salt-water poisoning" described by Critchley.

Another American, William Willis, who in 1954 crossed the Pacific on a large wooden raft, covering 6,700 miles, claimed afterward to have drunk about two pints of sea water a day—but then he had periodically supplemented this with fresh water.

In any case it is highly dangerous for a castaway to drink nothing but salt water. This can easily be appreciated if we consider the chemicophysical processes which go on in a man's body when he drinks sea water. With it he absorbs a certain quantity of dissolved salt, especially sodium chloride. But the human body needs very little salt, and has to get rid of any salt it has absorbed above this small amount. (That is why properly composed emergency rations for castaways should contain no salt.) The work of excreting superfluous salt from the body is done by the kidneys, which remove from the blood all waste products in the form of urine. For this the kidneys need water, at least a pint of water a day.

Assuming, then, that a castaway drinks a pint of sea water a day (which anyhow is all his stomach would tolerate), and does not supplement it with other, salt-free fluids; because of the dissolved salt in the sea water, this pint will give less than ten cubic inches of salt-free water, far too little to allow the kidneys to excrete the salt it has absorbed with the water. The kidneys react by taking from the body tissue the water reserves needed to form urine and excrete salt. (Smith noticed himself that he excreted more urine than he absorbed salt water, a clear sign that his kidneys had already broached his body's reserves of fresh water.)

If this fresh water in the body is not continually replenished, as occurs under normal conditions, the body begins literally to dry up from inside. The more salt water the castaway drinks, the faster this process takes place, with similar outward symptoms as when people die of thirst in the desert: dehydration of the skin, and its folds getting sore. Finally the kidneys are so full of salt that the effect is a fatal poisoning.

So if a castaway tries for more than ten days to satisfy his body's need for fluids exclusively by salt water, his chances of survival are nil. Any statements or suggestions to the contrary are wrong. Bombard quite realized this, but believed he could stretch his fresh-water supplies with some sea water, and keep his water economy balanced by drinking rain water and the body fluid of fishes. There have been experiments by the French Navy to test whether castaways short of fresh water can to a degree use salt water as a substitute; these experiments too have been unsuccessful.

Dr. Hans Lindemann, who since 1957 has crossed the South Atlantic in a canoe three times, doubted the effectiveness of Bombard's attempt to stretch his water supplies. On a trial voyage along the African coast, lasting only seventeen days, Lindemann noted the disadvantages of drinking salt water, though he only drank four glasses a day and was careful to drink fresh water as well. By the second day his feet were beginning to swell. "Gradually the swelling extended to my knees. Small blood vessels stood out on the skin of my feet, and when I pressed my thumb against my heel, it left a deep imprint. My ankles were hidden deep in swollen flesh. The nerve endings were no longer sensitive. Even massage didn't help." Yet on later voyages, when Lindemann drank no salt water, his legs were almost unaffected. His conclusions were as follows:

"I am firmly convinced that no one who wants to survive at sea should drink salt water. If there is enough fresh water on board, a small quantity of sea water may be drunk as a substitute for salt. That is all. Sea water can never replace fresh water. Should a castaway have milk or beer with him, he may count himself lucky; for both these fluids will give him the calories he needs. A practiced fisherman can get all the solid food he needs on a raft, but he must be careful to balance his intake with fluids. Only the eyes, blood, and fin-fluid of fishes gave me salt-free fluid. You need specially made presses to extract the fluid from the rest of a fish's body."

Some castaways in the war, however, managed to solve this problem by putting pieces of fish into a small linen "bag" (for instance the detached lining of a trouser pocket) and chewing it until they had squeezed every drop of precious fluid out of it; with bigger fish they would cut dents into the sides, which soon filled with fluid from the fish's lymphatic glands. "One can also press the juices out by twisting pieces of fish in a cloth, or, if the fish is large, cutting holes in its side, which soon become filled with ooze from the fish's lymphatic glands. It does not taste good if one has anything better to drink," says Thor Heyerdahl, "but the percentage of salt is so low that one's thirst is quenched."

But even expedients like these are taboo according to the American survival experts, who say: Never drink fishes' body fluid. Never drink urine. "And however desperate your thirst," they go on, "never, never drink salt water."

Without salt-free fluids a castaway at sea, as in the desert, has an expectation of life of eleven days at most. So, apart from the hope of land, or a ship or plane looking for him, he will be thinking night and day about the possibility of rain. By the ninth day of his ordeal even the most hardened agnostic, with sore lips and swollen tongue may find himself mumbling a prayer for rain.

Any castaway's life can be saved by "providential" rain: it is more important than all sources of solid food. Poon Lim, a Chinese sailor, drifted in the South Atlantic for one hundred and thirty-three days, almost four and a half months, and when rescued was scarcely suffering at all from dehydration.

Lim was a member of the crew of the SS *Ben Lomond,* which was sunk by a German submarine in the summer of 1942. He jumped into the sea with a life jacket and nothing else. After drifting on the waves for an hour, he discovered an unoccupied life-boat which had broken adrift from the sinking steamer. It carried food and water supplies for twenty-five men. Lim ate and drank moderate amounts, enough to keep his strength up. By using three and a half pints of water a day, he made the water supplies last fifty days. Meanwhile he collected every drop of rain in the empty food cans, set bait for and caught fish, ate seaweed and plankton. For the last eighty-three days he lived exclusively on rain and what the sea supplied. Then a Brazilian fishing boat found him and took him on board.

Bertram and Klausmann, after their crash landing on the shores of the Timor Sea, also hoped for rain and made appropriate preparations when the first storm clouds were gathering. "To the flat end of the wings we tied the fairings, long strips of metal which cover the gap between fuselage and wings. They were to carry every drop of water into empty film cartridges like a gutter. . . . We wait, trembling with excitement. Then the first drops come . . . and now its's raining. Wonderful! Eight to ten minutes . . . three cartridges of water . . . more than two gallons—and this is fresh water. Oh God!" (It was a pity they did not think of digging a hole on the beach near the water line, because brackish water fit for drinking would have collected in that hole, filtering through the sand.)

There are a great number of accounts of sea disasters referring to castaways who die despite plenty of rain. The reason for their death is that when rain comes, they have no containers to catch it in, and have to lap it up like animals. Or, if they think of catching the rain in a sail or a tarpaulin, they usually forget to wash this out in the sea first, so as to get rid of the salt crust and thus catch the rain water as salt-free as possible. Again, whether from panic or ignorance, scarcely any castaways think of cleaning the decks of their lifeboat or raft, in order to get rid of any pools of salt water; so the rain that falls there generally turns at once into a dirty or brackish mixture, in any case undrinkable.

Of course rain is a "gift from heaven," not something the casta-way can rely on. But industry has developed many devices for turning salt water into fresh by physical or chemical means, and every correctly equipped lifeboat will have one of the "watermakers" on board in due course. They will all be discussed in detail in a later chapter.

While the sea offers no direct substitute for salt-free fluids, it contains food in abundance for all castaways. Fishes, turtles, plankton, seaweed, and even sea birds will often parade past him within his reach, enough to sustain him for an unlimited period. However, the great majority of castaways do not realize this, and instead of looking for such food, they suffer agonies from hunger.

One of the most dreaded phenomena accompanying lack of food is scurvy, which, among other things, can cause teeth to become loose. Bertram and Klausmann found their teeth coming out after forty days fasting (although they were on a coast with plenty of fish). When their aboriginal rescuers gave them roast kangaroo meat, they couldn't chew it. The aborigines helped them by chewing up the meat first and then pushing it into the mouths of the exhausted men.

Scurvy, of course, is a vitamin deficiency. To overcome it, German prisoners of war captured after the fall of Stalingrad ate grass tips, flower blossoms, and leaves to quench their need of vitamins. The German doctor Hans Lindemann and his compatriot Wilfried Erdemann who singlehandedly sailed around the world in 1968 both took a good supply of onions aboard their vessels before they started out on their adventure. Onions, rich in vitamins, are an excellent protection against scurvy, and for that reason were also taken along by Columbus and his men when they started out to look for a sea route to India, only to discover America. The Koches, a married couple from Hamburg, West Germany, who returned in 1967 from a three-year sailing trip around the world, used vitamin pills and yeast whenever they were out of fresh fruit and vegetables.

If you are hungry, solid food, of course, is more important than vitamins—no matter what kind of food it may be. It is not surprising, then, that hunger among castaways has even led to cannibalism. For obvious reasons, those who survived by eating their companions have rarely talked about it. In the last century the crew of the American whaler *Essex,* lost in the Atlantic, ate each other almost to the last man. During World War II, there were plenty of cases where occupants of rafts or lifeboats ate the limbs of their companions who had died a natural death. In fact, it can probably be said that cannibalism among survivors of disasters has occured and is occurring more often than becomes officially known. The reason one does not hear about it more often is that those who finally get rescued are reluctant to talk about what kept them alive. A rare exception is the case of the Andes survivors, mentioned in the next chapter.

One of the most nightmarish castaway episodes of recent years took place early in 1953 near the Seychelles, a group of islands about a thousand miles off the coast of East Africa. Theodore Corgat was the owner of a boat called the *Mary Jeanne,* some thirty feet long, which was normally used as a ferry between ships at anchor and the various islands. At the beginning of February he hired it out to a party who wanted to go from the island of Praslin to Port Victoria on the island of Mahe, twenty miles away. He went on the trip himself with his fifteen-year-old son, Selby, and took an old sailor, Louis Laurence, to act as skipper. There were five other young men or boys and two women in the party. No one informed the harbor master at Praslin of their excursion.

Seven and a half miles from Port Victoria they began to have trouble with the old motor, a former car engine. It was impossible to get it out of second gear, in which the motor simply drank gasoline. Two and a half miles from their destination they were entirely out of gas. Confident that they would soon be found, they dropped anchor and waited. That night there was a storm, the anchor chain tore loose, and the *Mary Jeanne* began to drift. The next day, beneath a merciless equatorial sun, she drifted past Mahe, out into the open sea. The ten people on board had hardly anything to eat, and only nine pints of drinking water. The water was soon used up, and within ten days the food too. They still hoped to be rescued, but in fact a search for the missing boat had been abandoned after a few days.

Meanwhile twelve days passed. Most of the time the two women lay sweltering in the cabin below deck. On the thirteenth day it rained. The castaways managed to collect some twenty gallons of water in various containers, and this gave them new strength. They tried once to catch fish with a piece of bent wire and later on to harpoon them with a "homemade" spear. But after failing in their first attempts, they gave up. On the fifteenth day a flying fish landed on deck. It was divided between the two women, who ate it raw.

This did not help much, and their strength waned daily. They went without food till the thirty-third day, when a bird alighted on the deck. One of the men harpooned it, and cut it into ten parts. Two days later they caught two more birds, drank the blood while it was still warm, and ate up every bit of flesh. (If they had left some of the gut, they could have used it as bait for fishes.)

The sun blackened their bodies. The skin hung dry and loose round their emaciated limbs. On the thirty-sixth day, they sighted an island, but wind and current carried them past it. Losing heart and hope, they lay down to die. Then they caught two more birds, and again they sighted land, but again the wind carried them away from it. On March 11 one of the women died, and a little later, on the forty-third day, the other. On the fiftieth, the fifty-second, and the fifty-fourth day, three of the men died. Sharks fed on the bodies thrown overboard. (Macabre as it may sound, the *Mary Jeanne*'s last passengers might have used the bodies as bait to try to catch a shark.)

On the sixty-second day a fourth man died, his body burned black by the sun. There was suspicion among the four survivors that he had been "finished off" by one of them to provide food. Laurence, the captain, suddenly tore off his clothes, yelled: "I'm burning, I'm burning!" jumped overboard, and drowned. Eight days later Corgat died. Although unable to stand or sit, and suffering from acute abdominal bleeding, he kept up a logbook right to the end: its last entry is about his son Selby's condition. Corgat's body rotted on deck, Selby and Antoine Vidot (aged twenty) being too weak to throw it overboard.

On the seventy-fourth day, Selby and Vidot heard a ship's siren. They were too ill to shout for help. Just as the ship, an Italian tanker, was going to move off, Vidot half rose, with a terrific effort. He was seen, and the two of them were rescued, the only survivors.

Unlike the *Mary Jeanne* passengers, many castaways in an apparently hopeless situation have tried to get food out of the sea. It is difficult, of course, without the right equipment, although Barker in *Down in the Drink* speaks of "ditched" airmen who have shot sea birds with pistols: but they must have been master shots to have done this from a swaying dinghy. Birds can drive a man on a small boat to desperation. Many of them settle on the boat's side, tired after a long flight. Often they seem almost tame, so temptingly near do they come. But anyone who has tried to catch a bird can imagine how hard it must be for a weakened castaway, especially when a catch may be literally a matter of life and death. People on a lifeboat will scarcely ever have the patience to sit quietly and wait until the bird has folded its wings. Even then it is no good making a grab unless the bird is within reach.

Bombard tells of how, on a day which happened to be his twenty-eighth birthday, a big bird, a shearwater, pounced on a piece of flying fish in the hook of his homemade fishing line. "I pulled him slowly inboard . . . No sooner did I have him in the dinghy than he seemed to have an attack of seasickness, vomiting all over the deck. The creature was only half-conscious, and with a slight feeling of repugnance I wrung his neck . . . My strong advice to those who catch a sea bird is not to pluck it but to skin it, as the skin is very rich in fat. I cut my shearwater in two, ate one half immediately, and let the other dry in the sun. But I was disillusioned if I thought my birthday dinner was going to give me any respite from my imposed diet. The flesh was excellent, but it had an undeniable taste of fish."

During the war, the American long-distance runner, Louis Zamperini, who drifted in the Pacific for forty-seven days in a dinghy, lived off an albatross, small birds, fishes, and the liver of a small shark. Then he was rescued by Japanese sailors and was made a prisoner-of-war. Another castaway in the war succeeded in catching nine sea birds, not only enough to live on, but also to make from the feathers a pair of ear protectors, a hat, and ankle and foot protectors against the sun.

Turtles are as hard to catch as birds. Their liver and fat are edible and their tough muscles can at least be chewed. To quote again from *Down in the Drink*, "On the morning of the sixth day Bancroft pointed excitedly to a school of turtles which splashed within a few yards of the dinghy. Each man drew his revolver, and they began taking pot shots at the turtles, but all the guns had rusted up except Bell's. Bancroft was acknowledged to be the best shot, and he borrowed Bell's gun, but although he fired round after round the turtles seemed impervious to gunfire."

To be sure of killing a giant turtle, you have to shoot it in the head. If you have no firearm, you must try to cut through its neck with a knife, a hard task for a castaway in a weak condition; but some have done it. In June 1972, for instance, a forty-eight-year-old Englishman by the name of Dougal Robertson, his wife, three sons, and a male passenger were en route from the Galapagos Islands to the Marquesas with their thirty-six foot schooner *Lucette*. Two hundred miles off the Galapagos their yacht was struck and sunk by a group of whales. After an ordeal of thirty-eight days the Robertsons were picked up by a Japanese trawler.

One of their food supplies were turtles which Robertson caught barehanded during the many days at sea. After his rescue he told reporters: "One morning we awoke by pulls and tugs, a whole series of them. Looking out of the aft plastic window of our Elliot-Island [a rescue device], we saw the head of a giant turtle. The animal's legs were caught in the rope of our sea anchor."

Tying the rope to one of the turtle's hind legs, the survivors managed to pull the hundred-pound animal aboard the dinghy, rolling the turtle on its back. Grasping the head, they cut through the throat with a sharp knife.

"It took many hours to loosen the shell from the meat," Robertson reported later, "but then we had a great supply. Inside the body we found about one hundred eggs—delicious for hungry survivors."

In one case, at least, a turtle was not used for food but served as a life raft. This is what officers of the Philippine navy vessel *Kalantaio* reported in June 1974, anyway. The *Kalantaio* had been searching for survivors of a capsized ferryboat which had sunk on June 2 about six hundred miles off Manila. "On the second day of the search all of us aboard the *Kalantaio* saw a woman drifting dead ahead. She was clinging to something that looked like a big oil barrel. We threw her a life belt, and when she grasped it, the barrel went under. It was a giant turtle." The woman, as it turned out later, was fifty-two-year-old Candelaria Villanueva, and she claimed that she had been clinging to the turtle ever since the sinking of the ferryboat.

Sometimes, however, the efforts of castaways to get food from the sea without proper fishing gear are tragic-comic indeed. In June 1932, Stanley Hausner, an American transatlantic pilot on a nonstop flight from New Jersey to Warsaw, had to ditch his plane some distance off the coast of Portugal. The plane was fully fueled, but Hausner had no food or drinking water on board. In his desperation he bent the needle of his compass into a fishhook, and tied it to a line he had made out of his boot laces; then he peeled pieces of skin off his fingers and used them as bait. But he did not catch any fish! After eight days at sea he was rescued by a British tanker, in a very weak condition.

Some castaways have even developed the ability to catch by hand fishes which were swimming close to the side of their boat. Others have fed on half-digested fishes found in the belly of a bigger fish they have caught. Others again have held the barrel of a pistol under water and fired: the blast stunned some of the fishes swimming near, which they could then pick up without difficulty. Pacific Islanders who have managed to catch a remora fish alive use it as a fishhook, tying a line round its tail and then letting it swim again. The remora has a flat head on which there is a sucking disk. It makes confidently for the first large fish it meets, and attaches itself so firmly to this that with any luck both fishes can be pulled out of the water on the line.

Castaways have made fishhooks out of all sorts of unlikely "spare parts"—needles and pencil clips, shoe nails, and pocket knives, even bones of fish and birds—and their ingenuity has often been rewarded. They have made lines from shoelaces or even thread taken from the seams of their clothes. It is amazing how much some people's talent for improvisation is stimulated by hunger and adversity. Some American airmen who came down in the Pacific made little metal triangles out of the tops of food cans, wrapped some bait around them, put them out on a line, and caught several birds. Some castaways have succeeded in shaking shrimps and other small fishes out of seaweed drifting past them.

In the summer of 1962, nine men started out from the Spanish port of Palos in a newly built caravel, *Nina II,* for an Atlantic crossing to San Salvador, in imitation of Columbus. After they had covered a third of the distance, their supplies of food were already running short, and they took seventy-seven days to reach San Salvador, twice as long as Columbus had done. But they survived the last days with food supplies from the sea, eating seaweed, either raw or mixed with vinegar and oil, and catching fish—not many, but enough to satisfy the most acute pangs of hunger.

These are only a few examples to prove the point Bombard was first to make, and then successfully apply, that the sea will provide enough food for a castaway to live on indefinitely, including the necessary vitamins. The fish he caught contained the precious proteins and fat needed by the body, plus vitamins A, D (in cod-liver oil), B1 and B2. The plankton contained vitamin C, and sugar. Consequently Bombard reached his destination alive, even if in a weakened condition.

Lindemann too subsisted chiefly on food supplied by the sea; although (like Columbus before him) he took raw onions on his Atlantic crossings as a precaution against scurvy, and ate one every day: onions contain more vitamins than any other vegetable. On his first crossing he lost only twelve pounds in weight, which he attributed to the fact that he often had fish to eat. In fact, he and Bombard both went well-equipped on their solitary expeditions because they had the key to the ocean's "larder," fishing gear and a plankton net, as well as a knowledge of what the "larder" holds. Every castaway should have this key; indeed the idea that all lifeboats should be fitted out with fishing gear and harpoons was put forward by Alain Gerveault, who in 1923 sailed alone from Gibraltar to New York, and more recently by Jacques Yves-Cousteau, the famous deep-sea explorer.

While many castaways today still have to use parachute silk, mosquito nets or underwear instead of plankton nets, the *Kon Tiki* expedition (traveling by raft from Peru to Polynesia) made a point of taking such a net along. Thor Heyerdahl writes:

"The net was a silk net with almost 3,000 meshes per square inch. It was sewn in the shape of a funnel with a circular mouth behind an iron ring, 18 inches across, and was towed behind the raft . . . Where the cold Humboldt Current turned west of the Equator, we could pour several pounds of plankton porridge out of the bag every few hours . . . bad as it smelt, it tasted correspondingly good, if one just plucked up courage and put a spoonful of the stuff into one's mouth. If this consisted of many dwarf shrimps, it tasted like shrimp paste, lobster or crab. And if it was mostly deep-sea fish ova, it tasted like caviar, and now and then

like oysters . . . 'Snags' in the dish were single jelly-like coelen-
terates like glass balloons and jellyfish about half an inch long.
These were bitter and had to be thrown away. Otherwise everything could be eaten, either as it was, or cooked in fresh water as
purée or soup. Tastes differ. Two men on board thought the
plankton was quite good, and for two the sight of it was more than
enough. From a nutrition standpoint, plankton stands on a level
with the larger shellfish, and spiced and properly prepared it can
certainly be a first-class dish for all who like marine food. These
small organisms contain enough calories, as has been proved by
the blue whale, which is the largest animal in the world, and yet
lives on plankton."

Plankton, of course, is not found in all seas. Often it only rises
to the surface at night, and efforts to fish it out by day are wasted.
Those taking part in the *Nina II* expedition mistakenly took tiny
jellyfish for plankton. "After a few moments," reported Robert
Marx, one of the expedition members, "José said his tongue was
burning. Michel also complained of a sharp, stinging sensation,
ran to the side, and vomited. Then I got it too, feeling as if I had
eaten the strongest Mexican pepper."

Nor are there fish in all seas; yet experience shows that a castaway will always find enough to eat if he knows what to do. Thor
Heyerdahl notes: "Scarcely a day passed on our whole voyage on
which fish were not swimming round the raft and could not be easily caught . . . it even happened that large bonitos, delicious eating, were washed aboard with the masses of water that came from
astern, and lay kicking on the raft, when the water had vanished
down between the logs . . . To starve to death was impossible."

Sometimes, like the *Kon Tiki* crew, castaways have had the
good luck to get fish jumping "right into their hands"—the flying
fish which skim over the water at night, and may land by chance
on the deck of a lifeboat. The seafarers of past centuries called
them "manna from the sea." A sailor drifting in the Pacific during
World War II said after his rescue that from some distance away
he had seen a lot of fish jumping over the waves. "Some bigger fish
seemed to be after them. I rowed quickly towards the place, hoping that one of them would land on my dinghy—and it did."
(William Willis too found many flying fish on his raft, and
"feasted on them. Their flesh is tender and not as firm as that of

larger fish. They are six to eight inches long, and ten or twelve of them made a good meal. On the *Kon Tiki* "an ordinary day began with the last night watch shaking some life into the cook, who crawled out sleepily onto the dewy deck in the morning sun, and began to gather flying fish . . . There were often half a dozen or more. One morning we found twenty-six fat flying fish on the raft."

Following the reports by castaways of such "catches," the U. S. Navy started some interesting experiments on the collecting of flying fish. As a result, trainees at survival schools are advised in case of a shipwreck to spread out light-colored sails or clothes on the lifeboat, and at night either to shine torches on them or turn them toward the moon. The reflected light really does attract flying fish to them. After the jump they hit the canvas and drop stunned onto the deck, where the castaway has only to collect them.

Instead of eating all caught fish at once, a castaway should gut them, cut them into strips, and dry them on deck in the daytime; then he can keep a store of fish over a long period, and also use some pieces as bait for bigger fish. (This was, in fact, done by many airmen who came down on the water.) It is a bit unfortunate, of course, if instead of a nice ten-pounder some dolphin or swordfish comes on the line: with its hard skull, and rough skin, a big fellow like this can do serious damage to the lifeboat, and even overturn it, unless the line is cut at once or else the castaway manages to finish him off with a well-aimed shot or a powerful blow on the head.

Many castaways are frightened of unfamiliar big fish or mammals. They refrain from any attempt at fishing, thereby losing the chance of catching smaller fish, and their fear may also make them panic or lose their heads. A pilot drifting in a dinghy after ditching his plane, said of his encounter with a whale: "The sight of the enormous creature, exhaling with its long-drawn-out roaring bellow, gave me a terrible fright. When it beat its tail on the waves, it sounded like waves thundering over great breakwaters. I wondered whether to shoot at it. Then I decided to plug my ears with my fingers, and not look at it any more." Another pilot who heard the same noise at night took it for the waves breaking on an island. Thinking he was near land, he was on the point of jumping

into the water to swim to it, with the dinghy in tow. At the last
moment he saw the spray of the whale's breath.

Dougal Robertson, mentioned earlier, reported of his encounter
with killer whales: "Several bumps of unbelievable force struck
the ship. I lost all solid ground under my feet and was thrown
against the cabin wall. At the same time I heard the sound of
splintering wood and water rushing in. Through the earsplitting
noise, as if coming from a distance, I heard the desperate cries of
my wife from the cockpit." The boat sank within minutes after the
whale attack. Douglas, the oldest boy, recalled later: "There were
twenty of them, of different sizes. Three attacked simultaneously."

Some of these killer whales weigh up to three tons, and if they
attack they do it with a speed of up to thirty knots—like a ramrod.
No wooden vessel of medium size could resist such an impact.

Castaways, however, are usually left alone by whales and
dolphins. They must beware of sharks much more, and they also
must beware of eating fish that are poisonous. Of all the Japanese
airmen who came down in the Pacific during World War II, seven
hundred died from eating poisonous fish—and not from thirst,
hunger, or exhaustion. Between 1953 and 1958 such fish caused
acute poisoning in forty thousand people in the Western Pacific,
the symptoms being digestive disturbances such as nausea, diarrhea, and vomiting.

Many of these fish carry their poison only in the internal organs,
the gut, and above all, the roe. With others it is the flesh that is
dangerous to eat. Unfortunately there is even today no certain
method of telling beforehand whether a fish is poisonous or not—
unless you have the same sort of grounding as an expert
mushroom picker. Moreover, there are species which are sometimes edible and sometimes not, depending on the habitat or the
size. For instance, castaways have often eaten small barracudas
(up to three feet long), without aftereffects, whereas the flesh of
larger specimens may cause serious digestive troubles.

Survival experts try to give their trainees a few basic rules on
the subject: poisonous fish generally look very ugly, with deep-set
eyes, a small mouth like a parrot's beak, slimy gills, a ball- or box-
shaped body, hard scales, dangerous-looking prickles, or loose
whitish skin. Their ventral fins are stunted or completely missing.
Their flesh often has a repulsive odor, and if you press on it, the

dent remains for some time, as it does if you press on the legs of people suffering from leprosy or dropsy.

We do not yet know why these fish are poisonous. Perhaps they feed on a kind of algae which contain certain toxins. It is no good cooking such a fish, although its poison is soluble in water. To make it anywhere near edible, you would have to cut it into strips and soak them several times in fresh water.

There is one comfort for castaways: all fish to be found in the open sea are edible, and all poisonous fish live near islands and in tropical lagoons. The only exception is the mackerel-like oil fish, highly poisonous, and inhabiting the open sea as well, at a depth of between 200 and 400 fathoms.

Sharks, on the other hand, are to be found in all seas, bays, and river mouths. Many keep far below the surface, but others only just below, showing their terrifying dorsal fins. There are sharks in the Arctic and the Antarctic, in temperate zones and in the tropics, and there are sharks which (like tramp steamers) travel through all seas. They are always on the lookout for prey, and will avidly investigate any drifting object, even plastic nose cones of American rockets which come down off Florida.

Their monstrous greed is best illustrated by various fishermen's tales: they caught sharks, gutted them, threw sharks and entrails overboard; whereupon the sharks, already in their death throes, pounced on their own entrails and swallowed them greedily.

But although there are about 250 species of shark, very few of these—not even a dozen—are the "man-eating" variety. Those that are, however, are so formidable that a castaway may justifiably take avoiding action with any shark, rather than wait to find out whether it is the harmless kind or not! The common blue shark, for instance, is an extremely serious hazard on and near Australian bathing beaches, and every other bather attacked by sharks dies from injuries sustained.

Then there is the dreaded great white shark, infinitely voracious and also unpredictable. The movie *Jaws,* after Peter Benchley's novel of the same title, filmed in 1974, gives a true and frightening idea of how terrible an attack of a "Great White" can be. Sometimes these sharks will circle round a swimmer in shoals before attacking him; at other times they will suddenly appear out of nowhere, pounce on their victim in a flash, and vanish again just as swiftly. Their acute sense of smell leads them unerringly toward the slightest trace of blood, or the vomit of seasick castaways. They are attracted even more quickly by the violent jerks of fish on the hook, another shark that has been injured, or a drowning man. And all the sharks anywhere near will immediately be drawn to the place where one shark has found something edible.

Benchley's novel certainly is no exaggeration. The year it was published, several tourists at various resort places again became victims of sharks: in Israel's Gulf of Eilat (Akaba) a twenty-year-old medical student from Germany, Beatrice Aronowixz, was severely injured by a shark which even attacked the rescue boat. And on the Adriatic Coast, only 150 yards from shore, twenty-one-year-old Rolf Schneider, also from Germany, was mangled by a shark.

In August 1960 a ship capsized in the mouth of the Komati River in Mozambique. Shoals of sharks swam up and caused a terrible bloodbath among the passengers struggling for their lives: in very quick time the sharks had mangled and dismembered forty-six people. Only three men got safely to shore.

During World War II, an American pilot was "down in the drink" with two other airmen off the coast of South America. After five hours one of these two died of exhaustion, and the pilot swam on, pushing the corpse ahead of him. Suddenly something tugged at it. The corpse ahead of him sank under the water and did not come up again. The two survivors swam on, but after a few hours the second man died. The pilot now pushed that body ahead of him. Meanwhile the moon had come up, and in the pale light he suddenly saw the dorsal fins of a great many sharks, which were circling around him. Again something tugged at the body. It went under for a short time, then came up again, but minus its feet. In horror the swimmer turned it round and caught it by the shoulders. The body immediately disappeared once more, then again and again. The sharks nibbled it up right to the shoulders. When dawn was breaking, they began to attack the pilot himself, but he saw he was now very near the shore. Yelling and thrashing around, he reached the coast unscathed.

A big shark can easily bite off the limbs of a grown man or tear great lumps out of his body. The bellies of some captured white sharks (many of which weighed up to 7,000 pounds, and reached a record length of thirty-six feet) were found to contain other sharks of four to seven feet in length, a twenty-five-pound sea lion, turtles, and the flesh of horses, pigs, lambs, and even a sled dog complete with harness.

A shark's bite leaves a wound shaped like a half-moon. The bite is very clean-cut, as if done with a line cutter, and in the first moment painless. One story which illustrates this was told by an American naval officer after his rescue from a battle with a shark in the waters round Guadalcanal.

After his destroyer had been sunk, he had drifted for twelve hours, when suddenly "I felt my left foot itching. I lifted it up out of the water. It was streaming with blood. I held my head under water, and then I saw the shark coming after me. I thrashed wildly about me, as the shark swam past, very close to me. Then it turned and came back. Again it was making straight for me. I clenched my first and punched it on the jaw with all my strength. It turned away—but I saw it had torn off a piece of my left hand. Again it swept up to me, again I pummeled its eyes and nose with my fist. When it turned away I found it had mangled my left arm. My heel had gone too. At that moment a lifeboat came toward me. I waved in excitement—and forgot the shark. It bit a piece out of my hip and exposed the hipbone. Then I was pulled into the boat . . ."

This story has been reported by Dr. George A. Llano, a scientist who developed survival equipment for the U. S. Air Force during the war: he thinks it is significant that the victim of the shark's attack was wearing no trousers, shoes, or socks. For experience shows that sharks first mangle parts of the body which are not covered. Perhaps they are frightened off by the darker color of the clothing, or they may see the lighter color of the skin from farther away. It is thought that they don't like blue, and the slave-traders of past centuries believed that no shark would attack a Negro. Even today, West Indians dye the light skin of their palms and soles a darker color, before they go fishing in shark-infested waters. This does not mean, of course, that fully clothed swimmers are immune from attacks by sharks—there are plenty of examples to the contrary; but in these cases the sharks seem at least to take some time before they dare attack.

In the summer of 1974, a private yacht sank during a storm

thirty-five miles off the Florida coast. Skipper Edward Horn, his wife Dianne, and their five children were clinging to life belts and to each other while the storm slowly subsided. Fortunately, Horn had been able to send out a "Mayday" signal before his yacht had sunk. Still, it was thirteen endless hours before a search plane spotted the seven persons and could direct a nearby fishing trawler to the scene.

It was then that the first sharks appeared, first circling the survivors at close distance. Ten-year-old Billy thought they were porpoises—until the first monster attacked: with one bite, it ripped the boy's leg wide open and bit off both his hands. By the time the trawler had arrived, the scene was swarming with sharks. The Horn family was finally dragged out of the water, but for Billy and his brother Edward, three, who died of exposure, all help had come too late.

The Horns had to fight the sharks for three to four hours. To them even minutes among the sharks must have seemed like an eternity. Still, other survivers had suffered even more. The longest time on record for people to hold out against attacking sharks is forty-two hours. It was a group of eight shipwrecked sailors who were adrift in the Pacific during World War II. Joining arms and swimming back to back, watching the sharks' movements, they managed to shoo them away by letting out shrill cries and flailing the water with their legs—until help finally arrived.

Sharks do not, however, confine their attentions to people in the water; they often attack castaways in their lifeboats. An American pilot, drifting in his dinghy in St. George's Channel between New Britain and New Ireland, had a sort of duel with a shark, which started prodding the dinghy with its snout. "I held my .45 (pistol) about six inches from its skull and pressed the trigger, but the pistol didn't fire—it had rusted up. The shark now really became mad (probably because it had smelled me), and attacked my dinghy from beneath, plunging us both under water. Then it came up again, and attacked me several times. With the butt of my pistol, I hit it in the eye, and on its hard skull. The blow flattened a steel ring on the pistol. Finally I got hold of the bag with the signaling dye, threw it in the shark's eyes, and it moved off. The battle had lasted about ten minutes. My dinghy sustained eighteen tears and holes, some quite extensive."

What about the common saying that even attacking sharks are cowards? Amateur divers often maintain that you only have to swim up to one, yell at it and show it you are not afraid—and it will leave you alone. Well, one cannot generalize from the experience of a few divers, although this was a mistake made by survival experts at the beginning of the war, when they told sailors and airmen about sharks being "harmless." Admittedly, in comparison with the number of castaways, there are very few cases known of people being attacked by sharks. Out of 2,500 reports from American survivors afloat, only thirty-eight refer to meeting sharks, and only twelve of those mention injuries. As against that, we still do not know how many castaways really fell victim to the sharks, since dead men tell no tales. Certainly, when the *Nova Scotia* was torpedoed during World War II off the coast of South Africa, many of the thousand and more sailors who died were killed by sharks. These were found by rescue ships the next morning, drifting in their life jackets, their legs bitten off.

At any rate, it is generally established today that sharks are a serious menace to castaways. Almost every year, a new research program is started somewhere in the world by institutions or individuals in order to find some sort of effective antishark weapon. A later chapter will deal with that subject in more detail.

Next to sharks and whales another dangerous sea creature can be lethal or at least highly dangerous to any survivor who decides to take a quick swim beside his raft or dinghy. Although it looks harmless and to some may even appear beautful, the Portuguese man-of-war is one of Atlantic's smallest and at the same time most poisonous monsters. When Thor Heyerdahl crossed the Atlantic in 1969 in *"Ra I,"* a replica of an ancient Egyptian papyrus boat, one of his crew members out for a swim became entangled in the stinging filaments of a man-of-war. Dragged into the cabin, the man was already in a coma and needed cardiac stimulants. Ammonia, the only remedy that helps to neutralize the caustic acid emitted by the filaments of that jellyfish, was not aboard. So the ship's doctor asked the crew to urinate into a container. "Urine is full of ammonia," he said, and for the next two hours the poor patient was massaged with a rag dipped into the urine until the convulsions finally stopped and he fell asleep. The red sting marks on his body were like welts, and it took him more than twenty-four hours to recover.

So the castaway at sea is beset with danger of all kinds. Surrounded by water he may die of thirst, and he may starve drifting over the world's greatest "larder." He may be killed or horribly mangled by sharks, often within sight of land and safety.

Yet all these dangers, however commonly they occur, are of secondary importance compared with the danger of death from exposure: exposure to wind and waves, heat, cold and damp, and all their attendant physical stresses when people are afloat in a small craft tossing on the ocean. A castaway's powers of resistance are weakened anyhow by fear, nerve-strain and his struggles at the time of the actual shipwreck or ditching. Those powers are reduced still more, and still more rapidly, by exposure.

Madden, an American, whose story is mentioned in various brochures of official survival literature, recalls how on the tenth day in a dinghy after his shipwreck in World War II he was so weak, despite supplies of water and food, that he could only work the bilge pump ten times an hour. During the war an aircraft carrying U. S. Air Force General Nathan F. Twining was ditched in the Pacific. Six days afterward the seventeen men on two dinghies had a sack of food dropped for them by a search plane, which then came down in the water near them. "But we couldn't even paddle the three yards to the rescue plane." When they were put down on land a little later, they were too weak to walk, too weak to eat without assistance. So it is no exaggeration to say that after a few days or even hours a castaway may be lying in his lifeboat completely helpless.

Many castaways have fallen over the side of their lifeboat or raft, and were then too weak to swim back and climb on again. Often they were in a strong current which carried the craft away from them too fast to catch up—like a bather chasing a ball in the sea which is carried away from him by wind and waves.

Willis describes how, meeting a shark, he fell off his raft while fishing and was soon sixteen yards astern of it. He knew that however hard he swam he could never catch up. Luckily he found the fishing line wrapped round his arm; its other end was tied to the raft. Hand over hand he pulled himself along the line to the raft, and at last "made it" with great difficulty. He remembered how in

New York he had promised his wife "to keep a rope or two trailing from the raft at all times. If I had, it would have been an easy matter to pull myself in on a line, especially with knots every foot or so. But I'd just never got around to doing it.

Several members of the *Kon Tiki* expedition were nearly lost at sea through similar carelessness. To have a look at their raft from a distance, they had climbed into a small dinghy, forgetting that it would be carried away from the raft by wind and current. Paddling desperately, they at last managed to get back to the raft. "From that day," writes Heyerdahl, "it was strictly forbidden to go out in the rubber dinghy without having a long line made fast to the bows, so that those who remained on board could haul the dinghy in if necessary. We never went far away from the raft, therefore, except when the wind was light and the Pacific curving in a gentle swell." And during his later *Ra* expeditions, lifelines were mandatory for every crew member.

Unless castaways tie their rafts together, they are almost invariably parted. If they do keep together, they are likely to have a much better chance of surviving; and the same goes for those swimming in their life jackets, if they link arms and form a circle. For one thing, it will help to keep the weaker people above water, and such a cluster is also easier to spot from a rescue plane than a solitary swimmer.

Death from exposure is more likely if a lifeboat or raft is overcrowded, which is usually the case. General Twining and seventeen others were in two dinghies made for four men each. In the first chapter, reference was made to the Superconstellation ditched off the coast of Ireland in September 1962. Its single dinghy made for twenty-five people carried fifty-one survivors, an inextricable mass of human bodies, all struggling to get to the middle, where it was warmest. But the boat had taken a foot or two of water, mixed with blood, oil, gasoline, and vomit; and it was very easy to be simply pressed down under the weight of the desperate crowd. A soldier was the first to drown, and soon afterward a young woman. After an hour in the overloaded boat, she was so weak that she couldn't put up any resistance against the bodies lying on top of her and simply slid down onto the bottom.

"To have no boat or raft can be disastrous (for a castaway)," says one American survival report, "but to have to sit in one is almost as much of a physical and mental torture." Sitting in a tossing craft for days on end produces painful calluses on thighs and buttocks. Lindemann said his buttocks ached so much from salt water and calluses that he could hardly sit. Calves and thigh muscles develop cramp, and the castaway can only stand up with difficulty.

To try to reach a human settlement, Bertram and Klausmann built a canoe from a float of their ditched hydroplane. The morning after they had put out to sea, the canoe began to toss about wildly on the waves. The paddle broke, sailing was impossible. "Hours passed, the sun blazed mercilessly. The sea got up more and more. The boat was seaworthy thanks to the ballast of sand we had taken, but pitched drunkenly from side to side. We kneeled in the narrow hold, not moving. Our legs ached from the unaccustomed strain, and became badly swollen. Again and again we had to block the openings in the canoe with our bodies, to avoid taking a lot of water."

Three days later: "In this unusual posture the blood circulation in the legs was restricted. Then the air in the canoe was foul from tar, so that the legs had soon swollen to shapeless lumps and were completely numb . . . feet and calves were soon as thick as thighs, water blisters formed all over the body. When they burst, dirt got into them. After two days we were covered with festering sores."

Another hardship is the sea's motion. The sea is very seldom completely calm; at best there will be a gentle swell. Considering how many people are seasick on the relative calm of a steamer deck, it is not surprising that seasickness is often a direct or indirect cause of death for castaways. Over half the occupants of lifeboats, even hardened sailors, go down with it, often in the first hours. Their bodies are racked by ceaseless attacks of vomiting, till they can spew up nothing but blood and gall, and finally lie helpless and exhausted. No pills will help then, and certainly no solid meal; only rest and getting used to the motion, which generally takes up to three days.

The tossing often stops a refreshing sleep, especially if the lifeboat is overcrowded. In his book *The Raft* Robert Trumbull quotes the castaway Dixon: "If I was off watch and lay on the deck of the dinghy trying to sleep, it was more than disturbing to get a douche of cold salt water in the face, like a blow from a club. This, and the smaller waves continually beating against the thin deck, made it quite impossible for me to get any sleep, except in the few hours of complete calm. The banging of the waves against the deck nearly drove me crazy. Every evening I thought: today I'm wearier than ever before, perhaps tonight I can sleep. But every night the same monotonous obtrusive hammering rang out beneath me, combined with getting unexpected soakings all the time, which kept making me sit up. I was soon in the grip of utter exhaustion."

The same trouble has set other castaways screaming with despair, or ranting and raging, or breaking into tearful prayers; a few have even used morphia so that they could at last get some sleep. On his trial voyage along the African coast, Lindemann used to get fits of fury after a long period with no sleep; when he calmed down, he found he had thrown overboard tins of food, torch batteries, rubber cushions, and other important things. "I came to the conclusion," he writes, "that these outbreaks were attributable to my lack of sleep, and that even a brief ten-minute nap would have kept me free from them." He solved the problem by learning, before he set out on his Atlantic crossing, to take such brief naps whenever possible. The difficulty of how to sleep on a small boat is also felt, of course, by many people who are not castaways.

"Constantly waking up was a nightmare," said Taberly, winner of the Observer Trophy Transatlantic Race in 1964, who could never sleep for more than ninety minutes at a time, when the main shaft of his automatic steering gear snapped after only eight days out of the twenty-seven of his crossing.

Sleep is not the only problem in a tossing lifeboat. When there is even a gentle swell, the slightest physical activity becomes a hazardous business, including the relieving of nature. A great many castaways when trying to do this, standing or kneeling at the side of the boat, have lost their balance, and fallen into the water. If there are several men in the boat, they may hold on to each other or else use all conceivable containers, from empty tins to their own shoes, which they afterward empty overboard. But many urinate directly onto the deck "because the warmth is so reviving." As a rule, the deck is anyhow quickly washed clean again, by the water continually pouring into the boat.

But this "automatic deck-washing" is also one of the greatest trials for the castaways: it turns their boats into half-filled bathtubs, and often makes them use up their last reserves of energy because the water constantly has to be baled out.

After the *Pamir* capsized, one group of naval cadets saw a lifeboat drifting on the waves about five hundred yards away. They were on lifebelts—it meant leaving these and swimming to the boat. Five boys were drowned trying to get there, the other ten made it, taking an hour over the distance. But when they at last reached the boat, their jubilation died. It was only a floating wreck, with bow and stern torn away, the deck knee-deep in water. But at least they could sit on the benches: the water came up to their chests. The box with the flares was gone, but under one bench they found a package of K rations and a small barrel of fresh water. While swimming they had got rid of their trousers and shoes so as to make better headway. Now they missed these bitterly. They were freezing and shivered all over. Every wave soaked them anew. That first night two boys died from the effects of exposure.

Sea water attacks clothing as well as the skin. It makes zippers and firearms go rusty, it spoils iron rations and can act like acid in corroding even canned food. Willis had almost all his food cans rusted through; the only ones unaffected were those he had dipped several times in asphalt before he left. The crew of the *Nina II* had most of their food spoiled by the salt water, when their boat was no longer watertight. "Everything began to have a taste of brackish water . . . and in the end the food tasted so repulsive that we ate it in the dark so as not to have to look . . . After only five days at sea, over half of our stores of melons, bananas, oranges, and tomatoes were so rotten that we had to throw them overboard. . . ."

But it is the castaway himself who suffers worst from the corrosive salt water. After twenty days on a raft an American pilot said: "The sea water painfully ate its way into all the bruises on my elbows, back, and buttocks. My feet were wrinkled and white from continuous contact with salt water. My skin was peeling . . ."

Water removes the natural moisture of the skin. A few dry hours later, the skin will start to become brittle and will crack. The lips will get sore. The German couple Jürgen and Elga Koch who circumnavigated the world in a little sailboat later reported: "The ocean water soaked our clothing and acted like an acid. It caused oozing sores over the entire body." Elga Koch tried to protect herself by wearing a man's shirt under her oilskins. "The sleeves were so long they covered my hands . . . I also covered my face with a self-mixed paste of lanolin ointment which I had mixed out of sheep's lard and perfume." One castaway had rubbed his face and lips successfully with the fat of an albatross he had shot. Others have tried engine oil, but that only bit deeper into their wounds, already hurting from the salt of the sea.

The salt also crusts over a castaway's hair, covers his eyebrows and his rapidly growing beard like hoarfrost. Head, face, and body begin to itch. The eyes become inflamed. A stinking paste-like layer of food-remains forms in between and on the teeth—and a forefinger dipped in salt water has to be used as a poor substitute for a toothbrush.

The salt penetrates into everything, and the smallest scratch is horribly painful. If there is no fresh water or clean dressings, such a scratch will not heal and within forty-eight hours turns into an ugly sore. Lindemann says at one point: "My hands were in a shocking state. The calluses had rubbed off and were now sore and open. I had to wrap a towel or a sock round them before I could touch anything. My skin was peeling, and boils were bursting all over me. Two of them made it impossible for me to sit comfortably, while another on my hip made my foot swell up."

Jürgen Koch, his clothing repeatedly soaked by salt water, felt equally bad: "Although I could 'drysleep' them, the crystallized salt formed sores on my skin . . . After a few days I could neither sit nor lie down . . ."

The desire for a bath in clean water becomes overwhelming, and most castaways try desperately to keep their bodies clean with the miserable means at their disposal. But salt water is also a poor substitute for a bath in fresh or brackish water. And the rain which castaways long for and pray for is a double-edged gift after several days at sea.

Most castaways would agree with General Twining's observations: "The rain lashes down like drum fire. The big drops strike so hard that it hurts. They hammer on the brain till you feel you must hit back."

A pilot, who survived nine days' continuous rainfall in the Sulu Sea in the Philippines, said afterward that his limbs were as swollen from it as the hands of a laundry woman condemned to forced labor. Lindemann's fingertips were thick, the skin raw from handling wet things and constantly baling water out of the boat. The rain had soon bleached them white, and the calluses on them were soaked with water. "When I carried out minor repairs, I at once got cuts on my sensitive skin. These healed afterward, however, without complications."

General Twining declared that the rain was as bad for him and his men as the sun: which is saying a good deal, because many castaways find that the sun is like "hell fire." Even the reflection of the light on calm water is painfully dazzling to the eyes; and a few minutes under a scorching sun in southern latitudes will take a heavy toll. Castaways who rashly took off their clothes, for various reasons, perhaps even "sun-bathing," suffered such burns that they couldn't sleep at night for the pain. The American flying ace Eddie Rickenbacker describes the effects as follows: "Faces, hands, arm joints, legs and ankles were full of blisters, in some places exposed right to the raw flesh—and this was roasted again by the sun. The sun turned even the soles of the feet into raw flesh."

Shade or a bath in the sea are the only things that can protect a castaway against the scorching rays of the sun—though he will do well to look round first to see if there are sharks. Clothes soaked in sea water and put on again also have some cooling effect when the water evaporates; and a sail may cast a protective shadow. Where there is no sail, the castaway can only protect every exposed part of the body by clothing, regardless of the extra heat this will produce. It is at least better than being roasted alive!

The human body is a sensitive structure. It functions only in an environment of moderate temperatures. Too much heat, and it shrivels like a leaf the wind has blown off a tree. Too much cold, and it freezes. The seas extend over all latitudes, so plenty of castaways are exposed to great cold. What are *their* chances of survival?

Most of the pilots who were shot down over the Atlantic in the winter months knew they had scarcely any hope of being rescued in time. For though a man can hold out for quite a while in water between 59° and 64° F., his expectations of life at freezing point or under are little more than half an hour. When the *Titanic* went down, a great many of the 1,490 fatal casualties (some sources even give 1,635) died within the first half hour of cold. In Walter Lord's account in *A Night to Remember,* the water temperature was 28°, "and the Second Officer, Lightoller, felt as if a thousand knives were being plunged into his body. In such water life jackets were no use at all."

The passengers of the ditched Superconstellation mentioned earlier also had to jump into ice-cold water—and at wind force 8. Anyone who did not reach the one dinghy soon died. The cold attacks heart and breathing muscles like a severe shock. For a moment that seems like eternity, the castaway cannot get his breath. Sometimes, his lungs filled to bursting, he cannot even exhale. Only gradually does the choking abate, and very gradually he regains the power of movement. But the cold has already seeped into his body and limbs. The beginning of numbness, which gives an illusion of comforting warmth, is really the onset of death.

The numb fingers are usually the first to "refuse service." Their slightest movement, which may be decisive for life or death, becomes an almost superhuman effort. Many ditched airmen were drowned because with their numbed hands they could not operate the inflation mechanism of their dinghies. Others were almost choked by their own ties or shirt collars, which contracted in the water—and couldn't be undone fast enough with the cold fingers.

The first symptoms of frostbite in ice-cold water occur almost invariably after only a few minutes: Tony Sulak, a fighter pilot, who crashed in Alaska and went through the ice, said: "My frozen hands swelled up (soon after the rescue) to double their normal size. They became black and were covered with great frost blisters. They stayed like this for several weeks. I lost all ten finger-nails, but they grew again. The doctors told me I was lucky my hands had bled so much (from an injury) while I was swimming in icy water. That had stopped the blood vessels freezing."

During the war William Peters, an American sailor, spent half an hour in water below freezing point, drifting between ice floes, and survived. This is the only known case of a man surviving for that period in these conditions, without any protective clothing. Very few of the 641 American airmen who came down in Arctic waters during the war survived the great cold, even when they were drifting in dinghies. But whereas death in freezing water comes very quickly, it is a much slower business in a lifeboat. There have been castaways who went mad before they froze to death; others died in their sleep. In February 1963 two schoolboys on Germany's Lake Constance drifted on an ice floe out into the lake. With night coming on, no search was possible. The next morning, when the boys were found near the Swiss bank, they were so badly frozen that they died on the way to the hospital.

The survivors in the *Titanic*'s lifeboats were also hard hit by the cold. "A stoker in No. 6 sat beside Mrs. Brown, his teeth chattering with the cold. Finally she wrapped her sable stole about his legs, tying the tails around his ankles. In No. 16 a man in white pajamas looked so cold that he reminded the other passengers of a snow man. Mrs. Charlot Collyer was so numb she toppled over in No. 14; her hair caught in an oarlock and a big tuft came out by the roots."

But there are quite a few castaways who have worked to keep themselves alive in cold latitudes: for instance, by massaging each other's bodies, or doing exercises in the tossing boat or even on pitching ice floes. One man ran round in circles on an ice floe for all of twenty hours to keep himself warm. Others have sung loud and lustily to beat the cold. Rain and high seas pour into the lifeboats, the castaways shudder and shiver from wetness, and also from the wind, which blows through zippers and buttonholes and seams, and brings up sores in all exposed parts of the body. Instead of salt, they now have frost on hair, beards, and eyebrows, and the foam forms a crackling layer of ice on the lifeboats' canvas, like a starched white shroud.

So castaways may drift on the waves for days and often weeks —tiny atoms in the vast ocean. In every shadow on the horizon they fancy they see land; from every cloud in the sky they expect the longed-for rain, and even a drifting ice floe becomes an island of hope. The night falls, however, almost always cold, often accompanied by spray to soak them, sometimes with another storm; and after it comes morning, ice-cold or with a merciless sun blazing from a leaden sky. It is an irony of fate that a castaway's optimism increases, the more the prospect of his being found wanes. He will call for help to a jet plane flying 40,000 feet above, as a British sailor, afterward rescued, relates of his shipmate:

"Wilkes spotted the plane first. It was as small as a fly, high above in the blue sky. He jumped up and nearly capsized the dinghy. Then he began to yell and wave, until the plane had disappeared from sight. He stared at me in dismay, saying: 'The bastards. They never turned. Can you beat it? They didn't want to save us.'"

In fact you can scarcely make out a dinghy on the crests of the waves even from 1,500 feet. Unless a systematic search is being made for it, it will only be discovered by pure chance. Such was the case in March 1960 when two American airmen, Flight Lieutenants Glen Conrad and David Mericle, saw a raft on the waves of the Pacific. Coming down lower, they saw four men on it waving. Mericle at once alerted the aircraft carrier *Kearsarge,* and after a few hours the castaways were safely taken on board.

They were four young Russian soldiers, taking part in Soviet maneuvers on the Kuriles, who had been carried out into the open sea with their landing craft. Without radio, with only three tins of dried meat, a loaf of bread, a bottle of vodka, and three flasks of water, they survived for forty-nine days and drifted 1,020 miles from the original place. Since it had rained a good deal, they did not go thirsty, but as for hunger—they had begun to eat the leather of their boots. Philip Poplavsky, one of the four, confirmed a point that countless men have brought up after their rescue: the three ships which passed very close to them did not notice them. "It was like a spell. We saw *them,* but they couldn't see us."

The same, although a systematic search was being made, applies with the rescue of the *Pamir* survivors, where sixty-seven ships and eleven planes were engaged in the operation. Dummer, the leader of the rescued cadets, said afterward: "Many (ships) came up several times to within 250 yards of us." One of the survivors was first noticed by the lookout of "his" rescue ship, the SS *Abescone*, when he was drifting two hundred yards away.

Bombard fired two flares as an experiment to attract a passing ship—without success. "So I reached for my heliograph, an apparatus with which I could reflect the sun into the observer's eye . . . and tried to attract the steamer's attention by flashing it in the rhythm of an SOS message. The ship moved on . . ." For Bombard, of course, it was not a matter of life and death to be spotted by a lookout; he simply registered the steamer's passing as an interesting fact. It is different with castaways banking desperately on this one moment of possible rescue. If the ship passes, that is the end for them, most lose the last glimmer of will to live. In their desperation, they may even try to swim after the ship.

Sixteen days after their crash landing Bertram and Klausmann sighted a ship. "I yelled and laughed and prayed, and lost my head completely. The ship came nearer, heading directly for our boat, clearly they had already seen us . . . Now only another three-quarters of a mile or so! I fired the first red flare, Klausmann waved the white flag of distress. A second flare, a third and a fourth. But the ship passed—600 to 700 yards away. Klausmann dropped his head on his arms and wept."

American investigations show that in fact even castaways for whom a systematic search is being made have little prospect of being rescued except in the first twelve hours; after that the chances diminish fast. For one thing they are drifting farther and farther from the place of the disaster, which greatly increases the area to be searched. For instance, if they drift at only three miles an hour, they will be seventy-two miles off within twenty-four hours: so the search would have to be over a diameter of 144 miles, more than the area of Switzerland. Secondly, and even more important, their strength is ebbing every minute. After a certain period their rescue apparatus, affected by salt water, becomes unserviceable. Food and water give out.

Very few castaways are rescued after ten days at sea. Either the search is abandoned, or they are found dead. Those who survive often have themselves to thank, and their own resources: the most important being good equipment (with which we shall deal in a later chapter), the basic ideas of survival technique, and the will to survive. That survival at sea is possible in such circumstances is shown not only by what happened to Bombard, the volunteer castaway, but by such cases as those of Poon Lim and the four Russian soldiers.

One recent and dramatic example is that of a group of castaways who survived for over a hundred days on a lonely coral reef on the South Seas. The world heard of them for the first time on October 16, 1962. On that day two bearded savages dragged themselves with their last strength onto the beach at Kandavu in the Fiji Islands. They were the captain and one sailor of the two-master *Tuaikaepau,* a fishing boat which had disappeared without trace three months before; the search for it had long been abandoned. Stammering, weeping, and having to pause from weakness now and then, the two men told the Kandavu police a hair-raising story.

On July 4 the *Tauikaepau* had put out to sea from Nukualofa, the main port of the Tonga Islands. The vessel was heading for Auckland, over three thousand miles away. After three days, three hundred miles from the home port, the forty-foot two-master ran into a murderous storm, hit the treacherous Minerva reef, and capsized. Then she broke up and sank. The captain, Tevita Fifita, and the sixteen other men managed to get out of the raging waves onto the jagged coral rocks. But all they had with them was a few cans of food and a completely sodden box of matches.

But with such miserable resources, stranded on a barren coral reef, these men showed they could do more than some castaways surrounded by fish. When the storm had stopped, they first dried their matches in the sun, while some of them began to explore the reef. They discovered the wreck of a Japanese fishing boat which had also been stranded there years before.

With their bare hands the men broke the first planks from the hulk, piled up the wood and tried to get a fire lit. They succeeded with their last match. A watch was set to keep this fire going. With some iron bars torn from the wreck, they systematically chopped up the inside of it and fed the fire with the wood—so as not to let their precious flame go out. On top of the wreck they laid out two big SOS signs from shells and pieces of coral, which could be clearly seen from the air.

The contents of the cans of food lasted only seven days. But the castaways did not give up. They made fishhooks from the tops of cans, and used the iron bars as harpoons to try for fish. They built a small dike into the sea from pieces of coral, and repeatedly some fish got trapped behind it. They collected prawns and mussels (carefully avoiding clinging mussels, because these may be poisonous). They fried their catch over the flames, and boiled sea water in an aluminum pot. The covered the lid with pieces of metal so that no steam could escape. They took it through a rubber tube, which they cooled with sea water, into empty food cans—to make condensed fresh water. In this way they obtained nearly a quart of drinking water a day, not enough to keep all of them alive, but enough for the strongest ones.

The days crept by, turned into weeks, and on the twenty-fourth day after the shipwreck the first man died. Two more died almost simultaneously a few days later. The remaining fourteen men had given up hope of any search still being made for them. So at the end of September the captain decided to go off for help with his son and another man. It seemed a hopeless venture, for Fiji the nearest land, was over three hundred miles away. But the three men set about their task very thoroughly. From the biggest parts of the wrecked Japanese boat they built a primitive raft. Having no saws, they used a nail, with which they laboriously cut the planks into suitable lengths. But when they put to sea on the raft, it rolled so dangerously that they had to turn back. Patiently they built a second raft, tied it to the first, and put to sea again. The only provisions they took on it were a few cups of distilled water and some fish.

The three men had no compass to keep them on course, they had to steer by the stars. For seven days they drifted over the sea, then at last sighted land on the eighth, October 16. But within reach of the shore their raft capsized in the surf. It was still a mile and a half to the beach. They fought desperately against the current, had to struggle on yard for yard. It was too much for the captain's son. "My son began to sink," Fifita said afterward, "but I knew I had to swim on, or none of us would reach the shore. My son knew that too. He sacrificed himself. We kissed each other and I swam away from him. When I turned round, he had disappeared."

The Kandavu police alerted the New Zealand coast guards, and three days later a flying boat landed at the Minerva reef. Since Fifita had left it, another man had died of hunger and exhaustion, but the remaining ten were still alive. Weeping for joy they had enough strength left to run toward their rescuers. "It's a miracle," sobbed one of them. But the rescue was no miracle; they had made it possible by their courage, good sense, and ability to help themselves.

Chapter 5
Survival in Snow and Ice

Today the "White Hell" has lost its terrors.
From a "travelogue" on the Arctic and Antarctic

On Thursday, April 15, 1954, a party of pupils between the ages of fourteen and seventeen from the Federal Training School at Obertraun (on Lake Halstatt) in Austria, set out to climb the Gjaidalm on the Dachstein mountain. There were ten of them, led by a teacher of forty, Hans Seiler, and a younger colleague with his fiancée who was also a teacher.

Several bad mistakes were made before they started. None of them had anything hot for breakfast. Seiler changed the itinerary without informing anyone at the school. The party was quite unsuitably dressed; most of the boys were wearing shorts, and shoes instead of boots. One was wearing a track suit and short socks, another had put on his Sunday-best trousers, a sweater, and a sports coat; later he was to wrap the sweater round his head to keep his ears arm.

It was raining when they set off in the early morning. At ten they reached the Schönbergalm, about five thousand feet above sea level. They were pretty well soaked, already rather exhausted and quite cold. They drank hot tea, warmed their fingers on the hot cups, and set off again—not back into the valley, but farther up toward the Gjaidalm in the direction of the Krippenstein, at an altitude of about 6,500 feet.

The owner of the mountain lodge warned the teachers against

going on, but they took no notice. At 11:30 the climbers met one of the men working on the cable railway. He had started for the valley because of the growing storm. He stared in amazement at the party passing him. One of the boys waved cheerfully at him, another was already cursing under his breath about his soaked hair and shirt.

An hour later it began to snow on the Gjaidalm level. Farther down, where the party was still plodding upward, the slopes were wrapped in thick mist. The Dachstein had swallowed its victims.

The next morning—Good Friday—saw the greatest search undertaken in the history of the Obertraun district. One hundred and sixty men were on it, from the Austrian military police and the volunteer mountain rescue service, ski instructors, mountain guides, and mountain lodge keepers. The area where the missing party was presumed to be is rugged, full of gorges and caves, and extends over eight square miles. For many hours the snow had been falling at wind speeds of almost sixty miles an hour. The American forces stationed in the area offered helicopters for the operation, but they couldn't take off. The first day's search was fruitless.

The following day the weather had scarcely changed, and once more the search was in vain. The ground was covered everywhere with fresh snow, and the mist made things still more difficult. A diviner was called in, who had twice before given correct information about the scene of accidents. He asked for a map of the Dachstein area, set his divining rod in motion, and eventually said: "It must be here." The area he designated covered several hundred square yards. The searchers combed it feverishly. Without success. Their ten-foot poles were too short to reach the ground through the fresh snow which had fallen everywhere.

Professor Waldner, a well-known Austrian cave explorer, offered his assistance. He had spent years mapping all the caves in the Dachstein area, and they were now systematically searched from the Mammoth Cave down to the smallest hollow. Still no result.

On Sunday evening, three full days after their disappearance, no trace of the missing party had been found, although the number of helpers had now grown to three hundred and fifty. But they didn't give up. On Monday, search headquarters announced: "We will go on searching till we know for certain what has happened to them." There was little hope of finding them alive. Seven feet of fresh snow had fallen in the area, and even day temperatures were below freezing point.

The papers were already speaking of the "Dachstein Tragedy." Reports of other mountain-climbing accidents occurring during that period faded into the background: the one at Piz Bernin, for instance, where a search party found the bodies of two mountain climbers; one had fallen down the crevasse of a glacier, the other had frozen to death in the snowstorm trying to fetch help, and a mountain guide had already lost his life in that search. In the French Alps too, five climbers were missing for three days and nights, and were then found frozen to death.

During the afternoon of April 20 one group of searchers discovered the first trace of the missing school party. On the Speikberg, at about 6,600 feet, a man pulled a provisions bag out of the snow. In it there were some scraps of newspaper, and some biscuit and chocolate wrappings. On the ground underneath there were some torn-off dwarf-fir branches. The avalanche probes were plunged into the snow, but only hit firm ground ten feet down. The searchers scoured this hollow right to its bottom, and found nothing but an empty film packet, and a food can. A few hours later, northeast of this, a walking stick was discovered on which a woman's hair was found. This probably belonged to the young teacher's fiancée.

Here too the snow was so deep that the searchers had to screw four probes together in order to reach firm ground. When these were pulled up again, some fluff of white wool was hanging to one. Where did it come from—a pullover, a glove, or what? That day it was too late to dig farther.

The next morning the fifteen search parties, who had now been on their feet almost continuously for five days, were concentrated again in the area of the two finds. In the thick mist, which limited visibility to fifteen yards, and in an area which was full of ski-tracks, they searched as thoroughly as possible, again without success. Another day passed. German shepherd dogs which had also been used in the search were now withdrawn: their paws, roughened by continual scratching in the snow, showed cuts and calluses.

On the Thursday night another nine inches of snow fell. Then the weather cleared at last. Over a week after the party's disappearance, on Saturday, the sun came out again for the first time. At six in the morning new helpers arrived at the Schönbergalm by cable railway, climbed from there to the area of the search, and trudged through the snow, on which small puddles had already formed under the sun's rays. Again every square yard was tested with probes, and this time something macabre was seen: one of the missing party himself pointed the way. Half an hour northwest of the place where the provisions bag had been found, a human hand stuck out of the thawing snow, as if it were trying to beckon to the rescue party. It was bare and frozen white. The rescuers dug off the snow and exposed the first body, which they took to be that of Seiler, the older teacher. The features of the face were distorted, reflecting the terrible suffering of his last hours. A chart of the mountains was found in his anorak pocket. The searchers sent a message down into the valley that the leader of the party had been found. But when the body was later identified, it proved to be that of one of the oldest boys in the party (he was seventeen): the ordeals he had been through had so disfigured his face that he looked like a man of forty.

The searchers dug further, and a foot and a half under snow found the bodies of the younger teacher and his fiancée. Her shoes were torn, the soles in shreds. Probably the man and the boy had dragged her for some way until they couldn't go on themselves. Then they must have taken off their gloves and tried to cut off some fir branches to protect themselves and the girl from the storm; then, in exhaustion, they had fallen asleep. There was an open pocket knife lying near them. The same afternoon a probe revealed the bodies of six more boys one hundred and fifty yards southeast. They lay side by side, as if they had gone to sleep together. The bodies of the rest of the party were found a day later.

The Dachstein tragedy was the worst the district had known since ten workmen had perished in the snow a century before. The victims then had been buried by an avalanche, whereas now the teachers and their party were themselves to blame. They were quite inadequately dressed and equipped for such an expedition, and they had ignored warnings by local inhabitants that a storm was approaching. When it was too late to turn back, they pitched their camp in the flat hollow where the provisions bag was later found. But instead of building it up with fir branches into a real shelter, they tried the next day to find their way back to the Schönbergalm—while the search parties passed only a few yards from their abandoned camp. In thick mist, and the snowstorm which followed, they kept wandering at random over the slopes, instead of waiting for the storm to abate. They could probably have lasted out in a snow hole for several days, because when the bodies were found some of the boys still had cheese, fruit, and chocolate in their pockets. But they exhausted their strength fighting the elements, and probably died that second day, Good Friday, when the search parties were already on the way to them.

It might have been thought that such a tragedy would at least stop others, but the figures for mountain accidents show the contrary (an average of two thousand people are rescued annually in the Bavarian Alps alone, while the number of people killed in the entire Alps reached 760 in 1973). Many amateur climbers still set out as if they were going for a walk on the beach. They overrate their own powers, and do not realize that their hearts and circulations will already be affected by the change of atmosphere after going up by cable railway or ski lift; above all, they don't know that temperatures in the mountains can sink abruptly by 36° F.

Summer clothes offer no protection against the cold. In May 1960 four German boys in light jackets and thin trousers climbed the Gimpel in the Tyrol (over seven thousand feet). There they met a front of bad weather with heavy snowfall and low temperatures. All four froze to death. A year later three boys between fifteen and eighteen climbed the Wilde Kaiser. They set off in bright sunshine, and were dressed accordingly. At six thousand feet they encountered fresh snow. Eight men of the Mountain Watch looked for them all night, and eventually found them, half frozen. In the summer of 1961 a man went for an afternoon walk on the Traunstein mountain (2,500 feet) wearing shorts and a T-shirt. While he was out, a storm blew up, the sky darkened, he lost his way and spent the night in the open. The next day a search party looked for him, without success. The pilot of a rescue plane eventually discovered him lying under a tree completely exhausted and nearly dead.

Every winter many tourists in the Alps and other mountain regions lose their lives through their own extraordinary carelessness. Some are buried under avalanches because they go to particular danger zones despite express warnings. One party, overwhelmed by an avalanche in the Sellrain Valley (Tyrol) during April 1963, had listened only the day before to an address on the danger of avalanches given by an expert from the Mountain Rescue Service. Another party, quite undeterred, took the same route directly after this disaster.

In the United States, and increasingly in Europe too, many people travel for pleasure or business in small private planes, often flying over snowed-up forests or lonely mountain country. In their cockpits it is pleasantly warm. Bound for Florida, California, or the Mediterranean, or at least to an airport with all the comforts of modern civilization, they do not take along gloves or winter clothing. If they have to make an emergency landing, a disaster is unavoidable. Here are two of the more striking examples.

On June 14, 1956, a two-seater plane in Lebanon, Oregon, set out on a flight to Minneapolis, carrying Ralph Johnston, a dentist, and Hartwick Hanson, a clergyman. The plane never arrived, and for two weeks helicopters searched in vain for the wreck. In August 1957 a party of scouts, crossing a valley at the foot of the Sister mountain (6,600 feet), discovered the missing plane behind withered, burned bushes. It had not been much damaged in the landing and was half-hanging over a deep abyss. The two men had presumbly let themselves down to the ground by a rope, which was fastened to one of the cabin windows. The skeleton of the dentist lay between the plane's two wheels; Hanson's remains were found a few miles farther down into the valley. He must have been unhurt and set off to fetch help, probably freezing to death on a particularly cold night. Investigations showed that he was wearing a very light summer suit, the jacket of which he had left behind when he went off for help.

In May 1959 another private plane, for which weeks of fruitless search had been made, was found by two workmen in a thick pinewood in New Hampshire. About a hundred yards away lay the body of the sixty-year-old pilot, Dr. Ralph E. Miller, a professor of pathology. After days of waiting in a snowstorm, he had set out in his thin business suit to fetch help, and had frozen to death. So had his passenger, Dr. Robert E. Quinn (aged thirty-two), who was also wearing only a suit and a light overcoat. Before his death, Miller had stuck in a plastic container some closely written pages on which they had described their last hours (my comments in brackets):

"When we had to make an emergency landing here on Saturday [February 21] because of an iced-up carburetor, it was 4:30 in the afternoon. We pitched camp. Minus 7.6° F. We cut a lot of wood with the saw [a bone saw from Miller's surgical kit]. On Sunday we made ourselves snowshoes and set out to try to reach a human settlement. But the track petered out in the forest and we came back. Still had strength left to look for firewood. The night was fairly tolerable. Minus 6.8° F. in the morning, but at night minus 22° F. The sky is overcast, and I have no hope that a search plane will find us today. We shall head for the north. Let's hope this railway line [near which they had landed] leads somewhere. My [air] maps don't give enough information about where we are, but we'll try our utmost."

From Quinn [on February 23]: "Till today were still hoping we should be found. But no rescue plane in sight. [Many patrols were looking for them, but saw no SOS signals.] I am extremely weak. The fight against the cold is hard."

A few days later it began to snow. Miller wrote: "We won't go off again on snowshoes, but stay where we are. Spending our whole energy chopping wood. I have little hope." And then the last words: "This is my last and most important message. The will to survive can conquer pain. Good-bye everyone."

In the war, too, pilots were often too easygoing and didn't bother to put on their flying suits when crossing over Arctic areas. In 1943 the pilot of a training plane took off from a military airport in Alaska for a flight of 120 miles, wearing only a warm track suit and gym shoes. After forty minutes flying he had to come down halfway with engine trouble. He radioed for help, and when the rescue party found him shortly afterward, he already had frostbite on both feet.

As in the Dachstein tragedy, amateur climbers are often as careless about their footwear as about their clothing generally. One day in the summer of 1953 I myself was climbing to the Zugspitze, Germany's highest peak, by way of the Höllental (Gorge of Hell), when I met three teenage boys climbing barefoot; their ordinary shoes had fallen to pieces en route. A few years ago men of the Bavarian Mountain Watch had to bring down into the valley a woman who had tried to climb the Grasberg, quite a testing mountain, in shoes with stiletto heels. First the heels broke off, then the soles came away from the shoes. Finally, when she was standing in her bare feet, she began to call for help.

Anyone who climbs up the Partnach gorge to the Knorr Alpine Hut (also in Bavaria), can see shoe nails and complete heels lying among the stones and pebbles, a sign of the trials attendant on inadequate footwear in the mountains. But there are fatal casualties time and again among such foolhardy climbers who do not appreciate these facts. One victim was a nineteen-year-old American who, in 1962, tried to climb the 7,500-foot Faulhorn peak in sneakers. He slipped on a smooth stone, fell into a ravine, and broke his neck.

Few amateur climbers realize that they are often risking not only their own lives but those of their prospective rescuers. Perhaps this realization can scarcely be expected of them, but there are also ambitious mountain climbers who seem to take it for granted that others will risk life and limb to rescue them if they fail in some record-breaking climb. From 1953 to the end of 1962, for instance, there were twenty fatal casualties on the north face of the Eiger. But individuals and roped parties are always going up the "Wall of Death." They like the idea of showing off their skill and "courage" before hundreds of thrilled spectators following their climb through binoculars from the hotel terraces of Grindelwald. The spectators generally get double their money's worth, because they may also be eyewitnesses of dramatic rescue attempts.

In August 1957, for instance, rescue parties with men from six countries had to dash to the rescue of four mountain climbers, two Italian and two German, who had met with an accident on that north face. After laborious and extremely dangerous efforts they succeeded in finding one of the Italians—seriously injured and frozen stiff. The corpse of the other Italian remained hanging upside down on the "Wall" for two years. The two Germans were not discovered till four years later, lying in a stone gully on the west side of the Eiger range.

Not long after that tragedy, a Swiss mountain guide tried to conquer the "Wall of Death" alone, despite express warnings: he was killed in a fall. Karl Frantz, head of the Bavarian Mountain Watch, has justifiably called such climbs "a sporting method of suicide."

At least those who climb in such difficult regions as the Eiger face are practiced mountain climbers, and according to Georg Frey, an expert in the Mountain Watch, they make up only 5 percent of the casualties needing rescue in the Alps every year. The remaining 95 percent are the amateurs who have come for the weekend or a holiday "to do a bit of mountain climbing." They may not realize that climbs in high mountains are divided into six grades of difficulty, and that even in grade one an amateur will have to use his hands to grip with when climbing.

Nevertheless, Dr. Neureuther, a German doctor in the Mountain Watch who is also an explorer of the Karakoram Mountains in India, maintains that if amateur climbers could master the basic rules for all mountaineers, there would be only a fraction of the present number of casualties. Besides wearing warm clothing and strong boots, one of the most important of these rules is always to inform the hotel proprietor in the valley, or the keeper of the mountain lodge where you are going on the mountains and when you expect to be back. In the Dachstein tragedy, it will be remembered, the teacher leading the party changed the route without telling anybody; and there was another tragedy seven years later (1961) which was at first thought to have occurred in the same area. A Stuttgart lawyer sent his relatives a picture postcard giving his plans for a climbing holiday in the Dachstein range, and then disappeared without trace. The relatives alerted the Mountain Watch, who thereupon combed every hut in the area for two weeks, without success. Then a boardinghouse keeper told them that the lawyer had changed his plan at the last minute and gone to the Julian Alps in Yugoslavia. The Mountain Watch there searched all possible places for the missing man—and found nothing. In the summer of 1962 climbers discovered a human skeleton on a promontory of the east face of the Watzmann (5,500 feet). The rucksack lying by it showed that this was the remains of the Stuttgart lawyer. He had probably fallen, been injured in the fall, and then frozen to death.

The possibility of this happening is one very good reason why amateur climbers should never venture alone into remote mountain districts. Even an injury which would be slight under normal conditions (like a sprained ankle) may prove to have total results in the mountains. Year after year lone climbers in the mountains of Europe and America disappear without trace among the stones, gorges, and gullies. Often this fate overtakes them because they abandon well-marked paths, sometimes in favor of what looks like an easy short cut and then proves a treacherous mountain trap.

But even if you get into difficulties on the mountains despite taking the above simple precautions, you still do not need to despair, according to American survival experts. Even at a great height, in great cold, and with the most scanty equipment, you can hold out unscathed for a long time, they maintain, as long as you know a few "survival tricks"—like the building of an igloo, for instance.

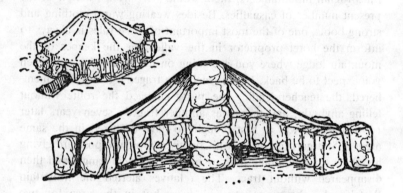

Shelter from blocks of snow or stone and a parachute.

An igloo built from blocks of snow.

These Eskimo snow huts are certainly the best protection against wind and cold. According to the latest researchers of the Arctic Aeromedical Laboratory in Alaska, they can be built not only from solid blocks of Polar snow, pressed together, but also from freshly fallen snow—as is the practice of the Nunamiut Eskimos in Alaska. When the Eskimos of this tribe want to pitch camp, they pile up branches and bushes and cover them with skins or tarpaulins, then heap the loose snow on top. After about an hour it hardens, and the leaves and branches can be taken away. The igloo is ready.

It is even simpler in deep snow to make a snow hole round a tree trunk. Put some branches over it, and your shelter is built. The party in the Dachstein tragedy passed a great many trees which would have served for such a purpose; had this possibility occurred to them in time, they might have survived.

Many mountain climbers could have saved themselves from freezing to death by staying in a snow hole. It is dug in loose snow round a tree trunk and then covered with branches.

Robert W. Elsner and William Pruitt, Jr., scientists in the U. S. Aeromedical Laboratory, have established that the temperature within such a shelter, even excluding the bodily warmth of those occupying it, can be 18° F. higher than outside, where storms may be raging at 36° below freezing point. If there are several people in an igloo, the temperature will rise even further: this seems the only explanation for the fact that when people are buried in an avalanche, their death is more often due to suffocation than exposure. (With "dust avalanches" the fine powdered snow at once gets into lungs and breathing passages; with "wet avalanches" the snow presses round the victim like concrete.)

In his book, *S.O.S. in den Bergen,* (*S.O.S. in the Mountains*), Georg Frey writes: "The study of avalanche disasters striking tourists . . . shows that they could almost all have been avoided, had those involved recognized the danger." A few people have indeed succeeded in freeing themselves from the clutches of an avalanche by taking the right action. Among them are Bernt Pederson, a Norwegian schoolboy of fifteen, who in 1962 spent twenty-four grim hours fighting his way out of such a "snow grave," and Evert Stenmark, a Swede of twenty-five who in 1957 spent eight days in an avalanche.

Stenmark was out shooting sand grouse when the avalanche caught him. Sinking gradually deeper, he slid down into the valley with the avalanche, and suddenly disappeared in powdery snow. Knowing the dangers of the mountains he at once did the right thing: while the snow was still carrying him down, he tried frantically to make swimming strokes. When the sliding mass eventually came to rest, he had thus secured a small hollow round his body, and could soon move his head a bit. But after a while there was no air left for him to breathe, he lost consciousness, and only came round seven hours later.

He found that the sun's rays had made a small channel into the open. Through the layers of snow he could see a bluish sky above him. He immediately began trying to free his legs and trunk. But as his legs were still in their ski bindings, with the snow weighing them down heavily, there was no chance of freeing the lower half of his body. With great difficulty, he got his knife off his belt, and gave himself some more space. When night came, he pulled the hood of his parka over his head, and slept till the next morning.

After an hour's laborious effort, he got his rucksack off his back, and pulled out four birds he had shot the day before—so now he had something to eat. He warmed himself with the rucksack and drank snow water, which he had first warmed in his mouth. He knew that his brother and a friend, whom he was going to meet for the shoot, would be looking for him. But when?

Suddenly he discovered that on the moss-covered ground right beside him was a birch branch. He cleaned it, and pushed it carefully through the snow into the open. Cold, fresh air came through to him, the blue sky suddenly seemed within reach. It occurred to him that no one would notice the branch as it was, so he pulled it back, got out of his wallet some red movie theater ticket stubs (which he collected as a hobby), stuck them on the end of the stick, and then pushed the stick out again.

The next day or two some of the snow thawed off, which made his hole even bigger; but he still couldn't move his legs, and was afraid they would get frostbitten. He tried to banish this fear by deliberately recalling all sorts of events in his past life, looking at and sorting all his belongings, and reading through an old newspaper from beginning to end. He ate birchbark, and when the last sand grouse began to smell, he tried to eat ski wax. His fingers were so stiff that he had to wind his watch with his teeth.

He still did not know whether anyone was searching for him, and in fact a whole week had passed before his brother and friend decided to do so. It was his brother who first noticed the red ticket stubs on the stick, so that after eight days Evert Stenmark was at last rescued. He lost one foot, except for the heel part, and all the toes on the other foot, but that was the extent of his injuries. With a bit more clear space he could have survived this period unscathed, protected by his "natural" igloo.

To build such a snow shelter is only profitable, of course, if the victim of an accident does not wait till he is too exhausted, but starts on it the moment danger is imminent: like the two men and a young woman who (at Easter 1959) ran into a heavy snowstorm on a peak in the Alps nearly 10,000 feet up. The storm lasted for five days, and the Mountain Watch had given up all hope of rescue. When the storm was over, the telephone suddenly rang in the valley station. One of the men believed dead was on the line. "We are alive and well," he said. Then he reported how

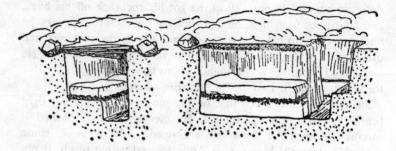

In deep snow this simple shelter gives protection against great cold.
A hole is covered with branches and a tarpaulin, except for the en-
trance. A little snow is put on top. Inside this primitive shelter the
temperature will soon rise.

they had built themselves a shelter out of branches and snow, and
with this relative protection had survived the storm, which had
blown with a force of sixty miles an hour. When it had died down,
they struggled through to a mountain but, from where the man
was now speaking.

In the winter of 1959–60 some Antarctic explorers who had run
into a storm during a scientific expedition saved themselves in a
similar way. The wind was so strong that they could not put up a
tent, and only erected a makeshift "barricade" against the wind
with blocks of ice. They held out without food or water for two
days and three nights, to be rescued thereafter, in good shape, by a
helicopter crew.

In the spring of 1963 eighteen German and Austrian skiers ran
into mist and then snowstorms in the area of the "Stone Sea"
above Berchtesgaden. They, too, crept into quickly dug snow
holes. The search parties in the valley gave up hope of finding
them alive, but after three days the skiers came down from the
mountains safe and sound. Significantly, several of them were soldiers and knew something about the correct behavior at temperatures below freezing point. There are, too, many accounts of pilots
who crashed in the Antarctic and owed their lives to the makeshift
snow shelters they made themselves. For this reason, the survival
manuals in use by the U. S. Air Force give the most important

types of shelter, which are also the simplest to build. They should offer protection against even the most severe cold.

People who managed to keep their heads cool and their bodies warm sometimes managed to survive almost hopeless situations even though they had no previous survival training at all. One example is the case of the South Vietnamese student Vincent Vinh-Hung who, at the age of eighteen, went on a winter hike through the Ardennes forest in December 1969. When fog, followed by a blizzard, set in, he and his three companions lost their way back to the bus where thirty-six other students were waiting for them.

Soon enough, Vincent's companions—the sisters Janine (nineteen) and Claudine (seventeen) Piroton, and Tony Gonzales (twenty), a student from Colombia, were about to give up. The girls started crying.

Vincent called for a break, and all four of them sat down under a snow-covered tree in freezing temperatures. Vincent asked everyone to produce whatever food he was carrying. The result were a couple of sugar lumps and a bit of dried meat which Vincent, according to Vietnamese custom, had been carrying in a small bag around his waist.

Vincent divided the food into four equal parts, and made everyone promise to ration it. After a meager meal they all lay down in the snow huddling close together to keep each other warm. None of them could sleep, however. When the next morning broke, they all got to their feet, shivering and tired, and started to walk on.

It was still snowing, and soon enough the snow covered the ground more than two feet deep. Despite frequent stops the girls became so exhausted that they could not go on. Vincent suddenly remembered a story about Eskimo igloos which he had read some time before. He asked everyone to look for branches under the snow or rip them off the trees. After leaning the branches against one especially thick fir tree, they piled loose snow all around and on top of them. When night came, their igloo was ready and they all crawled inside. Here Vincent—although he came from a country where cold and snow are practically unknown—had a new idea: he ordered each one to take off his boots and socks, and warm his naked feet on the warm abdomen of another. The next morning, the boots and socks were frozen stiff—they had forgotten to keep them warm, too. But nobody was suffering from frostbite. With some trouble, only Vincent managed to put his boots back on. Alone, he started out to look for help.

Meanwhile more than seven hundred soldiers, policemen, and volunteers had arrived looking for the missing students. Sixty hours after their disappearance, a couple of French paratroopers spotted Vincent on a snow-covered field, waving for help. He managed to lead the "paras" back to the igloo, where the other three students were waiting. "It's incredible they had managed to survive that kind of weather," an officer of the paratroopers stated later. "Without the clear thinking of the Vietnamese they certainly would all have perished within the first twenty-four hours."

Staying in an igloo has its dangers, of course. Usually it is the protective warmth itself which gives the occupants trouble. During a long stay, snow and ice can thaw under the sleeping bags, and turn the ground into a swamp; so fir branches must be put underneath as substitute mattresses. The occupant's exhalations are another problem. "All of us were so scared of the cold that we had tightly closed all openings," said a member of an American bomber crew which held out in an igloo in Labrador until they were rescued. "Naturally the air was soon very stale. All of us suddenly got headaches. Then we began vomiting in turn, which polluted the air still more. It was some days before it occurred to us to leave a big air hole open now and then on the leeward side."

It is even more dangerous if the survivors keep a smoking fire going in their shelter, without seeing that there is a constant supply of fresh air. During the war several pilots died in this way from carbon-monoxide poisoning. Admiral Richard E. Byrd, the famous American explorer, who in the twenties spent the whole winter alone in a hut on McMurdo Sound in the Antarctic, developed acute poisoning, and at the last moment crept out into the open.

Anyone talking of cold as a danger does not, of course, think first of the mountains, where it claims more victims than anywhere else, but of Polar regions. An American colonel who landed at the South Pole in the spring of 1958, said afterward: "The cold hit me like a sledgehammer. The temperature was minus 68° F." The record for Antarctic cold, however, is held by the Russian station "Sovietskaie" which (also in spring 1958) registered a temperature of minus 127°.

These are really temperatures "which freeze the tongue in your mouth," as a Rumanian saying has it, or, as the Eskimos put it, "where the urine flows upwards"—that is to say it freezes before reaching the ground. Such cold preserves all organic substances better than the most efficient refrigerator: they remain "farm-fresh," as it were. This was first recognized in dramatic circumstances on August 6, 1930, when the *Bratvaag*, carrying a Norwegian geological expedition (under Dr. Gunnar Horn), dropped anchor off the island of Vitö. Some members of the expedition went ashore to look for drinking water. On the beach they suddenly discovered a boat, and not far away, in a ravine, the frozen bodies of three men. They looked as if they had died only a few days before. But their clothes were old-fashioned, and their equipment had all the marks of the last century. A boathook which was found solved the riddle. It carried the inscription *Andrée Polar Expedition 1897*.

This was a Swedish expedition. Salomon Andrée and his two companions (Fränkel and Strindberg) had started from Dane's Islands, Spitsbergen, on the first Arctic flight in a balloon. Several times his homing pigeons had reached a human settlement with the message that the three men were well; after that contact with them was lost. All searches were fruitless; but then chance brought the Norwegians to the island of Vitö thirty-three years later.

They found Strindberg covered over with stones—so he must have died first. By the bodies of the other two lay supplies of food, as fresh as on the first day, and some exposed films, which were successfully developed. There were also supplies of fuel, and the sleeping bags were still in excellent condition: so they had not died of cold or starvation. Until recently it was thought that the flesh of Polar bears they had eaten was infected by trichinae; but American experts today believe all three explorers died of carbon-monoxide poisoning.

Equally fresh were the supplies of food forty-six years old discovered in the Antarctic in 1957 by American explorers. They came from one of Scott's supply camps on his return from the South Pole before he froze to death. The cans were given to his son, Peter, as a memento, and when Peter Scott opened some, he found they contained sheep's tongues, marmalade, and baked beans, all in excellent condition.

But despite these preserving qualities the extreme cold is the scourge of Polar regions. Many pilots who came down there said after their rescue that their bodies were instantaneously paralyzed by the cold, especially when it was accompanied by a biting wind. One man said: "When we came down in the water, my gloves got wet, and within a few minutes turned into blocks of ice as hard as stone."

In such cases frostbite is almost inevitable, unless the hands can be dried at once and somehow protected from the cold. However, the severest frostbite is often caused by carelessness rather than unavoidable accident. Greenstreet, for instance, a member of the Shackleton Expedition, lost his gloves and had to row with his hands uncovered. "His hands began to freeze. Soon frost blisters came up on the palms, in which the water also froze. As he went on rowing, it felt as if hard pebbles were embedded in his flesh." Afterward Greenstreet did the only sensible thing he could have done—he sank his hands into the warm entrails of a seal they had just killed. Experienced Polar travelers say with reason: "Lose your gloves in these latitudes, and you lose your life."

Even the slightest negligence can lead to severe frostbite. In the summer of 1959 fuel shortage forced an American pilot in a jet fighter down in the Arctic. After radioing to the nearest airport for help, he climbed out of the plane, had a look at his landing gear, and stamped up and down several times in the deep snow. Having had a promise that he would be picked up the next morning, he felt completely safe. At dusk he climbed back into his cockpit, and slept soundly. When his rescuers found him next day, all his toes were frozen. During his little stroll around the plane he had got some snow into his boots. The snow melted, the feet became wet, and the Arctic cold did the rest. All his toes had to be amputated.

Richard Howard, the American who investigated many accounts of airmen rescued from Polar regions, writes in his survey *Down in the North:* "Most of them did everything wrong they possibly could." They wore wet clothes, especially gloves, socks, and shoes, even when these could have been dried. Many used their bare hands to take snow to their mouths in place of water, which often led to increased thirst, a dry and burning throat, chapped lips, a sore tongue—and on top of that, frostbite on the hands (they swelled up and painful frost sores formed). Others tried to remove snow from the wings of their planes or handled tools, and when their unprotected hands touched the ice-cold metal, the skin was literally shredded off.

One pilot said after his rescue: "When the rescue parachute dropped emergency rations from the sky, I was so excited I ran through the deep snow in my socks to get to it quickly. A few hours later, when the doctor arrived by helicopter, he had to amputate three of my toes."

Wet shoes may quickly lead to wet feet. If that happens at a temperature a few degrees below freezing-point, frostbite does not set in at once when the temperature goes down, but the feet go white and numb, and walking becomes an effort: these are the first danger signals. Survivors who did not heed them soon found their feet swelling up to shapeless lumps. In some cases the tissues rotted away, and gangrene set in, making an amputation unavoidable.

Frozen limbs rarely feel numb, not at the start, anyway. A deep stabbing pain rages in them. There are reports of parties with frost sores groaning for hours in chorus. The danger of frostbite is even greater with broken limbs. Unless the injured person can be kept extremely warm, the frost penetrates rapidly because the circulation is restricted, and because of the lack of movement.

Many survivors have had their eyes water from the cold. "The tears ran down a man's nose," says Lansing in his biography of Shackleton, "and formed an icicle on the end, which sooner or later had to be broken off, and no matter how carefully it was done, a little patch of skin invariably came off with it, leaving a chronically unhealed sore on the end of his nose."

If most frost sores are caused by carelessness, they are often made worse by negligent or incorrect treatment. For instance (as has been mentioned earlier), rubbing frozen limbs down with snow is quite wrong, and so is doing it with alcohol, oil, or gasoline, a treatment many airmen coming down in Polar regions have resorted to.

Even massaging the limbs does more harm than good. William Everts, a pilot who had to make an emergency landing in Alaska in 1954, said: "I had frost-bite on both feet, and at once began giving them a vigorous massage. For two hours I belabored them frantically, and the pain was almost unbearable when the blood pulsed back into the veins. Then I thought I'd got over it. But the next morning instead of feet I had two half-raw lumps of flesh, on which all the toes had to be amputated."

Skin and tissues get very vulnerable in the cold, and Everts had injured them with his massage. Others will inflict the same suffering on themselves if they try to thaw their frozen limbs by physical jerks or running up and down—instead of protecting the limbs from frostbite by taking such exercises beforehand.

Some survivors have urinated on their frost sores, bringing a warmth which has led to a slight improvement. Some have warmed their hands under their armpits or held their feet against the bare skin of a companion's stomach or between his thighs. This method, in fact, is recommended by survival experts, who also teach their trainees that they can make "warming pans" by heating stones, and that the most effective first-aid measure where possible is to thaw a frozen hand or foot slowly in a hot bath.

Everyone knows how hard it is to get to sleep in a cold room with not enough bedclothes on. Either you curl up tight or you lie stiff as a board trying to avoid all contact with cold pajamas and sheet; and even then, with cold face and nose, sleep becomes almost impossible. The same phenomenon occurs even more, of course, in Polar regions.

Many pilots marooned there have not dared sleep in case they missed a rescue plane; but as a rule even those who tried have not succeeded—their sleep was stopped by the wind, by the snow blowing against their shelter, and above all by the appalling cold. Many covered themselves with parachute panels, spare sleeping bags, blankets, or newspapers. If there were not enough blankets, some of the crew would sleep by day and others by night— although this meant the beds could not be aired. Others slept snuggling up to each other, dove-tailed like a set of spoons (warmest for the man in the middle!) or with up to three men one on top of the other.

In 1957, Dr. M. B. Kreider and Dr. R. Buskirk of the U. S. Army discovered another means of helping the tired body to sleep despite low outside temperatures. It consists of taking a few mouthfuls of food with as many calories as possible before retiring; this stimulates the metabolism and increases body heat. In one experiment three out of six men took such a snack at a late hour (as well as their usual meals). Then all six lay down in sleeping bags at a temperature of minus 22.8° F. The three who had had the snack slept better and woke less often.

While cold can prevent a man from sleeping in comfort, it can also destroy all his normal routine habits. No one likes washing in great cold, which means exposing parts of the body you have been trying hard to keep warm. In 1915 the members of Shackleton's Antarctic expedition built themselves a makeshift shelter of stones, snow, and their upturned boats. Lack of ventilation soon made it stink so much that they always talked of it as "the Sty." Others occupying such shelters have for the same reasons suffered from headaches—which they preferred, however, to cold fresh air. Very few think of shaving, not only because a beard keeps the face warm, (although it usually soon crusts over with snow and ice), but because they are afraid they may get frost sores by not drying their faces properly.

When you stop washing and shaving, etc., you often lose all feeling for cleanliness and hygiene. An American pilot injured in a crash during the war was found in northern Canada in a disgusting condition: he had used his own sleeping bag as a lavatory, and for fear of the cold had not let his companions get him out of it.

Even the uninjured may behave little better. Many have used the nearest place in their camp or shelter as a lavatory. In the daytime Shackleton and his men used to "go behind a nearby pressure ridge, more for protection against the weather than for privacy, and get the job done as quickly as possible." They had long run out of paper, and had to make do with pieces of ice, which led to painful frost sores on the buttocks—and all their medicaments were at the bottom of the Weddell Sea.

In another camp the prospect of going outside at night to relieve themselves was "possibly the most disagreeable aspect of their existence" (says Lansing), and the men practiced bladder control "to the limits of bodily endurance." After a time, a two-gallon gasoline can was made into a urinal for use at night. The rule was that the man who raised its level to within two inches of the top, had to carry the can outside and empty it. If a man felt the need and the weather outside was too bad, he would lie awake waiting for someone else to go, so that he might judge from the sound the level of the can's contents. "If it sounded ominously close to the top, he would try to hold out until morning. But it was not always possible to do so, and he might be forced to get up. More than once a man would fill the can as silently as possible, then steal back into his sleeping bag. The next man to get up would find to his fury that the can was full—and had to be emptied before it could be used!"

Anyone exposed to extreme cold naturally has an overwhelming desire for fire and comforting warmth, which are indeed of vital importance to him. There is an unwritten law among all bush pilots in the far north of Alaska and Canada, that they should light a fire directly after an emergency landing. Very few of them have any difficulties with this. A former Air Force man who had been through a thorough survival training set about saving himself when his small transport plane crashed in the tundra during the winter.

"At first I wanted to creep into the fuselage. It was undamaged and looked so inviting, but I remembered that its metal exterior would soon exhibit the same qualities as the cooling unit of a refrigerator." (Survival trainers do, in fact, advise against staying in the fuselage of a crashed plane in winter time. Any damp condenses as ice on the interior walls, and the floor soon turns into a dangerous slide, four to six inches deep.) "So I built a camp beside the plane, using just the one wing as a roof. Then, after providing for an air hole, I tried to scrape the snow off the frozen floor with a tin can. I was unsuccessful, so I used the can as foundation for a fire. I took out cleaning rags, lubricating oil, and all the plane's wooden parts, and lit a small fire. Then I swept some places clear of snow, and collected moss, leaves and small green branches, which I dried by the fire. Later I built a second fire next to the first, and squatted in between them. In this way I kept nice and warm, until I was rescued."

Survivors lacking other fuel have sometimes burned the wooden parts of their planes, or they have collected dry peat, which is to be found under previously flooded river beds in an Arctic summer. Dung has been used as a wood substitute, also the bones and tallow of killed animals. Occasionally survivors risk lighting their last match, or draw sparks out of flints. As tinder, they have used string, birds' down, birds' nests, gunpowder, and very often in

The tarpaulin roof gives protection from wind and rain. The tree trunks behind the fire serve to reflect the heat into the snow shelter, which has an open front.

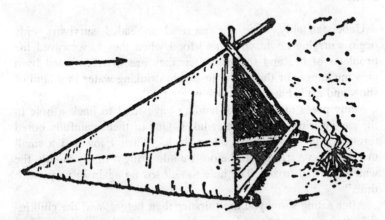

Many people have survived snowstorms and below-zero temperatures in such simple tents.

summer the fine woodmeal of woodworms—most of these usually mixed with a few drops of gasoline.

The radio operator of an air crew which had made a crash landing, after unsuccessful efforts with a flint, eventually had the idea of using a battery and two conducting wires with the insulation scraped off, to produce the sparks which did in fact set the tinder alight. "Then," he reported, after his rescue, "we filled some food cans half full of sand, soaked the sand in gasoline, cut a slit in the sides of the cans, lit the sand, and used the cans as a stove. We filled other cans with oil—and the black smoke was seen by the search planes." Even oil-lamps have been constructed out of food cans, with string as wick.

Bertram and Klausmann, who lost their matches in their landing, invented a "patent fire-lighter." Its ingenious component parts: "The engine's magneto, half a gallon of gasoline, an empty medicine bottle, and cotton-wool. We filled the bottle with cotton-wool, poured in a few drops of gasoline, saturating the cotton-wool with it, stuck the two cables of the magneto into the neck of the bottle, a few turns of the crank—and a spark between the cable ends lit the cotton-wool. This fire-lighter would last for years, since it uses only a few drops of gasoline. It is a wonderful invention."

Understandably, even the most clear-headed survivors only begin worrying about water and food when they have solved the problems of fire and shelter. Often they are first reminded by a growing hunger or thirst. But to obtain drinking water in a land of snow and ice is harder than one might think.

Many pilots after a crash landing have tried to hack a hole in the ice covering of fresh-water lakes. One of them painfully bored through a layer of ice three-feet thick. "Then I lowered a small metal cup on a string. But before I could bring it to my mouth, the water in it had frozen. The hole too closed up again in very quick time."

After eating snow you are thirstier than before, and the chill inside makes many people feel doubly miserable. Even when melted and heated, snow had often produced flatulence and diarrhea, very likely because of its lack of minerals. Yet the members of Shackleton's expedition satisfied their requirements of water wholly from

If the ground underneath is wet or covered with snow, a fire is built on logs of wood.

If the wood itself is wet, big logs are put near the fire to dry them.

snow and ice, though admittedly they boiled it with tea or soup cubes.

Research stations in the Antarctic today dig deep shafts to collect "drinking snow." In Camp Century (Greenland), an American "ice station," an atomic reactor conducts hot steam deep into the glacier ice, and melted ice is pumped up through another pipe. But this water has to be specially prepared for drinking, either with tea (as was done by the Shackleton expedition), or through the addition of minerals.

Whereas a survivor in the desert or at sea can get on without food for a long period, in cold latitudes the body needs fuel to maintain its resistance and produce warmth in the metabolism—food, that is to say, as rich in calories as possible. If this should be lacking or insufficient, a man's working powers sink more rapidly in extreme cold than anywhere else. This explains the exhaustion symptoms of people who have been exposed to extreme cold even for a few hours.

At great heights the first stages of exhaustion occur soon after the last meal has been taken. A pilot who landed on the Greenland Glacier (about seven thousand feet), could very soon cover distances of no more than fifty yards at a time, with long rests in between. A few days after his crash he would only walk for ten yards an hour. Other survivors have reported that this physical weakness, increased by lack of food, has led to "Long hours of doing nothing. We had to limit all physical activity to a few hours a day, sometimes even to less than an hour."

Evert Stenmark, the Swede caught in an avalanche, said that the hungrier he grew, the more apathetic he also became. "Decisions I would ordinarily have reached within a few seconds, took hours to ripen in my head—and hours more to carry out. It took me five hours, once I had decided to do this, merely to bring my head and hands out of the warmth of my rucksack."

Many victims of the cold, weakened by hunger, have stumbled into the snow from exhaustion and then been too apathetic to pick themselves up. They froze to death in the same position as they had fallen.

When parties of airmen or explorers have supplies of food, they usually ration it very strictly; but when the supplies are extremely scanty, as is often the case, this does not help much. Some American airmen subsisted for fifteen days on their iron rations, growing weaker and weaker. The crew of a bomber which made a forced landing in Greenland divided up their rations in such a miserly way that each man received a quarter of a biscuit a day.

Hungry men get the most curious ideas for making as much of their food as possible. A British pilot, too weak from Greenland's cold to go foraging, pushed a peanut around in his mouth for a whole day before chewing it up with relish. Another man in a similar situation sucked a toffee for twenty-four hours, taking it out of his mouth every few minutes, putting it away for a while, and then bringing it out again. Three starving American airmen in the Arctic, who had nothing at all to eat, but did have five thousand cigarettes, dulled their hunger by chain-smoking—which made them feel so ill, however, that they were cured of smoking once and for all.

The American explorer Adolphus Greely, who spent from 1881 to 1884 at one of the eleven "international circum-Polar stations" in the Arctic, was let down by his supply ships, after which his expedition was left in appalling hunger. Two thirds of the men died of starvation, and another man was court-martialed and shot for stealing some of the meager supplies left.

"Moldy hard bread, and two cans of soup had to serve as supper for twelve men," Greely wrote in his diary. ". . . To stretch our scanty fuel supplies, we are burning hemp ropes, which produce a thick smoke irritating to eyes and throat. . . . When the hurricane lamp is put out, there is always someone furtively pouncing on the rancid seal-oil inside, and finishing it off. . . . At present we are burning the soles of our boots to keep ourselves warm." And later: "We are eating the outer (seal) skins of our sleeping bags, roasted or boiled, according to taste. Today we divided up the last piece." When the supply ship *Bear* finally reached Greely, only he and six others out of the original twenty-four were still alive.

Some members of the Italian Nobile expedition also suffered agonizing hunger. In 1928 Colonel Umberto Nobile had tried to land at the North Pole with the airship *Italia*. But the attempt was abandoned, and on the return flight the airship had to make a forced landing about two hundred miles north of Spitsbergen. A little later a small Swedish search plane landed near the survivors.

Nobile yielded to pressure from his men and allowed himself to be rescued first—for which he was afterward degraded in rank.

On May 30 three of the *Italia* crew remaining behind—Malmgren (a Swede), Mariano, and Zappi—left their companions in an attempt to reach Spitsbergen on foot across the pack-ice, which they thought would give them a better chance of survival. Amost six weeks later, in the early morning of July 12, they were sighted on an ice floe by the pilot of the Russian ice-breaker *Krassin*. One of them was lying on the floe with his arms spread out. They were only about twelve miles from where the *Italia* had landed; that was all the distance they had been able to cover over the difficult pack-ice. The same evening the *Krassin* worked its way toward the floe, which was ten yards long by eight yards wide. But there were only two men on it, Mariano and Zappi; Malmgren had disappeared.

Zappi dragged himself unaided onto the deck of the *Krassin,* but Mariano had frostbite on both legs and had to be carried; he died soon afterward. And Malmgren? "He must be dead. We left him a month ago on an ice-block near the island of Broc," said Zappi, and went on to relate how the Swede had fallen several times in the pack-ice, breaking an arm and a hand and sustaining severe internal injuries. Finally he could go no farther, and asked the other two to put him in an ice-hole. They did so, and took his Polar equipment and all his supplies with them—again, allegedly, at his request. On June 30, according to Zappi, these supplies too were exhausted. Dead beat, and almost fainting from hunger, they drifted on their tiny ice-floe, without hope of rescue, until the *Krassin* pilot sighted them twelve days later. As he afterward maintained quite definitely that he had seen *three* men on the ice-floe, the rumor soon got about that the two Italians had killed Malmgren and eaten him. The truth, presumably, will never be known.

A more recent case is that of the Canadian bush pilot Martin Hartwell who crashed north of the Polar Circle in the Northwest Territory on November 8, 1972, with his Beechcraft 18. He was rescued thirty-one days later. The other passengers—a pregnant Eskimo, an Eskimo boy and a twenty-seven-year-old British nurse, Judy Hill, were dead. It was many weeks later that Hartwell admitted of having eaten some flesh that he had cut out of Judy's thighs, preparing a sort of stew for himself. When reporters got wind of Hartwell's deed (for which even Judy's parents showed a certain understanding), the full, horrible truth about a survival drama involving mass-cannibalism became known. It was early in 1973 when a group of Uruguayan students was rescued from a snow-covered, windswept 11,500-foot plateau on the Argentine side of the Andes. There, on October 13, 1972, their plane had crashed, due to a navigational error, killing thirteen of the forty-five persons on board—including the pilot.

The survivors, some of them injured, found themselves in what was left of the plane: namely, part of the forward fuselage with a big hole instead of the tail, with no wings and, what was worse, no galley. The only food that could be mustered among the wreckage were a few lumps of sugar, eight chocolate bars, candies, three jars of marmalade, a few crackers, some bottles of Coke, some liquor —and several cartons of cigarettes.

After moving the dead into the open, the survivors—most of them boys aged twenty to twenty-three—settled inside the plane as best as they could, trying to protect themselves from the bitter cold with blankets, and all the clothing they could muster, hoping for a quick rescue. They had rationed their food, and used melted snow for drink. But as day after day passed, their supply of food was quickly coming to an end. Soon, the first survivors who had escaped the crash itself died of exhaustion, or as a result of the severe injuries they had suffered during the actual disaster. They, too, were dragged out of the fuselage and put down in the snow outside.

On the tenth day of their ordeal, most of the boys were so weak already that they felt listless, cold, and found it difficult to move. They preferred to stay inside the plane, hoping for rescue, but at the same time preparing themselves to die.

It will never be known who first thought of the possibility of eating the flesh of those whose bodies lay frozen outside in the snow. But with the gnawing hunger, the thought had crept into everyone's mind—until one of the boys, nineteen-year-old Roberto Canessa, brought it out into the open.

To him—and to his friends, some of whom were deeply religious—it seemed inhumane to think or even talk about such a possibility. But Canessa tried to convince everyone, including himself, with logical and even religious arguments, that eating their dead friends would be the only chance to keep alive until they could be rescued. "If we wait any further, we will be too weak to cut the meat off the bodies. Then all of us will die. Besides, don't you realize that the souls have long left the bodies, and all that's left are the carcasses which are just dead flesh—flesh that could keep us alive?"

And so, after a deep struggle against moral and ethical scruples and, last, but not least, a fight against revulsion, they took the decisive step that ultimately saved their lives. With a piece of broken glass Canessa cut the first thin strips of meat from the buttocks of a frozen body. He put it on the plane's roof to dry in the sun. A short while later, after a final struggle, he swallowed a piece of the dried, human flesh. And suddenly his feeling was that of triumph: he knew he would survive. God will only help those who help themselves, he kept telling himself.

Gradually, the other boys followed Canessa's example. Once they had broken the taboo, it was a logical step for them to set certain rules. They all agreed that the bodies of relatives were to be touched only as a last resort. Spring was coming in the Andes, and if a rescue party did not find them soon, the bodies had to keep them alive until the snow had melted sufficiently so that they could find some moss or other plants between the rocks as another source of food. It was further agreed to eat all parts of a body except the skull and the genitals. Also, the bodies of the dead female passengers were not to be touched.

But as time dragged on and the hopes for rescue dwindled, most of these agreements were anulled by silent or open consent. Finally, after having consumed most of the easy accessible "outer" flesh, the boys ate every "edible" part of the human body— sometimes cooked, but mostly raw: the inner organs, including the liver, kidneys, stomach, heart and lungs, the fat, intestines, and bone marrow, as well as some blood clots that had collected in some of the limbs. When an avalanche hit the plane, killing another eight of the survivors, their bodies too were eaten. Finally, when only the skulls of the eaten bodies were left, they cracked them open and ate the brains—including some of the meat that had started to rot. It tasted like cheese, reportedly.

All during that time of mental and physical agony, the strongest and fittest of the students, fed with extra rations of human flesh, set out for exploratory expeditions trying to find a way out of the mountains and get help. But invariably they returned after one or two days, completely exhausted. There did not seem to be a way out—there were only mountains upon mountains stretching all the way to the horizon, and all of them, snow-covered.

After almost nine weeks—and the death of two more boys (one from injuries, the other from exhaustion)—there was to be a final attempt to reach help: three of the students started out for a final try. One soon gave up and returned to the plane wreck, but the other two went on. They climbed a mountain which—as it later turned out—was around 13,500 feet high, hoping that somewhere beyond it rescue would be waiting. This time, at last, their hope proved to be right: Roberto Canessa and Nando Parrado reached a river farther down the base of the mountain, and nine days after the start of their expedition they stumbled upon the first sign of civilization: a corral with several cows and horses. The same evening they spotted three men on horses across the river—and were themselves spotted. But it was not until the next morning, December 21, exactly seventy days after their plane had crashed, that one of the horsemen returned and the two boys were finally rescued.

Less than forty-eight hours later a group of Chilean helicopters, following Parrado's directions, picked up the rest of the survivors near the wreck of the Fairchild. All were still alive and—considering the circumstances—quite well. Still, they were immediately rushed to the nearest hospital. There, after a careful examination, the doctors were amazed to find that none of their patients was in critical physical condition. True, all of them had lost weight (Parrado as much as fifty pounds, for instance), but all of them insisted they felt fine. They refused to stay in bed, and immediately asked for big dinners which they not only devoured with great appetite but also kept down without harm, quite unusual for half-starved survivors.

Then, gradually the truth came out as to what had kept the students alive during the past seventy days. The doctors, if they were shocked, said nothing. Friends, parents—even the parents of those whose corpses had kept the survivors alive—tried to understand. Nobody who has not been in a similar situation should indeed condemn out of his easy chair what the Uruguayan students had done. Actually, they had done nothing else but break a taboo erected by "civilized" man, the same man who postulates that it is wrong to eat human flesh even if it is a question of survival, but who at the same time finds hundreds of moral justifications to kill his fellow man in battle or on the electric chair. Even the Catholic Church showed a great understanding for the act of cannibalism committed out of sheer desperation and the will to stay alive: "Morally I see no objection," said the Archbishop of Montevideo. "It is always necessary to eat whatever is at hand . . ."

Some of the most horrifying stories of death by starvation in the Arctic—a fate the Andes survivors escaped—have been told by the great Polar explorer Peter Freuchen. One concerned an Eskimo woman who had to kill four of her five starving children. The eldest girl was old enough to understand, and helped her mother to hang three younger brothers or sisters; then she put the noose round her own neck. After pulling it tight, the mother herself ran out into the icy cold. Only a boy of seven was left, who refused to die, saying he would live on grass and hare excrement. He survived, but was stunted in growth.

Freuchen's wife, an Eskimo, had in childhood suffered such hunger with her mother and three-year-old brother that they had eaten old leather straps and then their own clothes. The starving boy bit off one of his mother's nipples, and when she realized she couldn't keep him alive, she hanged him. During the summer, mother and daughter ate grass, hare excrement, old leather objects and the walrus-hide strips under the sleigh runners.

When Polar explorers find their food supplies running out, they often have to kill the sledge-dogs for food. Macklin, a member of Shackleton's expedition, said in anticipation of this: "I would have no hesitation in eating dog cooked, but I do not look forward to eating it raw." When it came to it, however, "the meat of the dogs was universally acclaimed. 'Their flesh tastes a treat,' McNeish remarked. 'It is a big treat for us after being so long on seal meat.' James found it 'surprisingly good and tasty.' Worsley said that the piece of Grus (one of the dogs) he ate 'had a better flavour than the sea leopard.' And Hurley went so far as to say it was 'exqui-

1. In February 1957, Chester Simpson (sixteen) set off from Amarillo, Texas, during a severe snowstorm to visit his girl friend. After twelve miles he got caught in a barbed-wire fence. Already too weak to free himself, he froze to death. (*Photo: H. W. Hilton*)

2. Near Silver Creek, New York, flood waters left these chunks of ice and stranded many residents. (*Wide World Photo*)

3. The correct use of rescue and survival equipment is now part of the basic training of armed forces all over the world.

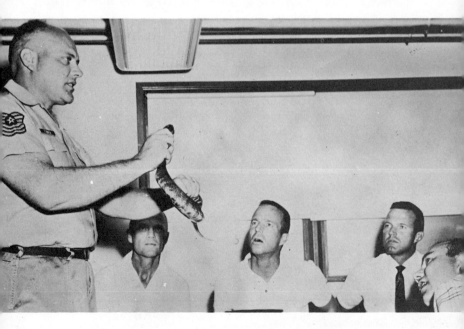

4. How to deal with snakes is one of many subjects on which survival trainees are instructed. Here the trainees are America's astronauts: (from left to right) Glenn, Carpenter, Cooper, and Grissom. *(Photos: U. S. Air Force)*

5. A member of the search party with the World War II bomber *Lady Be Good* which crashed in 1943 in the Libyan Desert and was not found until years later by a geological party. *(Wide World Photo)*

6. Sandstorm approaching Khartoum. *(Photo: Ullstein)*

7. In an experiment called "SOS Sahara" (in 1960), some Frenchmen tried to prove that survival in the desert was possible.

8. Three of them irresponsibly separated from the main party. They were found, nearly dead with thirst, in the shadow of a corrugated iron screen. (*Photos: Lutetia*)

9. A sailor from the *Jeanne Gougy* is hoisted to the top of a cliff with a breeches buoy. *(Photo: Deutsche Presse-Agentur)*

10. Two members of the U. S. Coast Guard cutter *Yakutat* saved sailors from the tanker S.S. *Mercer* who were injured and numb with cold. *(Photo: U. S. Coast Guard)*

11. Fourteen dead lay beneath the snow of this avalanche in the Bavarian Alps in 1957, and four hundred volunteers took part in the search for the missing.

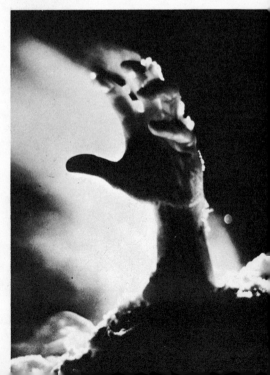

12. RIGHT: The hand of one of the victims sticking out of the snow. *(Photos: Rieder)*

13. Three of the five dead Viennese schoolboys who ran into a front of bad weather on the slopes of a 10,000-foot-high mountain range. They continued walking aimlessly, exhausting their strength, instead of building a shelter. *(Photo:Sz-Archiv)*

14. Help from the air for a pilot "down in the drink." The helicopter pulls him out of the water by means of a rope with a life belt attached to it; he is later taken, unhurt, on board the U.S. aircraft carrier *Bearss* (in background). *(Photo: U.S. Navy)*

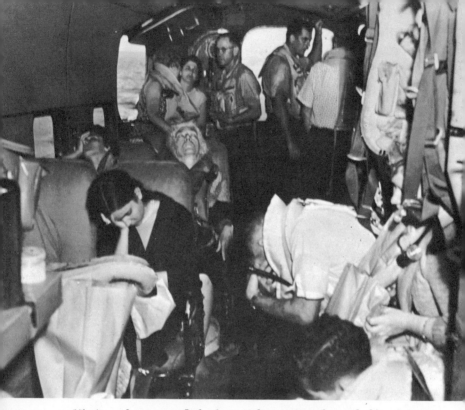

15. An airliner on a flight from Tokyo to Manila, with fifty-nine passengers, had to come down on the water with one of its wings on fire. The passengers were terrified and thought their last hour had come, but all except one woman were saved. *(Photo: U. S. Coast Guard)*

16. BELOW: With only one of its four engines still working, the passenger plane *Sovereign of the Skies* comes down in the Pacific.

17. OPPOSITE TOP: On hitting the waves, the rear part breaks off and sinks.

18. CENTER: Soon afterward the passengers climb onto the plane's rafts, while a lifeboat from a nearby weather ship hurries to the scene. All twenty-four passengers leave the sinking plane unhurt. *(Photos: U. S. Coast Guard)*

19. BOTTOM: A photograph taken by Albert Spear, one of the passengers, during the rescue operation.

20. A castaway could never rig up this aerial for distress signals unless there was no wind or swell at all. Yet it is still part of the standard equipment in many lifeboats. *(Photo: U. S. Navy)*

21. The arrangements for putting lifeboats to sea are outdated in most ships and therefore not always operable. In July 1956, when the *Andrea Doria* sank off the island of Nantucket, she took half her lifeboats down with her into the sea. *(Photo: U. S. Coast Guard)*

22. When wooden lifeboats are lowered from a sinking ship, they are often shattered against her side by a heavy sea. Some of the *Pamir* lifeboats fished out of the water. Note that they are quite open, so that the occupants were completely exposed to wind and weather. *(Photo: Ullstein)*

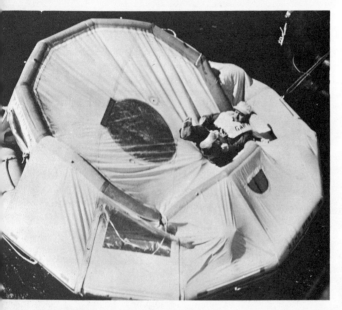

23. TOP: A castaway can make his presence known to rescuers by torches which emit colored smoke. *(Photo: U. S. Navy)*

24. CENTER: These inflatable life rafts are stable, warm, and cannot capsize. They can be boarded from the deck of a sinking ship by just jumping onto the roof.

25. BOTTOM: Interior of an inflatable life raft. *(Photos: U. S. Coast Guard)*

26. Helicopters can reach a castaway quicker than rescue ships. He is then fished out of the water with a net and pulled into the helicopter by a winch. *(Photo: Ullstein)*

27. In the future, pilots flying faster than the speed of sound will be able to detach themselves with the nose section from their crippled plane. The "rescue capsule" then sinks to the ground on a parachute. Since it is completely watertight, the pilot can also come down on the sea and call for rescue with his own radio. *(Photo: Lockheed Corporation)*

28. SOS in snow—the message Ralph Flores tracked out when he and Helen Klaben, after their plane crashed, spent fifty days in below freezing weather. *(Wide World Photo)*

sitely tender and flavorous, especially Nelson (another dog), which equalled veal.'"

Natural food in the Antarctic is always very scanty. It consists chiefly of seals and penguins. Shackleton and his men lived for weeks on seal. On April 10, 1916, they collected five thousand pounds of seal, enough for ninety days. They used the oil for burning, and also for cleaning their filthy tools—and playing cards. Penguins were a welcome alternative, and you could have a real Antarctic feast from "boiled penguin hearts, livers, eyes, tongues, toes, and Lord-knows-what else besides, mixed with a cup of water to wash it down."

Eskimos, too, are not very squeamish in their choice of food. Peter Freuchen mentions in his memoirs that they made a so-called "givac" from auks, a small Arctic bird. *Givac* means steeped, and the dead auks are wrapped into the whole fatty skin of a newly killed seal, then put in the shade to stop the fat turning rancid. In the mild warmth of the Arctic summer the fat gradually seeps out of the skin and penetrates the flesh of the birds, making it tasty and tender.

Another Eskimo delicacy is the flesh of reindeer, chewed, and mixed with spittle and snow-grouse excrement. It is said to taste like Roquefort cheese, and is offered to guests of honor. The Indians of North Canada take a special delight in half-rotten flesh of musk oxen roasted almost black in the fire.

If such things are delicacies for the natives of Polar regions, they should be all right (say survival instructors) for anyone from moderate latitudes marooned in these regions. Most likely, they will not have to rely on them for too long. The reason is that modern victims of that fate have better chances of being rescued than they would have had in earlier times, exceptions granted. People in an airliner can be sure that a search will be started within twenty-four hours of the plane being missed. Even if the plane comes down in the Canadian tundra, they can usually send out an SOS giving their approximate position. Whereas Scott, Greely, and Shackleton had to survive for weeks or months without contact with the outside world, passengers in the plane that crashes in snow and ice only have to hold out till rescue arrives; and if they find any sort of food to help them do so, it will greatly increase the chances of the rescue party coming on them alive.

The areas on the edge of the Arctic, which are anyhow much more frequented than other Polar regions, contain a relative abundance of plant and animal life. "Nobody needs to starve in the North," the survival experts say.

Although the water is cold and almost always covered with ice, it has in it enough lobsters, fish, seals, walruses, whales, and even some species of shark. On the coasts there are many water birds, reindeer, musk oxen and Polar bears; and in the Arctic summer, even up to 80° North Latitude, you can find bees and wasps, flies, butterflies, grasshoppers, insects living in trees, and several species of worms. It is all the more amazing that very few servicemen marooned in the Arctic during the war had the idea of going "hunting," looking for animals or setting traps for them.

In December 1942 a B-26, with its engines shot to pieces and its fuselage riddled, made a crash landing on the edge of a large snowfield in Labrador. None of the seven members of the crew knew the exact position. The radio had broken down, and it was assumed at home that they had been shot down over enemy territory. So no one knew where they were and no one thought it worth looking for them.

On the day after the crash, radio operator, rear-gunner and co-pilot took a dinghy and set off to find help somewhere. They were never seen again. The other four men, instead of pitching a camp outside, huddled together in the fuselage, and tried to protect themselves as best they could against the bitter cold. Then they waited.

On the third day they saw fifty seals, but did not think of shooting them. It was not till hunger was almost overwhelming that two men tried to catch fish, without success. At last they caught a small bird, and made a soup from it. But they spent most of the time in their sleeping bags inactive. Gradually they ate through their K rations: candy, Coca-Cola, dates, and canned chicken.

On the fifteenth day after the crash the officer wrote in his log: "It is really surprising how much pleasure a tiny toffee can give. We wait greedily for it from one day to the next."

On the twenty-sixth day: "We should have starved already if we hadn't had plenty of coffee." *Three days later:* "Each of us had a cough lozenge, three and a half dates, a level teaspoonful of peanuts and some coffee. That's damned little for a whole day, but our spirits are revived again despite the bad weather."

Thirty-seventh day: "None of us is specially hungry, but we are growing weaker and weaker, and also colder, because our bodies aren't producing enough warmth."

Thirty-eighth day: "Our food supplies are at an end."

Fortieth day (January 26, 1943): "We are overstrained, but still very calm. Every day we think we can't go on, but the next day we're still alive. We each smoked a pipe of tobacco, and it made G. feel sick. I don't feel too good myself—but we've survived it."

In the days between there are repeated sentences like "Bad weather. We went to bed early." "Didn't get up till noon, cleaned the place, went to bed again—too much wind." "Wind—stayed in bed all day." The last entry is for February 3: "We have spent a whole week in bed. W. died today. He hasn't been quite all there the last few days. We are all very weak, can't go on more than a few days longer."

No one knows exactly when the last three died. Some hunting Eskimos found the bodies in early March. By an irony of fate, they came from the village of Hebron, only a few miles from the crash.

There are many other examples of people starving to death in the Arctic because they didn't do any of the sensible things which might have led to their rescue. Scarcely any of them thought of even producing distress signals, such as a smoking fire, patches of ground conspicuously cleared of grass or snow, or a big SOS sign trodden deep into the snow at a suitable angle to the sun so that its rays would cast black shadows into the letters. Trainees at Stead were often told of an American pilot who (like the B-26 crew) made a crash landing in Labrador. The plane was hardly damaged, but the radio was out of action. Two months later, a search party discovered the plane. Beside it the pilot lay dead (of starvation). For days and perhaps weeks he had simply waited to be found. He had never ventured more than 150 yards from his plane. Once he had lit a fire only ten yards from a marked but seldom-used track. If he had walked along this track, he would have reached a village after ten miles.

It is understandable, of course, that people marooned in the

Arctic rarely go far from their camp (which is usually their plane). Not having learned the best way to survive in the Arctic, they feel safest there; but it doesn't do them much good, unless before their landing they have managed to send out a distress signal, giving their approximate position. The prospect of being found by chance in the thinly populated Arctic areas, is small indeed. Except with the passengers of an airliner (who can count on a big search operation starting immediately the plane is missed), the people with most chance of survival are those who try to get back to civilization "under their own steam," or at least explore the immediate surroundings where they have crashed.

The former was done by the pilot of a Canadian plane which in January 1963 landed on the edge of a lake north of the Arctic Circle, on a flight from Payne City to Fort Chimo. As the radio had broken down, and the plane had gone off course, owing to a front of bad weather, there was little hope of any help being sent. The pilot told the passengers to make camp outside the plane in the shelter of the fuselage; then he set off with one of them, an Eskimo, to fetch help. After five days, despite biting wind and Arctic cold, they arrived safely at Fort Chimo, sixty miles away. A ski plane left at once for the other six passengers, and a little later they also were rescued safe and sound.

Even isolated individuals, if they adapt themselves to their environment, can "march out of the cold" (a Stead phrase) of their own accord. One of the best examples of this is the story of Flight Lieutenant David Steeves.

On May 9, 1957, Steeves, then twenty-three, started from Oakland Airport, California, in a T-33 jet, making for his home airport of Selma, Alabama. The flight took him over the Sierra Nevada. Although this is in California, the climatic conditions in the early spring are subarctic; at great heights there is deep snow, some of which lasts into the summer; night temperatures there sink far below freezing point. Walking over the fields of scree and through the deep gorges is tremendously difficult.

Steeves was just flying over one of the tremendously precipitous gorges when there was suddenly a loud explosion inside the T-33. He lost consciousness. When he came to, his cockpit was full of smoke, and the plane was hurtling down through the clouds toward the Sierra. He pulled the joy stick, but the plane did not react. There was nothing for it but to use his ejector seat. The time was 11:45.

A little later Steeves landed by parachute on a rocky promontory in the middle of a steep snowfield, twisting both ankles. His plane crashed somewhere on a mountain slope dozens of miles away.

Steeves could see snow right to the horizon, with bare mountaintops behind, a few trees here and there. At this height, about ten thousand feet, there was no sign of human life. He knew a search for him would only start a day later, and as he could not give his position by radio, it was improbable that he would be found. He decided to strike out on his own.

The rescue operation did not start for four days, because of heavy clouds over the Sierra, and it was fruitless. The Air Force search crews were informed by a local expert: "In this Sierra region, you wouldn't even find the wrecks of twenty heavy bombers. It is the wildest area in the United States." On the eighth day the search was abandoned, and a week later, Steeves's mother received a letter from Air Force Headquarters saying: "There is no hope that a man might survive in the Sierra Nevada at this time of year." Soon afterward a death certificate was signed, Steeves's records were removed from Air Force files, and he was now officially dead.

In point of fact Steeves was far from dead. After his landing on the promontory he at first tried to get his bearings, without much success. He only knew that there was no human being anywhere near him and that he had several mountain ranges around him which must be well over ten thousand feet. It was the same region in which one of his friends, Flight Lieutenant Glen Sutton, had disappeared with his plane a few weeks before. After that Steeves had taken some precautions which now proved very useful. He had got a cobbler to sew into his flying boots a sheath for a small butcher's knife, and a holster for his service revolver: so he was carrying both these weapons on him. Since Sutton's crash he had also been careful to take several boxes of matches on any flight. His K rations, however, were in the crashed plane.

The first thing now was to get out of the snow, to avoid freezing to death. He rolled up his parachute, "the pilot's best friend," tied it up, then threw it over the promontory. It fell three hundred feet, landing near some snow-covered trees—the first objective he set himself to reach. By now it was noon. He scraped holes with his knife in the ice under the promontory and climbed down the slope foot by foot. His hands were freezing in the soaked gloves, and he stopped repeatedly to warm them under his armpits. After four hours he had at last reached his parachute.

A short rest, then he tied the nylon panels on his back, and tried to walk to the edge of the snowfield, which was much farther down. But now his swollen ankles gave out: With a cry of pain, he collapsed.

A few minutes later he had the idea of using his parachute as a sledge. He sat down on the nylon bundle, with his legs extended in front of him, and slid cautiously down the field, which had a surface of hard snow. When he reached a pit, he would crawl on elbows and knees. By evening he had reached some stunted pines deep in snow.

He dug himself a hole beneath them, put his parachute over it, and crawled in. He used the empty parachute case as a seat. With the aid of some paper money, family photos, and his identity card, he lit a small fire, which he fed with the wood of a dead tree stump. The temperature had sunk to 14° F., but in his hole it was at least endurable.

The next morning it began to snow, and got only slightly warmer. He decided to stay near his camp till the weather changed. Wrapped in his parachute, he spent two more days and nights in the snow hole. Then the swellings on his ankles had gone down far enough for him to be able to hobble on after a fashion. He rested often. In the evening he dug himself a hole in a snowdrift and spent the night in it. He ate snow, but warmed it thoroughly in his mouth before swallowing it.

After three days he had reached the edge of the snowfield and found himself in a sparse forest. Here, under the trees, he made his first big fire, dried his clothes and slept for over twelve hours.

The next day he reached a stream and followed its course. He discovered a path on which headway was easier, but soon lost it again in deep snow. He struggled on over large boulders, through waist-high snowdrifts and over iced-up tree roots.

Fourteen days after the crash he came to a small fenced-off clearing, a picnic place for mountain climbers who sometimes

came to this region in the midsummer. Discovering some rusty
cans in a litter bin, he picked out the cleanest and found some
marmalade at the bottom, which he scraped out with his knife and
gratefully swallowed.

Four hours later, just before nightfall, something dark loomed
up before him—a hut! The door was locked, and he was so weak
that it took him three hours of laborious effort to smash the hinge.
Opening the door, the first thing he set eyes on was a big notice
saying FOOD. He stumbled over to the shelves on the wall facing
him, while dozens of mice hastily made off, and began a feverish
search for the hoped-for supplies. What he found was not much,
but it was enough to make him break down and weep tears of
thankfulness: a can of beans, a can of corned beef, a can of tomatoes, two packages of gelatin, half a box of lump sugar, a can of
rice a third full, another can of beans half full, soup cubes, tea,
ketchup, and at least twenty different spices.

Although he was feeling tremendously hungry, he confined
himself to the beans, chewing each bean with deliberate slowness,
drinking some ketchup from the bottle with them, and frequently
pausing in between. In fact, his shrunken stomach did not rebel.
Although he would like to have gone on eating, he forced himself
to leave most of the food untouched, and not to eat again until he
had digested the first meal. He got some water from the river, and
quenched his thirst.

Then he made a bed from an old mattress. Tarpaulins, gnawed
by mice, had to serve as blankets. He put the remains of the food
and enough water within reach, then started on an agonizing
"operation": inch by inch he pulled off his boots. The pain was
terrible, and he could almost see his ankles swelling up before his
eyes; the bluish red of the bruises stretched right up to the calves
on both legs. With cold sweat on his brow, he crept under his tarpaulins. For two days, he lay there delirious. In his few waking
moments he ate from his store, but had enough will power not to
eat too much. His stomach tolerated the small quantities without
any trouble.

On the third morning he was over the worst. Outside the hut
snow had fallen again, so he didn't need to hobble to the river to
fetch drinking water. He cooked himself a rice dish on a grill in
the open. Then he went over his hut for further treasures, and

found a map, which showed that this hut was about six thousand feet above sea level, surrounded by mountains of about twelve thousand feet. There was no human settlement marked on the map.

The next morning, carrying a rucksack crammed with the remains of the food, firewood, and paper, Steeves struck out from the hut, meaning to follow the river, which must somewhere lead out of this range of mountains. After about a hundred yards he had to cross the river. He took off all his clothes, tied his things on his back and waded into the ice-cold water. Seconds later he lost his footing, got carried away, and was swept over a waterfall ten feet high. But happily he reached the opposite bank. The matches, well packed in nylon and protected inside his rolled-up jacket, had remained dry. He made a fire, dried his things, then trudged on. But after a day's walking his way was blocked by a sheer rock face, and he had to turn back.

He got back to the hut just before a snowstorm set in. He started on the tomatoes, which he had left behind as a precaution, and didn't stir outside for five days, while storm and snow were doing their worst. He found a cookery book and read through it three times. To use his "leisure" productively, he made a fishing line out of some threads, rusty hooks, and a switch. When the weather cleared, he broke up a rotten tree trunk from which he got some woodworms as bait. An hour later he had caught a six-inch trout with this improvised fishing line.

Every day now he caught from two to four trout. He boiled them or roasted them on wooden spits over his fire, which he kept going continuously. From the fork of a branch, his revolver and some ropes, he skillfully constructed a trap on a game path. Steeves was a townsman, with no idea of hunting, and before his crash had never slept in the open; yet his trap was a masterpiece of improvisation. Its chief element was a block of salt which he found in the hut. If a deer moved the block, this pulled a string, firing the revolver, which had its safety catch released. When he tried out the trap, the first shot went into a tree right by the block of salt. To make doubly sure, he tied round the bullet hole some sticks of dynamite, which he also found in the hut, and loaded the revolver. For two days nothing happened, and the catch of fish was also very poor. On the third day, he hobbled over to his trap and found a roebuck in it.

The meat lasted for only five days, because for the first time he ate his fill. He kept resetting the trap, and almost every morning found fresh blood on the game path, but the wounded animals must have dragged themselves away. Meanwhile four weeks had passed since his crash. The ground began to show its first green. He ate dandelion leaves and small snails, which he cooked with his stocks of spice, and supplemented this dish with fresh trout.

But he felt that such food would not be enough to return him to his full strength: he must move on. So he prepared a stock of smoked fish, collected the first ripening wild strawberries, and set off toward the ten-thousand-foot Granite Pass. He reached the top about midday, rested for a short time in knee-deep snow, ate two fish, then walked down a path toward the valley.

In the late afternoon he took a second rest. Just as he was going to revive himself with some strawberries, he heard a woman's voice call out: "Hallo, what are *you* doing here?" The woman rode up on a horse, followed by some men.

"What's the date of today?" asked Steeves.

"The ninth of July," she answered.

When he worked it out, it was fifty-four days since his crash. In those fifty-four days, he had walked a hundred miles, negotiating height levels differing by up to five thousand feet, had climbed a pass of ten thousand feet—and only lost forty pounds in weight. He was in such good condition physically that there were people who doubted the genuineness of his story. Stead, however, accepted it as further proof that one can "survive below freezing point." At the recommendation of Major General LeMay, Steeves visited the survival school to talk to the instructors and trainees about his experience. This was an impressive illustration of the fact that when there is no more hope of help from the outside world, it is best to "march out of the cold" of your own accord. It also makes the chances of finding something to eat better than if you merely look in the immediate surroundings of your camp.

But pilots who crashed during the war in Labrador, north Alaska, and north Canada sometimes discovered, within a mile of their wrecked aircraft, food stores and huts, stocks of fuel, and also paths leading to a settlement. Then there were rivers; rivers in the Arctic invariably lead to the coast and so to a settlement.

Two members of a crew baled out over Newfoundland "by mistake" (because they thought their officer had given them the order to do so). One was injured in landing. The same evening his companion set some nooses and caught a hare. The next day, after a hearty meal, he loaded his injured friend on his shoulders and stamped southward through the snow. During the next forty-eight days(!) he caught eight more hares, which kept up his strength sufficiently to let him cover one hundred and fifty miles with the other man still on his shoulders, till he reached a settlement.

Another pilot, who also left his wrecked plane, walked along a lonely path and so came on the huts (and food store) of Arctic hunters. Eighty-four days later he met a group of Eskimos, who led him back to civilization. Both the above cases occurred during an Arctic winter.

It is is interesting to learn that according to the survival experts and, of course, the experiences of survivors, winter is a good deal easier than summer for making headway in the Arctic. Apparently the ice covering of frozen lakes and rivers, and the ground being hard as stone, enable you to get on faster without big detours; whereas one party of airmen, for instance, after a crash landing in north Canada during the summer, took all of six hours to cross a piece of marshland half a mile wide, and several days to circumvent a bog.

The Arctic winter, of course, brings other dangers besides the extreme cold: storms, snowdrifts, and crevasses concealed by snow. Among the dangers is the remarkable and eerie phenomenon known as "whiteout," not to be confused (as it often is), with snow blindness. The exact causes of whiteout are not yet known, but it has already cost the lives of many airmen and explorers in Polar regions. After crossing the Antarctic in 1958, the explorer Sir Vivian Fuchs said: "If anyone wants to meet the big nothing, he only has to get into a whiteout."

It occurs when the light reflected by the snow has the same color as the sky overcast with light-gray cloud. Then all shadows disappear, and there is suddenly no more horizon, no height and depth, so that anybody in the whiteout loses all sense of "above" and "below." Pilots in a whiteout frequently make crash landings if they rely on their senses (which are deceived by the whiteout), instead of on their instruments. In one case, it is reported, in an official survival account, a bomber in a whiteout dived into a snowdrift, and stuck there. The pilot evidently did not realize anything was wrong until the rear-gunner suddenly stood in front of the cockpit, excitedly waving his arms.

The airmen at Arctic bases who have crashed in a whiteout found it hard to get their bearings because there was no horizon or any other landmark to guide them. One said: "I felt like a swimmer under water who had burst his eardrum. It was not till I discovered the wreck of a plane in the snow, and fixed my eyes rigidly on it, that I managed to stand up straight again."

Judgment of distances go too. A friend of mine who was investigating the whiteout phenomenon for the U. S. Air Force in Thule (Greenland) reported the following interesting experiment: "I painted some metal beer cans black and threw them into the snow during a whiteout. Then I had some airmen guess what these were. They all thought it was black oil drums several hundred yards away. The whiteout had completely taken away their ability for judging distances."

There are many stories of men in a whiteout in Alaska or Greenland who have seen their companions jump down a "small slope" which was really an abyss several hundred feet deep, and their rashness cost them their lives. Survival school trainees are recommended to wait calmly for the end of a whiteout, and only move on when things around them have resumed their shape and structure.

With reasonably thorough training, a healthy energy and will to live, anyone, instructors say, can survive in the Arctic. Even the Antarctic is no longer the White Hell it was once called. Although both Polar regions have lost none of their dangers, it should be quite possible, if you behave sensibly, to stay there for long periods, as is proved by increasing settlements in the most northerly and southerly latitudes.

In Greenland the Americans have planted complete villages in the perpetual ice, with billets, laboratories, wash- and bathrooms, a movie house, television station, and a fifty-mile tunnel connecting the ice station, Camp Century, with Thule Airport. Radar stations are strung along northern Canada, on the edge of the Arctic Circle, and in Alaska airfields and air bases have been established in the perpetual snow. Geologists and hunters travel through the Arctic today in growing numbers, and recent advertisements in American newspapers have offered amateur hunters a month's stay in an Eskimo igloo, including the services of a native guide.

In the Antarctic too one can speak of a regular "settlement." In the summer thousands of explorers and technicians with their teams, from twelve nations, travel through the White Continent to explore its last secrets. There are many small stations and forty big ones, one of which, McMurdo (on McMurdo Bay), is even equipped with an atomic reactor. In Amundsen-Scott, an American settlement a few yards from the South Pole, the men can go to the movies or have a hot bath even when the outside temperatures are at their most severe. There was even talk of the scientists there wanting to bring out their wives and children.

But such men have to have a thorough training in survival through their own resources without the technological aids provided by their bases. None of them has so far been lost, after an emergency landing or an unsuccessful expedition, through inability to "work out his own salvation."

Chapter 6
Survival in the Tropics

I felt like a snail with a beard—but I was alive. The Japanese corporal, Minagawa, who hid in the jungle of Guam, one of the Mariana Islands, for fifteen years and ten months

On May 24, 1959, two small Japanese ships dropped anchor off the tiny Philippine island of Lubang. Soon afterward fourteen workmen and four technicians stepped onto the dazzling white sand, dragging along two big telephone poles, with a huge loudspeaker hanging between. In the afternoon these men fought their way through the thick tropical vegetation to the island's interior. On their march one of the engineers was attacked by a swarm of bees, and stung so badly that he lost consciousness. Another, sitting down for a short rest, was tormented by hundreds of ants, but by evening they had at last reached their objective, a hill of about two thousand feet, in the middle of the overgrown island, still known from war days as Hill 600. The masts were set up, and soon the words of the party's leader, Yuzo Miuru, boomed through the loudspeaker:

"Lieutenant Onoda! Lieutenant Onoda! I hope you can hear me. We have an important message for you. The war has been over fourteen years. The United States of America and our Japanese nation are now allies. It is madness for you to hold out here any longer. Come out with your men and give yourself up. There is no one who will not approve. It would not sully your honor."

The only answer which came from the jungle was the screeching of frightened birds. For weeks Miuru went on shouting his message into the tangled thickets of the tropical island—without result. In November of that same year the strange search was abandoned. The Japanese Welfare Ministry, after having spent U.S. $400,000 for the search, listed Hiroo Onoda, lieutenant in the former Imperial Japanese Army, as dead. Yet, it remained quite probable that Onoda or one of his men was still hiding in the jungle of Lubang in the belief, of course, that the war between Japan and the United States was still in progress.

This assumption was revived once again in January 1972, when almost sensational news reached the welfare ministry: on the tiny (209 square miles) island of Guam in the Pacific, wire services reported, two local fishermen had caught a shabbily clad, elderly man trying to loot their fish traps in the Talofofo River. When they turned him over to the authorities, the man insisted in Japanese that he was to be treated as a prisoner of war. His name, he claimed, was Shoichi Yokoi, and his rank that of a sergeant in the Japanese Army.

A quick check in the files of the welfare ministry proved that a Shoichi Yokoi indeed was reported as missing on Guam—back since the summer of 1944, when U.S. forces had recaptured the island during a four-week-long bloody battle. If Yokoi was still alive after all these years—he was fifty-six meanwhile, and the war had been over for twenty-seven years—so might be Lieutenant Onoda. Conviction grew once Yokoi was brought back to Japan. Doctors and psychologists examining the former sergeant and trying to readjust him to life in modern Japan found him to be in remarkably good physical and mental health.

For the first nineteen years in the jungle, Yokoi reported, he did have the company of other Japanese soldiers. But one by one died until Yokoi was left alone. "For the past eight years I have been without company. Most of the time I was hiding in my home (a subterranean cave in the jungle). I kept time by carving a notch into my 'calendar tree' at each full moon. Since I was a tailor in civilian life, I could weave and sew my own clothes. For a light I used a home-built lamp which I fed with coconut oil. For food I used mangoes, crabs, nuts, snails, rats, fish, and birds—anything that grows or crawls in the jungle. Sometimes I also stole tools and food from villages."

Yokoi's greatest wish after his return to Japan was "to climb a tall mountain and meditate there alone for a long, long time." Well, the Japanese didn't give him much of a chance. After a tour of the country during which Yokoi was celebrated as a hero and showered with gifts, he got married and settled down in his home town of Nagoja.

Yokoi's return to Japan had raised new hopes and efforts in Japan eventually to determine also the fate of Lieutenant Onoda. So, in 1973 a young Japanese adventurer named Norio Suzuki took it upon himself to hunt down the lieutenant on the island of Lubang. Surprisingly enough, in a remote jungle area, Suzuki ran into a man wearing a battered Japanese army uniform and carrying a World War II Japanese rifle.

The man admitted to be Onoda but refused to be rescued. "I know the war is over," he said to Suzuki, "but I will only surrender if my commanding officer will tell me in person to do so."

Suzuki went back to Japan, fortunately found Onoda's former superior, and returned with him to Lubang. It was only then that Onoda indeed agreed to surrender to the Philippine authorities—twenty-nine years after the war. He also surrendered his .25-caliber rifle, 500 rounds of ammunition, and a sword his mother (still alive) had given him when he had left for Lubang at the age of twenty-two.

Onoda had survived almost half of a human lifespan in the jungle practically the same way as Yokoi: eating the fruit and animals he found, and pilfering from the villagers whatever else he needed. He, too, was in amazingly good shape when examined by doctors in Tokyo, by the same doctors who had examined Yokoi. What did they have to say about both men's survival feats?

After performing more than 200 different tests on Onoda, the doctors came to the conclusion that he, like Yokoi, was in remarkably good shape. In fact, his physical and mental states were far better than those of many of his countrymen living in urban areas of modern Japan.

Both men, as Dr. Yoichiro Orihashi said in a press conference, had one thing in common that had kept them alive in the jungle for amost three decades: "The will to survive." And his colleague, Dr. Tominaga, pointed out in the same conference: "How to survive was the most important thing for both of them . . . it was the fundamental motive that drove them . . ." Dr. Ishida, another member of the medical team: "Other men perished in the same environment because they did not have the character of Onoda and Yokoi. Those men had the sort of character that gives up. They had no will to survive—but Onoda and Yokoi did, because they also could make accurate judgments of their situation. They kept their wits about them and coolly planned what they had to do."

Onoda and Yokoi were perhaps the most widely publicized Japanese stragglers of World War II. But although both set amazing records of endurance, they were not the only modern Robinson Crusoes. How many Japanese soliders managed to hide out in the jungles of Pacific islands after the end of World War II nobody will ever know for certain, although traces of them were discovered for many years after 1945.

It was in those years that large-scale operations were conducted to bring home these *san-ryu-sha,* as they were called in Japan.

First, the Americans began to drop leaflets on every island and coral reef where Japanese servicemen were presumed to be. Later the Japanese government joined in these operations. In 1953, for instance, fifteen thousand leaflets were dropped over Guam. They were devised by former Lieutenant Colonel Touru Itagaki (then head of the Repatriation Section in the welfare ministry), and contained the following message:

"To the *san-ryu-sha* of Guam: your long, dark days of waiting are approaching their end. Happiness and joy lie ahead. This is no trick, no dream, but real and genuine. . . . Here is an example: eight men who had remained in hiding on Guam, just as you are doing now, gave themselves up in September 1951 to the American Forces. They were well treated. All of them returned to their homes, are now in good spirits, and enjoying life within their family circle. If you cannot believe this, please write a letter. You can use the enclosed paper and envelope. We promise to deliver it to your families, ask for an answer, and put that answer in the same place as we find your letters."

On occasions such appeals were answered, and some *san-ryu-sha* came out of hiding. Besides the eight mentioned in Itagaki's appeal, another group on one of the Marianas gave themselves up to the military police in 1952. The most famous *san-ryu-sha* were a party of thirty-one on the island of Anatahan, who had been joined by a woman. When this party laid down their arms in 1949, ten of them had died in the battle for the lady's favors. But the "rescuers" could not get over how well the party had otherwise survived their long years of isolation in tropical jungle with only the most primitive small arms and tools, without a supply column, without tents or a stock of clothing: without, in fact, any of the resources a soldier can usually count on, during a lull in the fighting, even in the most primitive conditions.

In 1944 fifteen Japanese soldiers fled deep into the jungle on the island of Mindoro. There they split up into two groups. Seven men settled on a mountain slope where all but one of them were killed not long afterward by some natives. The other group, eight men under a Lieutenant Yamamoto (in private life a teacher), climbed to the mountaintop. With almost nothing beyond their uniforms, a single ax and their Japanese swords, they decided to practice farming and stock breeding in the jungle. Yamamoto was sure the Emperor would "some time come and get them out." Till then they just had to hold on.

Living off snails, snakes, lizards, frogs, maggots, and even rats, they began clearing half an acre of wood, under Yamamoto's direction. Then they discovered, a day's march away, a settlement of natives, the ones who later killed their fellow soldiers. These were primitive savages, still living in stone-age civilization. Yamamoto traded them some watches in exchange for seeds, two pigs, and two chickens. But not trusting the natives, he avoided contact with them in the future, and concentrated on making a livelihood for his men.

He had corn and sweet potatoes sown, and in ground never cultivated before the first harvest surpassed all expectations. He decided to extend the cultivable land by half an acre every year. After two years, he and his men were leading a contented settlers' life. They had seventy chickens and twenty pigs. To supplement the food these provided, they often ate roast monkey. They sewed together monkey skins to make blankets. They had expanded the primitive wooden hut of the first year into a "luxury villa," which contained several bedrooms, plaited straw mats on the floor, and a bathroom with a big stone bath. There were armchairs on the veranda, and the large kitchen had a clay oven and running water, which Yamamoto had piped through bamboo stems from a spring some distance away. There was also a farm building with corn and potato mills and a distillery, in which one of the men brewed liquor.

These Japanese spent twelve years in their tropical hide-out. During this time five men, including the one from the other group spared by the natives, died of various illnesses, especially malaria. The last four were finally impelled by pure curiosity (not hunger, or other privations) to resume contact with the outside world. An American prospector brought the news of their small settlement to the coast. From there a party of Filipinos—former enemies of the Japanese—set off for the mountains to bring Yamamoto back to civilization. The initial mistrust of the Japanese was quickly overcome, and they gave the Filipinos a three-day feast with roast pork and banana liqueur which left the "rescuers" staggered.

Yamamoto's remarkable "record" was broken in 1960 by two corporals, Masashi Ito and Bunzo Minagawa, who returned to civilization on May 21 that year after spending fifteen years and ten months in conditions of amazing primitiveness in the jungles of Guam, the same island where Yokoi was hiding out. It is not known whether they ever met him, and Yokoi does not remember, for Guam's interior is covered with virgin forest so dense that even those who have lived on the island for years are apt to lose their way in it. The climate is mild, the temperature ranging between 68° and 90° F. There is a rainy season and a dry season, but the jungle never loses its foliage.

On July 21, 1944, when the United States Marines recovered Guam, Ito and Minagawa were twenty-four years old, both simple country boys. Admittedly they had grown up on the land, giving them a closeness to nature; but they had no sort of training in the art of survival.

During the first months they separated repeatedly, to live with various other *san-ryu-sha;* but they kept returning to each other, because they felt their fellow soldiers did not take enough care about avoiding discovery. Finally they stayed together for the rest of the fifteen years. Ito had nothing but his uniform, a sword and a cap, Minagawa had these, plus a mirror and a pair of gloves: this was all their original "equipment."

"The first nights," said Ito—telling his story after the return to

civilization—"we stole some chickens in a village. We swallowed
them raw on the spot. Soon afterward we caught a calf. We killed
it in the meadow, and ate its flesh, also raw. We wrapped what
was left in palm leaves and took it into the forest, to eat it up as
quickly as possible. We realize that raw flesh soon goes bad in the
tropics."

They supplemented this "liberated" food with coconuts,
breadfruit, bamboo shoots, lizards, snails and snakes, plus sea
food from the nearby coast: seaweed, lobsters, fat coconut crabs
and an abundance of other fish. (The Guamese say there are so
many fish on their shores "you can catch them with your bare
hands, if you're not too lazy to bend down for them.") After a few
months the two Japanese had got used to living like natives of the
jungle, even their senses becoming adapted to this existence:

"Although we were both smokers and missed tobacco, we took
care not to pick up stubs thrown away by American soldiers. We
were afraid if we smoked ourselves we should lose our power of
smelling others' smoke from a distance. Our sense of smell became
so sensitive that we often smelled the hair oil of American soldiers
before we heard them talking. It was vital for us to discover other
people before they discovered us."

Both men, and the others they were with from time to time,
went foraging only at night, always walking in single file. The first
man tested the ground ahead before putting his foot down; it was
the last man's business to see that all tracks were wiped out. They
took care not to tear off any grass or tread it down in a conspic-
uous way, or to break off branches of any height where no animal
could have done it. If they took fruit from a tree, they would never
take more than a few fruits, so that it shouldn't be noticed afterward. When they made a fire, they always buried the ashes or
scattered them in the sea. If they lost a tool or piece of clothing,
they went on searching until they had found it again, so as not to
leave any tokens which might betray them. And throughout the
sixteen years, it seems, Ito and Minagawa always talked in a whisper.

In 1949 they moved into a cave with their most valuable posses-
sions, which now included two rifles and some ammunition they
had found; several needles they had filed down from old metal
springs, thimbles and fishhooks made of empty cartridges, pots

and pans from gasoline tanks, daggers and hatchets from steel car springs.

"With the needles we mended our tattered uniforms, using threads pulled out of pieces of woven material. Having ground our swords as sharp as razors, we used them as scissors, and also to shave each other. At first we shaved our head as well, but soon gave this up when we realized that hair was a good protection against gnats."

In contrast to Yamamoto and his men, Ito and Minagawa did not go in for farming or stock-breeding, nor did they keep stores: like castaways at sea they lived from hand to mouth, on what they could find. Moreover, because of the constant danger of being discovered, they could hardly ever use their rifles—except when there was heavy rain to muffle the sound. In fifteen years Ito fired only seven of his eight cartridges, and did so to good purpose, as is shown by the fact that with them he killed six cows and a pig. "Anyhow, we caught more game in simple wire nooses. Or we would sit on a tree above a game track and wait till a deer ran past (there are plenty of them on Guam), then drop on it and stab it."

After the first months they felt safe enough to roast or boil the meat instead of eating it raw. Almost every day they lit a fire. They had no matches, but enough ingenuity to get over that. "When the sun shone, the bottom of a bottle served as a burning glass. When it was raining, we found an even simpler way of managing: we forced open a cartridge, and mixed some powder from it with paper, dry leaves and wood shavings. Then one of us rubbed a piece of wire along a piece of hardwood until it was red-hot, and simply pushed it into the tinder. The powder fired at once and set the wood shavings alight."

Whereas normal survivors relatively seldom fall ill in what is usually only a short period of isolation, Ito and Minagawa, like other *san-ryu-sha*, worried a lot about the chances of illness and set about finding natural remedies. When they killed an animal, they cut open its stomach, collected the gastric juice and dried this in the sun. They ground the solidified mass into a greenish-white powder and kept it in a bottle; it proved an excellent gastric tonic. They also made charcoal from animals' bones, ground it to powder and used it as a remedy for dysentery, diarrhea, and other stomach troubles.

Trainees of survival schools are told of the natural remedies a pilot may find after a forced landing: for instance, the leaves of the common coltsfoot reduce the swelling on a sprained ankle or wrist; and you can combat fevers, including malaria, with an infusion from the bark of willow branches from two or four years old. It is also an effective gargle for throat troubles. A few mouthfuls will alleviate abdominal or intestinal chills.

After eight years of voluntary banishment from civilization, the remaining *san-ryu-sha* on Guam were subjected to the "leaflet raid." Ito found one of the leaflets, but did not trust it: it might be an American trick to lure him into captivity. But he responded by carving his name-sign and that of three dead friends on various trees near a well-frequented track. The search parties discovered the signs, and the Japanese Welfare Ministry at once traced the families in Japan of the men with these names, including Ito's father. The father immediately wrote a letter to his son, who had been believed dead, asking him to come back since the war had long been over.

But the letter never reached Ito. A bundle of Tokyo daily papers had been dropped over the jungle with the leaflets, and Ito found one a few days after he had carved the four name-signs on the trees and was waiting for an answer from his relatives. He and Minagawa avidly devoured the news they had missed for so long. Everything seemed genuine: the pictures, the reports, the grammar. There was nothing which looked like enemy propaganda—until Ito discovered a small and insignificant item stating that the price of bean cake had been fixed at ten yen.

This immediately aroused their suspicions. It could only be a blatant piece of enemy propaganda. Their monthly pay had been twenty yen, and now the price of bean cake was ten yen! They could not know anything of the creeping inflation in Japan, and rejected the whole newspaper as a cheap trick to lure them into captivity. Without waiting for the promised letters from relatives, they withdrew still deeper into the jungle. Their life became even harder. "I soon felt like a snail with a beard," Minagawa recalled. "But I was alive, and that was the main thing."

Seven more years went by, 2,600 nights, in which the two men lived almost like animals. Then, at dawn on May 21, 1960, two Guamese fishermen got up from their palm-leaf beds to look at some crab traps which they had set on the shore. While they were walking along the beach, they saw a man a short way ahead of them, stepping through the water so that his foorprints would soon be washed away by the waves. He had long unkempt hair, and was wearing a loincloth—it was Minagawa. He stopped near a coconut palm, climbed up and pulled off some coconuts. Then he suddenly saw the two fishermen under the tree. He jumped down and began to run. They caught up with him and threw him to the ground. There was a fierce tussle, in which he reached for his knife. Finally they got the better of him and took him to police headquarters. The police realized at once that he was a *san-ryu-sha,* but wanted to find out his name and whether he was alone.

For forty-eight hours Minagawa refused to talk. "When they caught me, I thought they would wait two or three days before killing me. If I could keep silent that long about Ito, he would have enough time to get away from the place where I had been caught. . . ."

They shaved him and gave him a bath. He took this to be pre-execution ceremonial. When he was given a blood test, he thought they were doping him. Other police at once began looking for Ito, who in the end gave himself up voluntarily, unable to endure the idea of going on living in complete loneliness.

American doctors gave both men a medical examination. They found that neither had lost much weight after almost sixteen years in the tropics. Both were in good physical condition and had no deficiency symptoms like hair or teeth falling out from lack of vitamins.

The end of the story is a little pathetic. While in the police cells, they both tried to cut their wrists with springs from their beds. They showed no interest in current Japanese newspapers, and on seeing the photograph of a Japanese girl kissing a uniformed American soldier, they called it "a dirty lie. Our women wouldn't do such a thing." Even when Minagawa's sister telephoned from Japan, he didn't believe the war had ended. Not recognizing her voice, he slammed down the receiver in fury. The next time she called him, he asked her detailed questions, like how much land the family possessed, etc. Because in her agitation she gave a wrong answer to one of his questions, it confirmed his idea that the telephone calls had been engineered by the Americans. And Ito, who was almost convinced of the truth, started doubting again.

The only thing to do was to fly the two stubborn jungle warriors to Japan as quickly as possible. This was done, and Ito was quite convinced he was going to be thrown out into the Pacific during the flight. It was not till his and Minagawa's relations embraced them tearfully at a Japanese airport, that they both began to believe what people had been telling them for days.

Others, of course, besides the *san-ryu-sha,* have shown that it is possible to survive for years in the tropics living completely on their own resources. The model for Robinson Crusoe, for instance, was the Scottish sailor Alexander Selkirk, landed (by a shipmate with whom he had quarreled) on the uninhabited islands of Juan Fernández, and rescued five years later. But the *san-ryu-sha* had not only to overcome natural difficulties; they were also trying to escape from a presumed enemy whom they believed would capture or shoot them. Those of them who are known to have died, did so from illness, suicide (to avoid being taken prisoner), in quarrels with their fellows—or else they actually were shot by pursuers. (In the first eighteen months after Guam was reoccupied by the United States, 117 Japanese soldiers who forcibly resisted their "rescue" were killed in tussles with the Guam Combat Patrol, a team of Guamese in American uniforms.) None of the *san-ryu-sha,* however, died of starvation or thirst.

This fact alone refutes the common conception of the tropics held by most people in the Northern Hemisphere. A pilot in the war, rescued from the Burmese jungle, said: "I always thought of the tropics as a region where every step you took might be fatal. After my crash landing, I was constantly afraid of wild animals, snakes, and dangerous insects. From fear of poisoning myself, I ate neither fruit nor plants. I was soon at death's door." This idea stems from the last two centuries and the great, arduous explorations of South America and Central Africa and the Far East, when the tropics were considered uninhabitable or at least unsuitable to people of European stock.

A contrary conception, which is presumably due to Hollywood and similar fantasy-builders, is illustrated by another pilot who landed on an atoll overgrown with palms and after his rescue remarked wryly: "Where was the paradise I'd always pictured? Above all I missed my beautiful South Sea maidens."

Of course in particular places the tropics *may* be like hell or paradise, but not on the whole: their average yearly temperature is 70° F. This means that there are sometimes temperatures which can seem like hell; but at any rate it is possible, though not simple, to survive when marooned in these latitudes. Ito commented, after his return to civilization: "We only managed it because our race was born to a struggle for existence in the jungle. I don't think an American would have stood such hardships for even a year."

Ito's contention, however, is contradicted by the example of George R. Tweed, a radio engineer, one of the five hundred men in the American garrison of Guam who were driven out by five thousand Japanese at the beginning of the war. Tweed fled into the jungle and lived there for two and a half years under similar conditions to these of the *san-ryu-sha,* until the Americans retook the island in August 1944. Then he turned up again, was feted as a hero and wrote his book, *Robinson Crusoe, U.S.—NAVY.* His conclusion was: "Others could have done the same." In this the survival experts agree with him. "No other climatic zone offers such good chances of survival. In the tropics you find water, food, and enough raw materials to produce the essential things: tools, shelter, clothes."

But what about wild animals? People exposed to jungle conditions are scared of lions, tigers, elephants, and other big game, although unless you go out of your way to provoke them, the danger from this quarter is very small. In the dense jungle, say the survival experts, "you can live more safely today than in most large towns."

All accounts show that of the airmen who spent any time in the jungle during the war and were then rescued, hardly any came across a beast of prey. Those who did, it may be said, have not survived to tell the tale, and obviously people *have* been killed by wild animals; the same is going to happen again from time to time. But generally the case is as stated by Marston Bates, the American natural historian, who himself lived many years in South America: "I should have been frightened to death if I had ever met a jaguar in the virgin forest. But this has never yet happened to me, although I have often enough come across fresh-looking tracks."

Those who did come upon beasts of prey and survived the meeting found that the animals seemed almost as frightened as they were. A pilot who met a tiger in Hindustan said: "The tiger stood rooted to the spot. I yelled at him, whereupon he left the path in a great hurry." Another man was pushed out of the way by

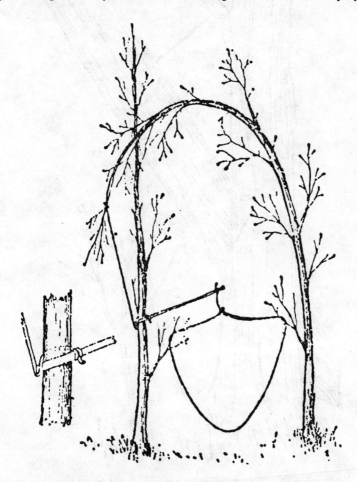

Trap for small game which has saved many people from starving to death. If a creature gets into the noose, it releases the simple loop fastening on the small tree on the left. The bent top of the right tree springs up and tightens the noose.

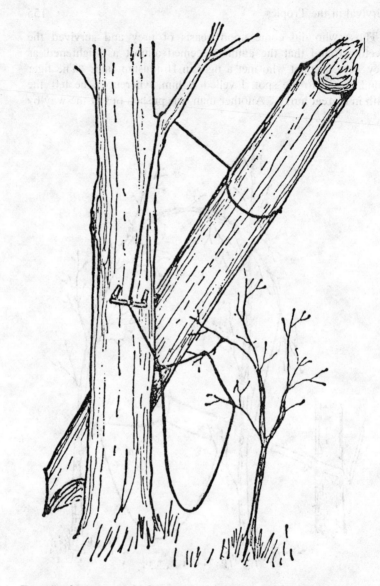

Trap for big game, which is secured by two pegs knocked into a tree, with a third peg under their ends, held in position by the pull of the heavy wooden pole. When the game runs into the noose, the peg is pulled out and the pole drops, tightening the noose by its weight.

an elephant who took to flight on seeing him. "I don't know which one of us was the more scared," the man commented afterward.

The real danger of the tropics are the insects. Many species carry parasites and spread epidemics, and are thus a greater menace than a whole zoo of wild animals turned loose. In 1939, for instance, only two hundred people in the whole of India were killed by tigers, while four million died of typhoid. The number of human victims devoured by wild animals during the past few hundred years is probably smaller than the number of malaria deaths in a year.

So the survivor in the tropics is more likely to succumb to an infectious disease or blood-poisoning than to hunger, thirst, or attack by wild animals. He must therefore take great care of his health and do everything to protect himself from insects. By all accounts the worst of the diseases they spread is malaria, which is carried by mosquitoes. The Stead trainees are given a long list of instructions on how best to avoid mosquitoes: for instance, never pitch your camp near swamps, the breeding places of mosquitoes; use your mosquito nets; use the ointments in your first-aid kit; take off as few clothes as possible.

Earlier it was mentioned how Bertram and Klausmann were plagued by mosquitoes. Ito and Minagawa were so badly stung that their faces and arms were constantly swollen. They could squash twenty mosquitoes every time they slapped their foreheads, but the spot would immediately be covered by a new lot. "Each morning our hands were bloody on both sides. This was another reason why we fled from the coast and deeper into the jungle. We were simply afraid of losing too much blood."

Then there was the American pilot who had to make a crash landing in New Guinea during World War II in a swamp only twenty miles from the airfield. He was sure he could get back on foot to his unit, so he set off eastward, leaving his emergency equipment in the wrecked plane. Soon he got into a bog, which quickly became very deep. After only three miles he was stuck and sank in it up to his shoulders. When a search party finally found him thirty-six hours later, he was covered with mosquitoes from the waterline to the top of his skull. They had bitten him so severely that his ears had swollen to shapeless lobes and he could hardly open his eyes. When he spoke, his nostrils and lips hurt. He was so much weakened that he could not walk unaided.

He had neglected to cover his face and the top of his body with mud, the simplest protection against mosquitoes (as the instructors of survival schools are always stressing). This, often mixed with burned cow dung or the dung of water buffalo, is used with great success by natives of the tropics. It also helps to rub in certain oils, from coconuts or lemon grass. Coconut oil is used too, by the natives of tropical islands to protect them against head lice, and so is tobacco juice; while the savages of New Guinea and New Caledonia rub lime juice into their hair. This makes the hair turn red, but castaways from the west who had tried it out say it is as effective as modern synthetic preparations.

To keep off flies and bugs, the natives in the Philippines take breadfruits to bed with them. The inhabitants of New Guinea rid themselves of ants by storing lemons in damp places till the fruit is covered with mold. Then they quarter the rotten fruit and put the

pieces on the tops of anthills. The ants clear off at once and don't go back there.

Some pilots after crash landing pitched their camp near an anthill or spent the night on an ant path: this was bad luck for they were naturally attacked by the ants and badly bitten. The South American fire ant, which has also penetrated into the southern states of North America, is so vicious that it makes calves and cows charge off lowing wildly, to save themselves from its bites; farmhands there refuse to work in fields where there is a mound of fire ants. Many tropical ants live in the branches of certain trees, so one should sleep neither in a tree nor on the bare ground. In fact survival trainees are told how to construct a bed several feet above the ground; they are also warned to keep their shoes on at night and always be careful where they put their hands.

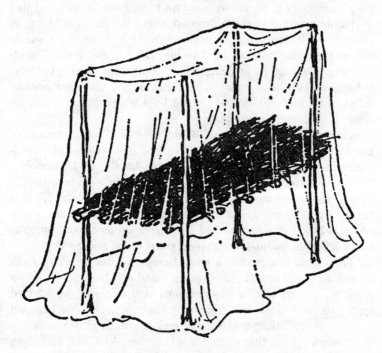

In the tropics you can make a bed from sticks and palm leaves, covering it with a mosquito net.

A man whose parachute got entangled in a tree in the Burmese jungle tried hastily to get to the ground, but lost his balance; one of his feet got caught in the noose, so that his head dangled a few inches above an anthill. Later, a rescue party found that with a little will power, and a realization that his situation was not hopeless, he could probably have freed himself from the noose. But the bites of the disturbed ants threw him into complete panic, and when a native party reached the place an hour later, he was already hanging dead from the tree—having put a bullet through his head.

Then there are the tropical parasites which bore into a man's skin to feed on his blood. "The ticks were terrible," said a pilot rescued in the tropics, "especially when I sat down on a place covered with grass. Sometimes I discovered dozens of these disgusting creatures on my body within a few minutes. Every day I had to strip completely to check my body for them from tip to toe. I had no iodine with me to put a drop on where the tick was biting, in order to get its head out of my skin. The only thing to do was to use a cigarette, holding its burning end to the insects hindquarters. They let go at once, and I could snip them off. Once, though, a tick's head came off in my skin, and the place became inflamed at once. When I was found by a search plane, it had already turned into an ugly wound."

Marston Bates, in *Where Winter Never Comes,* writes of another unpleasant creature: "I have had a great deal of experience with one tropical worm, the human bot-fly, or Dermatobia. This is the larva of a fly that develops in a boil-like sore on the skin of men or of various other animals (especially cattle)." It is carried by mosquitoes, and when the mosquito comes onto a man or warm-blooded animal to bite, "the larva drops off and burrows into the nearest sweat-sore, where it starts to eat and grow.

"The victim first notices a small bump like that resulting from some insect bite. But the bump persists and gets larger, and after a week or so there will be an occasional sharp pain at the infected spot. The little larva that is growing there is big at one end and tapering at the other; and the big end is armed with a series of sharp black spines, that make the whole thing look like an Indian war club. I suspect that the sharp pains result when the worm turns over, grating some nerve ends with these spines. If the spot is examined with a hand lens, it will be found to center in a tiny hole, where the worm periodically comes up for air.

"We got quite expert at getting the worms out, which is something of a trick, because they hang on inside with those spines. If the worm is broken and part of it left inside, infection is likely to result. We had many methods of extraction, but the neatest was to hold a lighted cigarette close to the skin, making the worm uncomfortably warm so that he relaxed his hold and, with an appropriately timed squeeze, could be popped out. This required considerable skill, and a more routine method was to cover the worm hole tightly with adhesive tape. The worm would then be smothered in about twenty-four hours and, dead, it could easily be squeezed out."

A person "attacked" by such worms may actually feel as though he is being eaten alive sometimes. At least this is what Juliane Koepcke felt, a seventeen-year-old German girl who on Christmas Day of 1971 was the sole survivor of a plane that crashed into the dense jungle of Peru. The plane, with ninety-two passengers on board, had been on a flight from Lima to Pucallpa when, apparently, it was hit by lightning. When Juliane came to, she found herself still strapped in her seat, but thrown clear of the wreckage. Her mother was dead, no other passengers were to be seen (although some did survive apparently for a few days), and so Juliane started to walk out of the jungle alone.

From her father, who for many years had directed a jungle research station, Juliane had learned: "If you get lost in the jungle, look for the watercourse. It will lead you to larger ones, and they in turn will lead you to rivers. Rivers are the highways of the jungle—and will lead you to safety." And Juliane had also learned that "in the jungle, danger does not come from big animals—like jaguars, or tapirs, but from small ones—like spiders, ants, mosquitoes, flies, and other insects."

Within hours Juliane was stung by dozens of flies. "After a few days I had worms everywhere in my skin, and they hurt with every movement. Every now and then I operated on myself with a wooden splint, once extracting thirty-five worms in one hour. Where I had hurt myself (during the crash) the worms were particularly nasty: they had eaten so much out of the cut that I could put a finger in it."

On the tenth day after the crash, struggling along a river, Juliane was found by two men. Her body was swollen from mosquito bites, and thirty more worms were pulled out of her skin, this time with the aid of a few drops of gasoline.

A "bed" consisting of a hammock and a tarpaulin offers protection from sun and rain.

Other survivors have reported that a favorite spot for fleas to settle and lay their eggs was under the toenails; they could only be scraped out with a sterilized knife, after which the wound had to be treated at once with iodine to stop an inflammation. One survivor of the Burma campaign recalled that "Mites also settled in our skin round our hips. They caused a terrible itching, but we knew we mustn't scratch. We covered the places with iodine, and the itch gradually stopped."

Of course there are a great many other tropical insects and parasites, which cannot all be listed here. But these few examples will show that survivors have often been able to protect themselves by simple methods (like tobacco juice and lighted cigarettes), and have also taken care to avoid inflammations. For in tropical heat even the smallest scratch can very quickly turn into an ugly wound. Cases of blood poisoning are quite common—although the natives are seldom affected by this.

Elisabeth Elliot, who during the fifties spent a year as a missionary among the Auca Indians of South America, writes in *The Savage My Kinsman:* "There were several people who displayed deep scars from spear wounds. They described to me how they had been pierced . . . They had either yanked out the spears tearing the flesh badly on the barbs, or left them in until the wounds festered, and maggots ate a hole large enough to enable them to remove the spears. The scars in these cases were as neat as a surgical incision."

The maggots in the wounds had fed on the pus-forming germs, and stopped an infection spreading. When there were no more pus formers, the maggots died and fell off. I have heard of the same phenomenon from a German woman doctor who worked in a field hospital on the Eastern front during World War II; many soldiers refused to have a new dressing put on, saying: "We're all right, we've got maggots." In the cold winter the maggots also had the effect of keeping the wound warm all the time, so that frostbite couldn't set in.

In tropical forests and swamps during the rainy season leeches can become a real scourge. Even when the body is covered all over, they find their way to the skin and start sucking. They creep through a pant's fly and even through the eyelets of boots. "During the rains they settled on every blade of grass and every bush," said a party of British airmen after a forced landing in Burma. "They dropped down our necks, crept into our ears and noses and over our heads. Every hour we had to stop and 'deleech' each other. We had no salt to put on their sucking disks, but lighted cigarettes again came in handy here."

According to the survival experts, poisonous spiders are not the menace they are often imagined to be. The tarantula, for instance, rarely does bite people. It is much more likely that when man comes into contact with it, some of its tough hair gets attached to his skin, causing a severe itch. The bite of most other tropical spiders has an effect similar to a wasp sting. Natives of tropical islands alleviate the pain with a mixture of salt and/or sea water, honey and vinegar. A pilot who made a crash landing in South America used a lighted cigarette, that survivors' panacea. "I held it near the bite. The heat apparently broke up the poison. At any rate the pain vanished immediately."

You can usually keep away from large centipedes, although their bite can be as painful as a wasp sting; but scorpions are very insidious creatures, often lurking in clothes or shoes not being worn, or an empty bed. If you happen to come in too close contact with them, they will sting you in a flash. Their poison can cause nausea and fainting. American cowboys still use mud packs and cold compresses as remedies, while in southern latitudes the wound is rubbed with grated coconut.

As to poisonous snakes, the experts hold that men in the jungle come upon them no more often than on beasts of prey. One survival leaflet on the danger of snakes says: "You will probably never see a poisonous snake, unless you try hard to find one. The thing that will scare you most in the tropics is the howling, shrieking and all the other jungle noises produced by monkeys, birds and giant trees toppling." And Marston Bates, in the book previously mentioned, writes: "I have seen more snakes, both poisonous and harmless, in Florida than I ever did in South America. Certainly there are some there . . . but as a rule they keep well hidden."

Nevertheless, the trainees at survival schools are, of course, told what you should do if bitten by a snake. One of the "simplest" things is also the hardest to carry out: to keep as still as possible, and just relax until help comes. Animals do this naturally. Dogs bitten by a rattlesnake have been observed lying on the ground and staying in the same place for several days, then getting up again as if nothing had happened.

When snake poison gets into the blood stream, it destroys the red corpuscles. It is not fatal till it reaches the heart. The more slowly the victim of a snake bite moves, the better his chances of survival. If there is no antidote available, those chances can be further increased by putting a tourniquet between the bite and the heart, as some American soldiers did with one of their party. "We loosened the tourniquet every twenty minutes, so as not to stop the circulation completely. We also disinfected a knife on an open flame, made a cross-shaped cut about half an inch deep into the wound, and sucked off some blood. The swelling slowly went down. Finally, when it had quite disappeared, we removed the tourniquet, and as this did not bring on nausea, we knew he was saved."

Alcohol as an antidote to snake bite is always wrong. It may calm the nerves, but it speeds up circulation, and so has exactly the opposite effect from that desired.

Apart from snake bites, you can also be badly poisoned in the tropics by contact with certain plants and types of wood. In 1950, when American space researchers set up their ground station in the West Indies, they had to clear large patches of bush. The labor force cheerfully heaped up the wood in stakes and set fire to it. Shortly afterward all those who had come in direct contact with the wood began to complain of severe itching, and their skin was soon covered with blisters. They developed a high temperature. Those who had inhaled the smoke of the wood fire, even at a distance of several hundred yards, sustained serious internal burns and had to be admitted to the hospital. The explanation of the mystery was that the wood contained a poisonous sap. Even minute quantities of it, such as were carried by the smoke, produced the symptoms described above.

Equally unpleasant, though less dangerous, are the effects of poison ivy, poison oak, and poison sumac. The sticky sap on the back of the leaves remains active for days. If a car drives through poison ivy, and its owner changes a tire within the next forty-eight hours, he may still be attacked by the ugly, itching rash. Scratching can easily lead to the fluid from the blisters affecting a wider area.

Those afflicted by such a rash have often got some alleviation by urinating on it. But the best advice here too is to watch out where you put your hands. Bushes which are dangerous to touch can best be recognized by their bark, which is usually resinous. A black sap often drops from fresh cuts. The fruits resemble cherries and have a stone in their center.

After their rescue from the jungle or tropical islands survivors say time and again: "It was only the fear of poisonous plants and fruits that kept us from eating what we found. We preferred to go hungry." If there was a group of survivors, they acted on this until one of them weakened and risked eating un unknown fruit or root. The rest would then generally hold out for two or three days "to see how he took it," before following his example.

Survival experts have established a basic rule (as with poisonous fish) which also derives partly from the customs of the natives in tropical islands: "Never eat black seeds from ears and grasses. Avoid plants with milky sap (except for wild figs, breadfruit, and papayas). Never eat large quantities of a strange fruit, before you have tested it."

How this is done can be seen from the account of a castaway stranded on a lonely beach in South America with his raft of gasoline barrels: "I found a fruit on a tree which looked like a potato. First I cut a piece off and boiled it. Then I chewed a bit and kept it in my mouth for about five minutes. As it still tasted good, I swallowed it. Had it been bitter or too sour, I should have spat it out." (A burning taste which causes nausea is always a danger sign.) "I waited a day, and as I didn't feel ill, I ate the rest of the fruit, on which I finally subsisted for three days." (This pre-tasting is no good for mushrooms, however; only experts can tell which of *them* are edible.)

Survivors in the tropics have safely eaten all fruits and parts of plants which were fed on by birds and mammals. Many have watched mice, rats, hares, beavers, or apes feeding, and then eaten the same food. "To be on the safe side," said one man, "I cooked the plants thoroughly. I first cut the roots into thin slices and let them soak for a few days in river water, thereby washing out possible poisons." The Indians of the American jungles do the same with poisonous tubers.

We are always reading that the natives of the tropics are undernourished (because they lack certain vitamins), but we rarely hear of one starving to death because he has nothing to eat. Even in regions where a townsman wouldn't be able to find anything edible, a "savage" can "help himself" (in both senses). A British pilot who made a forced landing on the coast of New Britain gives this account:

"After the landing, I wandered along the beach without finding anything edible. At last, in dire need, I met a native and indicated by signs that I was hungry. He promptly climbed up the nearest tree on the edge of the forest and returned with a bird's nest. Then he dug out a wild root near the tree, which looked like a sweet potato. Finally he pulled off a coconut, which he opened with skill. He also brought a mussel shell from the beach, while I made a fire. A little later he served me with a tasty meal; the bird's nest roasted in coconut oil and garnished with the root."

There is really an abundance of food in the tropics, you only have to know how to find it—and in many cases to overcome your repugnance. There are seven hundred different kinds of yam, the "South Seas" potato. The basic food of the South American natives is manioc, another tuber containing starch, which is very fortifying. "The women prepare a food drink by boiling and mashing the manioc," writes Elisabeth Elliot, "then chewing and spitting a small portion of the mass to start fermentation. Mixed with water, this is drunk. On the second day, a stringy, lumpy liquid of a milky consistency is produced which seems to be very nourishing."

The best-known tropical plant, of course, is the palm, described by botanists as "the princess of the plant world" and by survivors as "a gift of God." There are fifteen hundred species of palm, but much the most popular is the coconut palm. Its fruit is edible at almost every stage of ripeness, and the number of castaways who owe their lives to it is legion.

"Without the palms on my atoll I should be dead," declared an American pilot after his rescue from the South Seas. "Every day I picked my breakfast, lunch and dinner from the top of a coconut palm. The green fruit contained a gelatinous flesh, which immediately quenched the thirst. The ripe fruit contained the hard-shelled edible coconut, which had the cool milk in it. When I was found after fifteen days, I had eaten thirty-two coconuts and was in the best of health."

Another pilot came to enjoy coconuts less easily. He had ditched his plane one night off the coast of the Dutch East Indies (as it then was), and had to swim for an hour before he reached the shores of an island. There he found several nuts in the sand. He looked for his knife to open them, and was furious to find he must have lost it in the water. So with the aid of a propelling pencil he began to peel the thick husk off the first coconut fiber by fiber. He reached the nut proper after almost four hours of peeling, and then it was easy to break it up with a stone. Ravenously hungry, he was about to fall on the white flesh of the nut, when he realized to his horror that he had also lost his false teeth during his swim. Fortunately he found some pieces of coral with which he grated the nut to small flakes, and munched these up with relish.

The hard fibrous outer husk of the unripe coconut is the fruit's only disadvantage; opening it without a bush knife is quite a problem. American trainers have therefore developed the so-called "wedge method": you ram a stake into the ground and grind the top end to a wedge; grasping the coconut in both hands, you can bring it down on the wedge until the green husk is pared off.

The flesh and milk of a coconut, however, are not its only valuable products; coconut oil is equally useful. An American pilot who made a crash landing in Japanese territory during the war even managed to escape to freedom with the aid of coconut oil.

"After my landing I had stolen a boat and an outboard motor from a native village. But I only had gasoline from my plane engine. That, of course, had such a high octane rating that after a few minutes the motor would have burned out. Additional oil, to make up the right mixture for a two-stroke engine, was nowhere to be found. Then I thought of coconut oil. I broke up several nuts, made a crisscross score on the outsides of the kernels, and put the pieces onto some flat stones in the sun. The heat soon drew out the oil. It ran down a narrow gutter, from which I caught it in a tin. In two days I had collected a half-gallon of oil. I mixed one part of oil with three parts of gasoline—and the mixture was just right to take me to the nearest American-occupied island."

South Sea islanders get coconut oil in a similar way. Not for powering motorboats, of course, but as a protection against sunburn, insects, and parasites. Or they rub their legs with it up to the hips before standing in the water for hours with their fishing lines: this stops the salt water affecting their skins.

One survival report says: "The simplest way of getting this oil was by boiling the coconut meat. This brought the oil to the surface of the water, when it only had to be scooped off." Survivors have also used coconut oil for frying, cooking, and as lamp oil for earthenware lamps (this is still done regularly today in Africa and the South Pacific).

However, in ten castaways there will probably be one at most who knows all you can do with the palm—which according to a South Sea saying, can be used in 999 different ways. With palm resin you can polish cars, floors, furniture, and shoes, make carbon paper and phonograph records. Palm oil is used in the making of metal plating, e.g. in food cans, and of toilet soaps and other cosmetics, lubricants, varnishes, and weatherproof coatings. Palms serve as a basis for the manufacture of syrup, sweets, and aromatic substances.

No wonder, then, that the palm has become the most important plant for inhabitants of the tropics. They use palm leaves to roof their houses, and people cast up on their shores have done the same. The leaves of several species have a diameter of up to fifteen feet, while others even reach a length of fifty feet.

A party of Japanese soldiers stranded on a South Sea island for four months had not only lived the whole time entirely on palms, but had made the following things from fibers and kernels: loincloths and sandals, hammocks and floormats, shelters, a raft with floats (from coconuts sucked dry), water containers and climbing ropes. Their rescue was celebrated with palm wine!

Not everybody cast up on tropical shores is lucky enough to be near palms or even where pineapples, bananas, and citrus fruit are growing. They often have to make do with other, less appetizing foods. In New Guinea some airmen lived for weeks on flower buds. "We didn't like them much raw," said one of the men afterward, "but in the end we had the idea of baking them, and then the taste was excellent." Other survivors have eaten bamboo shoots, even using them for a goulash with the meat of a monkey they had killed.

Just as the natives of tropical regions are berry-gatherers, and mainly vegetarian, most survivors in the tropics have to get used to a vegetarian diet, since meat is hard to come by. Ito and Minagawa occasionally got meat by raiding the cattle herds and pigsties of the Guamese; the deer they sometimes caught were introduced into Guam by the Americans. But such delicacies are scarcely to be found on uninhabited tropical islands. For the Pygmies in the virgin forest of New Guinea the biggest "game" is the size of a rat; they live chiefly on caterpillars, beetles, larvae, and maggots—and so can survivors there.

What does this sort of food taste like? "I soon ceased to think about it," said an American rescued from the Burmese jungle, after twenty-two days. "At first I made up my mind to starve rather than eat such vermin. But I soon conquered these foolish inhibitions and started feverishly hunting for the things. I caught tree-insects large and small. After pulling off their legs and feelers, I gripped them by the wings and cheerfully bit off their bodies. I did just the same with grasshoppers. I ate larvae and butterflies whole. The butterflies' bodies had a slight aroma of meat and were best of all. The larvae, alas, were very hard to find, or I should have eaten more of them."

The Aucas in the forests of South America are better hunters of that "game." For them the big whitish larvae of the giant beetle are a great delicacy. The larvae feed on the heartwood of palms, and with an expert's eye the Aucas at once find the revealing bore holes in a trunk. They fell the tree and pick the larvae out of the trunk, often several dozens of them. They eat the larvae raw or baked in ashes.

Dietmar Carsten, an expert on South American Indians, told me that those living deep in the Amazon jungles will eat any bit of protein they can find. "Once on an expedition we ran out of food. While I stayed hungry I watched my Indian friends picking their toes and eating the tiny eggs deposited there by a certain kind of jungle insect. They ate maggots, too, of course, but I couldn't force myself to do the same—fortunately I was not starving."

In New Guinea survivors have lived on ants. One pilot said after his rescue: "I scoured old tree trunks and anthills, where the ants were positively swarming. So I could be choosy, and only looked for the biggest specimens." Another said: "Instead of snipping off the ants which crawled up my legs, I ate them. I enjoyed getting my own back for their greediness."

There is scarcely any kind of insect which a survivor could not safely eat, and in the countries of the Far East, as has been said, many of them are considered distinct delicacies. On the coast of China fried water beetles and water lice are as nourishing and as much enjoyed as peanuts with us. The crew of a transport plane which crashed in the hills of Burma lived for several days on water beetles, which they fished out of a pool and roasted. When they found this diet too monotonous, they copied some natives and varied it with roasted bees.

In India some soldiers who had got lost in the jungle were served by a mountain tribe with a dish of rice sprinkled with chopped cockchafers. Roast grasshoppers are much appreciated in Thailand and many parts of Africa. Cicadas are generally boiled, bees and wasps fried, ants and flying termites pickled, and some kinds of spider roasted, others eaten raw.

Of course insects are not much use for filling stomachs, and should be more of an hors-d'oeuvre for the survivor in the tropics. A good roast monkey, on the other hand, can provide food for two or three days. Elisabeth Elliot describes how the Aucas prepare it: "Monkeys are singed whole, and cooked with the skin on, so that the thin layer of fat under the skin is not lost. The tail is smoked and eaten, and heads are eaten with brains, eyes, ears, and all. Sometimes even the teeth are carefully pulled, and carefully sucked before being thrown away."

During the war many survivors in the tropical forests of the Far East were forced to do the same as the Aucas, though they all made a point of first skinning and gutting the monkeys they killed. Many who ate the meat raw found it tough, but the liver tasted extremely good. Only a few complained of the unfamiliar food. "The monkey looked like a roasted human. We felt like cannibals all through the meal."

Dog's flesh may not sound much more appetizing, but it has been eaten (as previously mentioned) by survivors in the Arctic and Antarctic, and also served as a delicacy to survivors in the tropics by their native rescuers. In certain Thailand restaurants diners can have a puppy picked out from a kennel, as we might select a special lobster or carp. Presumably they can then watch it being prepared.

Pilots who have come down in the jungle, once they had eaten a snake, could not praise the flesh highly enough: "It was as tender as a young chicken." One airman in Borneo lived for a whole week entirely on snakes, which he caught in wire nooses. After his rescue he insisted on going to an Asiatic restaurant, "to have a properly cooked dish of snake."

Starving survivors have even eaten nearly hatched birds' eggs, as long as the embryo hadn't started growing feathers. A British soldier in the rain forest of Burma loosened the many leeches on his legs with a cigarette, shut his eyes and swallowed them raw. "After all I did want to get back the blood they had taken off me," he remarked after his rescue. Apparently the leeches were very tasty.

An American airman who came down off the coast of Borneo during the war soon made contact with the natives. But they refused to feed him. When he realized that they had a craving for salt, he began to collect it on the shore, evaporating sea water on large, flat rocks. He offered it to the natives against food, and they agreed at once to the exchange. He was soon engaged in a vigorous trade and had more than enough to eat.

A party of Japanese soldiers on a Pacific island were in a similar position. Instead of collecting salt, they resorted to a distillery. They made such an intoxicating drink from fermented bananas that the natives couldn't get enough of it. The Japanese were almost worshiped and didn't need to worry about their further food supplies.

Just as men stranded in the desert during the war were able to quench their thirst from the radiators of wrecked cars, there were survivors in the tropics who could appease their hunger from the remains of food thrown away by men wandering in the jungle before them. An American soldier lived for a week on the remains of food cans which a patrol on the same jungle track had left behind a week earlier. Castaways on tropical islands have often found in the sand the rations from torpedoed ships. One man lived for a fortnight on canned fish he found in the wreck of a Japanese plane.

So finding food and drink in peaceful times or in war is no insoluble problem for the survivor in the tropics. But just as the uninitiated have wrong ideas about this, they also imagine a journey on foot through tropical terrain to be harder than it really is. For one thing, the "average castaway" is usually stranded only on the edge of tropical country—on the coast. Of course the case is different for the pilot who bails out deep in the jungle, when the coast (usually identified with civilization) is often hundreds of miles away.

But even in such circumstances he has great chances of survival, according to experts. A search is almost always made for him, and he can bring it to a successful conclusion if he gives distress signals to his rescuers, as all missing people should do. They were given, for instance, by some American pilots who bailed out in the Burmese jungle in April 1944. Their approximate position was known, but no search plane had been able to spot them because of the dense foliage of the treetops. Nor would any pilot have seen a signal fire. The men knew this and began to clear a patch of wood with swords and axes from their emergency kit. They lit a signal fire there, and were promptly sighted. Two weeks later a patrol reached them and led them back to the coast.

Another party, who had done the same thing, also waited for the search patrol, but soon became afraid the patrol would not find them. This fear reduced their morale more and more, until they suddenly had the idea of attracting their rescuers by shrill whistles. They cut off some bamboo stems and made them into flutes. Then the man on watch had to send out continuous SOS calls on the flute. Finally, with three more flutes, they all blew together. The shrill tone carried well. It attracted the attention of the rescuers, who were just about to pass the clearing where the missing men were.

In another case a pilot who bailed out in the Burmese jungle found three wrecked planes one after the other, among the trees. "I took their radios to pieces, 'cannibalized' the broken parts and made a new set with which I appealed for help. I was found the next day."

But in the tropics, whenever help cannot be expected from outside, it is best, say the survival experts, to leave the scene of the crash quickly and try to walk to the nearest settlement, generally the coast. This, according to survival experts, is easier than most people think. For most people picture the tropics as largely impenetrable jungle where you hack your way through the bush, and the undergrowth simply closes again behind you after each laboriously made path.

But the tropics are by no means all jungle, of course, and not all jungle is impenetrable. Talking of rain forests, Marston Bates says that there is very little vegetation on the forest floor since the light is too dim for plants ". . . basically the forest floor is open, with vistas of a hundred feet or more, vistas framed and closed by the straight trunks of the trees that disappear into the vaulted green canopy that they support above. The cliché often used for the forest, 'cathedral-like,' is inevitable . . ."

In every jungle are rivers, and every river leads "somewhere safe to sea." To find them, many survivors have followed a game track. In Burma two American airmen, having discovered a river, built a raft, loaded it with roast monkey meat, and drifted on it to the coast.

Certainly there are zones which can only be penetrated with great difficulty and loss of time: it is best to pass them by, even if it means a detour of several days. A party of airmen after a crash landing struggled for five days to get through a bamboo forest which they could comfortably have skirted in four hours. But of course if you have little detailed idea of direction, and especially if you are injured, weak, exhausted, miles behind enemy lines, the nervous strain of plunging on through the jungle can be almost intolerable.

Such was the narrator's situation in *The Wind Cannot Read,* by the British novelist Richard Mason (some of which is based on personal experience). On the second day after his escape from a Japanese prisoner-of-war camp, "I used the sun, and went south, still parallel to the Imphal Road. Later on I came upon an encampment of Japs. Luckily I heard them first and got down out of sight, but it took me a long time to skirt the area, cautiously crawling most of the way—and with one arm useless it was a terrible business that exhausted me. When at last I tried to stand up I collapsed and had to lie resting for a time. I was weaker than ever, with a pain spreading through my body like a poison from the shoulder of my wounded arm . . . All over the arm a dirty blue-green colour was spreading, and in places the flesh had been scratched and torn by thorny growths. The dysentery was nothing now. I had dried up with no food or water in my stomach, and there were only pains which didn't matter. But there was a burning pain round my head like a red-hot steel band. It was this that made me cry. I could have kept myself from crying, but this would have taken energy that I needed, and I let myself weep. It did not matter weeping in the jungle when there was nobody to see. Once I had started, enormous convulsions began in my breast, but there were only tiny tears at the end of them, squeezed out as though my body had not enough water to spare for this. I put my face on

the ground and bit the earth until the waves that shook me had
subsided. Then I got up and went on, but stumbling half blindly. I
felt utterly broken and hopeless.

"Yet something kept holding me up, some strength that no
longer seemed my own. . . ." And in the end this man, perhaps
Mason himself, got through and was saved, as many others before
him have somehow kept going in tropical jungle and been saved in
the end.

Chapter 7
Survival After Plane Crashes

The airplane is the safest means of transport in the world.
In five years of peace the United States lost more men in her
Air Force through crashes than during the whole of the Korean
War.
From two articles on aviation

"Mayday . . . Mayday . . . Mayday . . . This is Flight N 90943
from Honolulu to San Francisco 'Sovereign of the Skies' . . . This
is Flight N 90943 *Sovereign of the Skies* . . . This is Flight N
90943 'Sovereign of the Skies.' Engine number one out. Our position, course and speed are . . ."

On October 16, 1956, at 1:26 A.M. this emergency call went out
from the big stratocruiser of an American airline company. Here
is what had happened: the plane had left Honolulu in Hawaii on
the evening of the fifteenth at 8:26 P.M. There were twenty-four
passengers aboard, including three small children, and seven
members of the crew: Flight Captain Richard N. Ogg, his first
officer, flight engineer, navigation officer, and three stewardesses.
Stores, as well as two dogs and 3,300 canaries, were carried in the
unoccupied flight deck below. The flight was scheduled to take
eight hours and fifty-four minutes, and the plane carried fuel for
twelve hours and eighteen minutes.

As it took off, some of the passengers looked at the literature in
front of their seats and found instructions for emergencies, including what to do if the plane were forced down in the water. They
expressed wry amusement, especially as before the take-off they
had received a brief demonstration on how to put on a life jacket.

"You won't need it of course," they were assured. "But we have to give you this practice to comply with the regulations."

The plane had been flying for over four hours with engines humming monotonously. Most of the passengers had wrapped up in blankets and were asleep in their lean-back chairs. At 1:02 A.M. Ogg asked the ground control at Honolulu for permission to climb higher, which was granted, there being no other aircraft in this flight corridor. Four minutes later the first officer, Haaker, who was piloting the plane at the time, started climbing. In twenty-five minutes, they would be at "the point of no return," halfway to their destination.

At 1:19 A.M. the plane reached the desired height of 20,000 feet. Mary Daniel, the stewardess then on duty, came into the cockpit to see if the crew wanted anything to drink. Captain Ogg asked for a bottle of Coca-Cola, Brown (navigation officer) and Garcia (flight engineer) ordered coffee. Mary turned to go. It was just after 1:20 A.M.

Haaker was increasing the speed to 188 knots when he noticed a wobble in the steering column. Then they all heard the steady noise of the propellers taking on a higher pitch with a faint whining note. Mary and the others knew at once what it meant. The speedometer registered 2,900 revolutions a minute for engine number 1 (on the outside left) more than the maximum compatible with safety: this engine must be out of control. It began to turn even faster, and Haaker tried to cut it out, so as to let it cool off; the plane could fly on three engines for the time being.

Almost automatically, although he knew the plane's fate might depend on it, he carried out the first emergency maneuver: he pressed a button to "feather" the blades of the damaged engine's propeller, i.e. to put it in neutral; with the engine stopped, the blades would then offer least resistance to the current of air, and so not be turned by the wind. At the same time Garcia was working the fire-fighting equipment, to stop a fire in the damaged engine. He cut off the fuel and throttled the other three engines to reduce the plane's speed. At this point the speedometer needle had already gone beyond the highest figure registered on the gauge.

The terrible whine grew louder and louder, a sign that the propeller blades had refused to go into the neutral position. It was now the current of air (no longer the fuel) that was sending the engine's pistons up and down faster and faster, nearing the fatal moment. The engine might then burst apart, or one of the propeller blades might break off and crash into the plane.

Ogg had taken over from Haaker, and tried once more, but in vain, to get the blades into neutral. He told Garcia to cut off the oil feed as well to engine number 1; so that the engine should seize up before a blade could break off.

At 1:22 A.M. the needle of engine number 1's speedometer went down a bit—but only for a moment. Then there was a violent bang from the engine, and shortly afterward the propeller began to turn even faster, making an even shriller noise. The engine had seized up as planned, but connection between piston shaft and propeller seemed to be broken. The propeller was now turning in the air current like a mad windmill.

Mrs. Gordon, one of the passengers, in a window seat with one of her two young daughters, woke up at the bang and peered apprehensively into the night. The two other stewardesses, Pat Reynolds and Katherine Araki, also asleep in the passenger cabin, were awakened too. Pat, the chief stewardess, got up at once and went to the cockpit. A minute later she came back and whispered to Katherine: "Engine one has gone. The captain's trying to feather it."

Ogg was indeed making repeated attempts to get the propeller blades into neutral, but still could not do it. The speedometer meanwhile showed zero for revolutions, despite the frantic whirling of the propeller; the connection between cockpit and propeller was definitely broken. The plane's speed had now gone down to 150 knots. Gradually, at about a thousand feet a minute, she was diving toward the sea.

The other passengers were now waking up. They got out of their blankets and raised their lean-back chairs to a sitting position. The first anxious questions were heard. The stewardesses tried to calm them. "It can't be anything much, or the captain would have told you."

At 1:26 A.M. *Sovereign of the Skies* sent out her first call for help. It was directed especially at the coast guard ship *Pontchartrain,* the "Ocean Station November" for that night, the ship, that is, which is on rescue service halfway between Hawaii and the West Coast of the United States.

Contact with the *Pontchartrain* was established at once, and Ogg informed the coast guard of his situation: "Unable to feather propeller. Shall have to ditch. Require detailed information weather condition. Require further details my position in relation to you." A few seconds later he received the answer: "O.S. November to N 90943. Wind: eight knots, northeasterly. Sky: partly overcast. Main swell from 80 Deg., height of waves three to four feet, speed about twenty-four knots. Distance between crests 150 yards. Smaller swell from 130 Deg., height of waves two to three feet, speed thirteen knots, distance between crests twenty-two yards. Barometric pressure 30.28. Water temperature 73.4° F. Your present position according to our radar: thirty-eight miles away from us, on a course of 256 Deg." After that there were instructions on the most favorable approach for the "ditching" operation.

It was time to break it to the passengers. Ogg switched on the aircraft intercom, cleared his throat, and said in a quiet, unemotional voice: "Ladies and gentlemen, this is your captain speaking. I am sorry to have to wake you, but one of the engines has conked out, and it is possible we shall have to ditch. Please put on your life jackets, fasten your seat belts, and take all pointed objects, glasses, ballpoint pens, and so on out of your pockets."

While Ogg was slightly altering course so as to approach Ocean Station November, Pat Reynolds switched on the main lights in the passenger cabin. With a friendly smile she tried to disperse the passengers' growing anxieties. Standing in the gangway, she demonstrated again, with practiced assurance, how the life jackets were to be put on; then went down a list of other instructions:

"Please bring your seat into a vertical postion, and fasten your seat belts as tight as you can. No smoking please. Take off your shoes, and if you are wearing glasses or false teeth, please remove these too. As the captain has just said, you should take all sharp, pointed objects out of your pockets. We will keep them in plastic bags, which my colleague is now distributing to you." (One woman obediently tore the crucifix from her rosary and put it into the plastic bag.) "You will like to know the reason for these precautions. Well, a forced landing can be rather rough, and we don't want to have such things flying through the gangway. In case we have to make this landing, please bend right forward and press your face hard into the pillows and blankets which we shall now also be giving out to you. Cross your arms under your thighs. You should remain in this position until the plane has come completely to rest. The plane can float of course, and when we have alighted there is no cause for undue haste. We will show you which emergency exits to use. You should not blow up your life jackets till you are out of the plane." (This instruction is given because if the passengers were to blow up their life jackets in the plane and there were a panic, it would be very hard for them to get through the emergency exits.) "When I ask you to, you will please move up to the seats farthest forward, where it will be safest." (The captain had told her that he expected the rear of the plane to break off when they alighted.)

The passengers listened to her calmly. Nobody screamed or had hysterics, and it seemed almost like a harmless air drill. Ogg was trying to maintain a height of 5,000 feet, for which he had to increase the revolutions of the other three engines to 2,350 a minute. The plane's speed was now 135 knots.

At 1:26 the lights of the "Ocean Station" came in sight. Ogg brought the plane down to 3,000 feet. He could keep it at this height for a long while, but ditching was now inevitable. There was such a braking effect from the still turning propeller of engine number 1 that the fuel would only last out for another 750 miles, and it was 1,000 miles to San Francisco or back to Honolulu.

The passengers set about carrying out instructions given them. No children's life jackets had been brought, so adult ones had to be made to fit by trying some extra strings round them. Mr. and Mrs. Gordon's two small daughters began to cry as the yellow rubber jackets were put round them, but they soon quieted down.

Pat Reynolds showed the passengers where the lifeboats were stowed, and designated some of the men to help launch these after the landing. The plastic bags and all loose articles like suitcases and briefcases were stowed in the flight deck with the stores, dogs, and canaries. Then the passengers moved to the forward seats. The children were laid on the floor, and their parents instructed to press them tight between the feet. These preparations were completed in less than three minutes.

By 1:27 *Sovereign of the Skies* was flying over "Ocean Station November," where all was set to aid the plane after the ditching.

The rescue crews were ready in their motorboats, and a row of light buoys were set out to help the pilot judge the distance to the dark and choppy sea.

But the danger of ditching by night was too great. After circling twice over the *Pontchartrain,* Ogg decided to put it off till dawn. At 1:35 he informed the passengers: "You may unfasten your seat belts and walk about if you wish. We shall not be coming down till dawn."

The plane was now circling above the *Pontchartrain* at a radius of five miles. All ships within 300 miles were informed, and asked to come to the place where the plane was expected to come down.

The passengers talked in whispers with members of the crew. "You may smoke again," Pat Reynolds told them. The men lit up eagerly. Coffee, chewing gum, and orange juice were served. Everyone knew the forced landing was now certain, but the refreshments were welcome all the same. "What are we getting for our last breakfast?" one man asked her with a grin, and several of the passengers began making "sick" jokes on their situation. Nobody seemed unduly agitated, and Marcel Touze, a French doctor, even wrapped up his blanket and went to sleep again.

At 2:45 the plane was shaken by another violent bang, which made the passengers start up in their seats. It was engine number 4 (outside right) that was now giving trouble. After a few misfires its power went down rapidly—the cylinders were not firing properly. This engine too must be stopped: Ogg tried to feather the blades, and this time succeeded at once. For the next two and a half hours, flying with only two engines, the plane maintained a height of 2,000 feet and a speed of 140 knots. It was consuming about 220 gallons of gasoline an hour. Ogg was deliberately lightening the plane as much as possible before coming down on the water, so that it should float a good long time. Meanwhile he made some trial descents, without informing the passengers, so as not to alarm them.

At 5:15, after going up to 5,000 feet, he saw the first glimmer of dawn on the horizon. Far below him, the Ocean Station's motorboats were picking up the light buoys again. In the cockpit of the plane another radio message was received: "Please inform us ten minutes before you start coming down. We shall then have enough time to get all our men standing by."

At 5:40 Ogg advised the coast guard accordingly. In order to stop a fire in case the fuel tanks burst, their men at once began spraying the water with a layer of foam thirty yards wide and half a mile long to form a "landing strip." Then Ogg addressed his passengers: "Please take your seats. No smoking now. Fasten your seat belts again. We are about to come down on the water. The landing conditions are ideal, the sea couldn't be better. I shall presently give you a ten-minute warning, which means we shall be landing ten minutes from then. A minute before we reach the water I shall give another warning. Now will you please follow again the instructions of the stewardesses."

Some passengers began to pray softly. One child cried. Except for the whine from engine number 1, those were the only sounds to be heard. Everyone was highly disciplined, and readily obeyed the instructions given. The heavy plane gradually came down toward the waves.

"Ten minutes from now," said Ogg. The plane was 900 feet up. In the dawn twilight he could clearly make out the carpet of foam, which helped him judge the distance to the water. The strip had been laid out in the direction which would allow him to land against the wind. He would have to let the plane skim along the crest of a breaker, so that the waves shouldn't press it under water. "One minute more," he called into the microphone. Brown set the radio transmitter at automatic, so that he could send out a continuous SOS (which would allow rescue ships to locate the plane).

The stewardesses took seats in the passenger cabin. Forward in the cockpit, although the speedometer only registered ninety knots, the crew felt as if the deadly waves of the Pacific were rushing toward them with terrific speed. Ogg tilted the plane up a bit, bringing her nose about five degrees above the horizon. Then he yelled: "Here we go." The passengers put their heads down and bent double.

At 6:15 precisely the plane touched the water. There was a slight bump, then the fuselage bounded off the waves, glided through the air for about 125 yards, to come down again, this time with a terrible shattering crash. Cockpit and passenger cabin were pressed a little way under water, but bounced out of the waves again at once. The left wing, however, plunged a bit deeper into

the waves, and acted like a gigantic lever, pulling the plane round
to the left with tremendous force. The rear did not turn so quickly.
Within the fraction of a second the metal casing stretched to its
utmost limit—and directly afterward snapped with a horrible
crackling noise.

Just as Ogg had feared, the rear broke off close to the main
door. The seats in the separated part were unoccupied, but the
seats right by the break were torn from their fittings, hurling the
passengers to the floor. There was only one child lying on the
floor. He scarcely felt a thing. Two other mothers had taken their
daughters into their arms, thinking this would be safer. But the
two girls were now torn away from them by the force of the crash,
and were also hurled to the floor.

The water began splashing into the gaping fuselage, soaking
some of the passengers. The red plush carpet on the floor was
soon sodden from the waves. After a fairly short distance the
plane came completely to rest. The gurgle of the water was the only
noise to be heard. Water filled the storeroom below, and the two
dogs and 3,300 canaries were drowned.

The passengers, still dazed, could scarcely grasp that they themselves were alive; none of them was seriously injured, and only
five people had minor bruises. Members of the crew and some
passengers opened the emergency exits. Two rafts for twenty people each were carried over the remaining wing into the water. A
third was set afloat at the main door. All the passengers left the
plane one after another, calmly and with complete discipline, nobody showing excessive fear. While their traveling companions
were quietly boarding the rafts, two passengers actually stood on
the wing taking photographs of the scene.

Meanwhile the first motorboat from the coast guard was already
alongside, taking the passengers off the rafts. Thirteen minutes
after the plane touched the water, all its passengers and crew were
safely on board the *Pontchartrain*. At 6:35, seven minutes later,
the plane lowered its nose and the wreck sank into the Pacific.

This dramatic example might almost suggest that a crash landing on the water or on the ground is as simple as a normal landing
on a smooth runway. But of course it is a dangerous business even
in the most favorable conditions, for the plane is coming down on

its belly, not on the undercarriage, so as not to overturn where the landing surface is uneven.

Many pilots have compared the moment of touching the water or the ground to a violent explosion. One bomber pilot said: "The plane crashed onto the sea as if it were hitting a brick wall. The impact of the waves seemed to break the cockpit in two." (Often enough this does actually happen, and a waterfall descends into the cockpit with tremendous force.) Another pilot said: "There was an earsplitting crash. I thought the whole plane was going to shatter to pieces the next moment. It was the most terrifying thing I have ever heard."

Passengers sitting toward the rear of the plane have the same impression. After a Boeing 707 landed on its belly near New York, one passenger said: "I thought my last hour had come when I heard the crash. I could only assume there had been an explosion, and that a moment or two later we should be blown to the back of beyond." When a German passenger plane had made a crash landing near London, a boy of nineteen said: "It sounded as if we were sliding over a thick bed of large stones. I thought the whole floor would break up the next moment."

In emergency landings on concrete strips the runway is sprayed with foam, both to reduce the danger of sparks forming and causing a fire in case the fuel tanks explode, and also to increase the plane's gliding capacity and lessen the shock of braking. Where no even layer of spray can be put down, on a potato field, for instance, a plane will come to rest more quickly and violently. Water has an exceptionally strong braking power. At the sudden halt all objects in the plane which are not securely fastened down are dislodged and shoot off in the direction of their original momentum.

If before a crash landing the captain did not ask the passengers to take precautions, they would all be pulled off their seats and flung forward very violently as soon as the plane touched the ground (or the water)—the same as the occupants of a car which brakes suddenly. Some passengers who have failed to fasten their seat belts have sustained grave injuries or even broken their necks. (One reason, of course, why it is so important to use the seat belts and to take up a posture advised by the stewardesses, as shown in the accompanying diagrams.) Passengers have also been injured

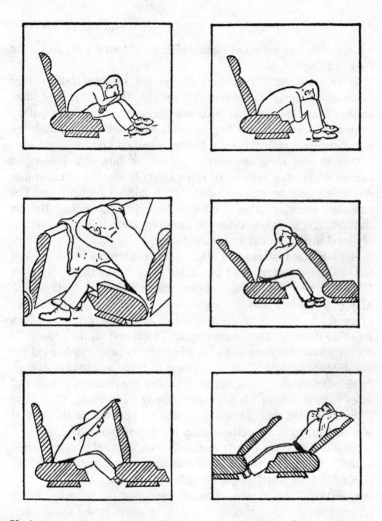

Various postures recommended to passengers for their protection when a plane has to make a crash landing.

(*U. S. Government Printing Office*)

by eyeglasses or ballpoint pens which people sitting behind them have not discarded.

Often, after first touching the ground or water, the plane bounces up again (as *Sovereign of the Skies* did), and then crashes down harder, shattering any passengers who have got up from their seats after the first impact: it is when people think the worst danger is over that most fractures and cuts occur.

One of the most interesting aspects is how the passengers behave during the minutes or often hours before the plane comes down. It might be expected that they would all be panic-stricken and the passenger cabin filled with hysterical screaming. But on the contrary, as in our dramatic example, there is almost invariably good discipline and an amazing calm.

Here are a few random examples from recent years. A few months after *Sovereign of the Skies* came down in the water, a U. S. Air Force C-97 transport plane faced a similar situation, with Major Samuel Tyson in command: on the flight from San Francisco to Honolulu the plane lost a propeller blade, which seriously damaged a second engine. Tyson had all the luggage of the sixty-seven passengers thrown into the Pacific, and headed for the military airfield of Hilo (Hawaii). With a smoking engine, flames sometimes coming out of it, he flew the remaining thousand miles without any of his passengers losing their nerve. They were naturally scared, but no one screamed or behaved in the sort of way that might be expected in such terrifying circumstances.

No doubt this was largely due to Tyson's own calmness: "I tried to make my voice sound quite dispassionate, and said over the intercom 'We are just losing a propeller. Everything will soon be all right again.' I saw no reason to tell them that the propeller might separate the cockpit from the fuselage or stove in the middle petrol tank and set it on fire. It could also, of course, have cut the electric wiring or the steering cables."

In 1958 a Curtiss plane was flying over the West German city of Mannheim during the night at 6,600 feet, when the electric equipment failed, putting all the instruments out of action, including the radio. The pilot, Eric Nilson, informed his thirty-three passengers that he would have to make a forced landing in the dark. Then he flew several times over a small military airfield, until the ground staff were alerted and turned on the landing lights. The plane landed safely. One of the people on board, Kage Sundermann, told reporters: "We were frightened to death. But all the passengers kept calm. There was no panic."

In July 1960 a DC-7 flying from Tokyo to Manila caught fire, with fifty-nine passengers on board. It was a pitch-dark night, and when the pilot came down on the water with a wing burning, they showed an exemplary calm. Crew and passengers were all saved, except for one woman who was killed by the impact when the plane hit the water. Wing-Commander F. Rall previously had told his passengers: "Ladies and gentlemen, this is your captain speaking. We are sorry to have to wake you up—but as some of you may have already guessed, we are having engine trouble. I would like to assure you that we are not expecting any worsening of the situation, but it would be quite a good thing if you would now pay attention to our stewardess, who is going to put through a drill on coming down in the water."

In fact Rall and his men had already decided on a "ditching." A little later the position became even more critical, when the fire in the wing began to spread to the fuselage of the plane. In a matter of minutes the wing was certain to break off, and the plane would plunge into the water like a stone. Rall still maintained his complete calm. "I think, ladies and gentlemen, that we shall soon be able to touch down. Prepare for the landing shock. Please don't be afraid, nothing will happen to us." Yet it was night, and the sea was stormy. Rall and his crew were not expecting to survive the next two minutes.

In October 1960 a Viking charter plane circled over Munich for ninety minutes with damaged undercarriage. After a successful landing the passengers climbed out pale and shivering—but throughout the hour and a half they had shown no signs of panic.

During the night of February 22–23, 1961, when a two-engine plane, also with a breakdown of the electrical equipment, was preparing for a forced landing in New Jersey, a father who was with his wife and daughter wrote to his two children not on the plane: "Darling Paul and Kathy, Mother and Sally and I are on this plane which has no electricity and its engines have stopped. So I can't see what I'm writing. It certainly doesn't look too good—but we love you, and if we are to die now, we know you will go on. Your mother is very brave. We have prayed, and our lives are in God's hands. We love you. Mother, Sal and Dad."(All survived unscathed.)

In September 1962, when the Superconstellation came down off the coast of Ireland with sixty-six passengers (as previously quoted), the panic did not start till they were all struggling to get on the only lifeboat; till then they had accepted the situation without undue excitement. The following month a DC-7 came down in the Pacific off the coast of Alaska, with 103 passengers on board, the largest number ever to experience a forced landing. There was no panic, and they were all picked up by a coast guard boat safe and sound.

On March 10, 1963, a Superconstellation with eighty-five people on board had a failure of two engines on a flight from Hawaii to California. It returned to Honolulu—no panic. Four days later a Boeing 707 flying from New York to Stockholm landed in Copenhagen with damaged undercarriage on a carpet of foam. The fifty passengers behaved admirably.

On March 21, 1970, a bomb planted by Arab terrorists exploded in the freight compartment of a "Caravelle" of the Austrian Airlines, tearing a man-sized hole into the fuselage of the plane which had just taken off from Frankfort in West Germany. Miraculously, the pilot managed to make a safe landing. Passenger Gert Merx, twenty-five, later recalled: "After the blast, smoke was pouring out from everywhere. Suddenly I couldn't see a thing. I had to cough. There was a terrible stench, I got sick and I was very afraid. All passengers were staring straight ahead, petrified. But there was no panic."

On September 6, 1971, a BAC Super 1-11, chartered for a group of tourists, made an emergency landing on a highway near the airport of Hamburg, after two of the plane's engines exploded in flight. The passengers, most of whom felt the explosions or even saw the flames coming out of the engines, knew that "something terrible must have happened." But, as one survivor later said: "There were no cries, no shouts—until we actually hit the Autobahn."

How is this surprising calm and good discipline to be explained? The chief reason is that in almost all emergency landings the captain and crew have enough time to take appropriate action and prepare the passengers for what to expect, as illustrated by Tyson and Rall. They always address the passengers in confident, almost conversational tones, having had a thorough training in all that has to be done in such cases. Without this training the stewardesses, for instance, could not keep enough self-control to conceal from the passengers their own fears (from which, of course, they are not free either) and even restore passenger morale. One American pilot said: "A good stewardess is often worth more than an extra engine. The passengers will confidently obey her instructions. If her voice does not tremble, that is half the battle." The same applies, of course, to every member of the crew.

Often some of the passengers are brave enough to try to make their fellows forget how serious things are. Red Skelton entertained the passengers on a plane for two hours with a continuous flow of anecdotes, jokes, and miming—when the plane was limping across the Atlantic with one of its engines gone haywire. It alighted successfully, and he confessed afterward: "That was my toughest performance ever. I was incredibly frightened the whole time, and couldn't think where my next crack was coming from— but I knew I mustn't dry up." Mickey Rooney rose to a similar occasion a few years later. In fact the U. S. Air Force has recently introduced a program of studies for its men which stresses the usefulness of humor in dangerous situations.

Strangely enough, most air travelers will be calmer on seeing a burning wing or propeller out of action, or even facing an emergency landing (where they are told what to expect) than when the plane suddenly shakes or jolts for no apparent reason or makes any unusual movement. They are not prepared for this, so they are more inclined to lose their nerve, start screaming, or get into a complete panic. A young woman in a jet plane which pitched from one side to the other a few times before landing at London Airport, said she had never been so frightened in her life. "Some people had begun to scream—but by then we were already on the ground."

On July 27, 1962, a B-707 only escaped colliding with a Dutch military plane because its pilot nose-dived. The seventy passengers had not got their seat belts fastened, which is not mandatory, although recommended during a flight, and the dive made some of them (literally) hit the ceiling with cries of horror. Those who had been sitting at the rear were completely soaked by the upsetting of the water tanks in the pantry. Some people were hurt, and the stewardess sustained a serious back injury. Altogether the chaos and panic were appalling.

On August 13, 1960, a British pilot had to tilt his plane down 40 degrees, so as to avoid colliding with another plane over Rome Airport. The fifty-two passengers were hurled into each other in wild confusion, suffering gashes and fractures, and the passenger cabin was filled with cries. "I screamed and screamed," said a young woman after the landing, "I couldn't control my fear. I simply thought: in a moment or two, we'll be smashed on the ground." After a smooth landing twenty-three passengers had to be sent to hospitals with serious injuries.

Accident-prevention experts, I might mention in this context, believe that air travelers should keep their seat belts fastened throughout the flight; since the danger of collisions between planes grows every year. Of course the passengers would die if there *were* a collision; but they might escape severe injuries in case of a near-collision, and statistics show that nowadays such near-collisions occur two or three times per day. The reactions of the passengers give some idea of the terror that must be felt inside a plane which is hurtling toward the ground—where there are no survivors to tell the tale.

The longest "near-crash" so far, occurred in early February 1959, when a Boeing 707 with 114 passengers (including actor Gene Kelly) dived nearly 30,000 feet. It was on a flight from Paris to New York, and was crossing the Atlantic at about 35,000 feet. The captain, Waldo Lynch, had switched on the autopilot, a routine matter on long flights, and had gone to have a chat with the passengers. Gene Kelly said afterward: "Suddenly there was a violent jolt forward—followed by screams of terror from the passengers. My God, was I scared!"

The passengers couldn't know that the autopilot had for some reason broken down. They only felt that the plane had turned on its nose. With ever-increasing speed it dived toward the Atlantic. Everyone saw death staring them in the face. Many were screaming for help, others praying out loud. "The shrieks were terrible," said another passenger. "Even worse was the chaos caused by the sudden and violent plunge. Anyone who happened to be standing was hurled down with terrific force. A stewardess was flung under a seat. Anyone seated was pressed into his seat as if by a giant's hand (i.e. the force of acceleration). I myself felt as though I had been hit on the chest with a sledgehammer."

After the first minute of the dive, nearly all the passengers were screaming. With all engines working at full power, the speed was now approaching sound level, so that most of the passengers could scarcely move a limb. "My arms seemed to be nailed down . . ." "I couldn't move legs or arms . . ." "The upper half of my body stayed immobile, however hard I strained . . ." "I felt as though all the blood had left my body and my lungs were being torn to shreds . . ." "I had broken my ankle skiing. It suddenly hurt like mad, and I tried to smash the plaster . . ." These were some of the impressions recorded afterward.

Children cried, women were in hysterics, and in between several men could be heard shouting. Captain Lynch too had been thrown to the ground. Fighting against the force of gravity, he now strained to get forward into the cockpit. Although actually moving downward, he had to crawl laboriously on all fours from seat to seat. Finally, after what seemed an age, he reached the cockpit and tried to force the plane back into a horizontal position. He succeeded at last, after stopping the engines—6,000 feet above the waves. Ten seconds more, and the history of flying would have had one more mysterious crash.

In view of the periodical emergency landings by passenger planes, many people wonder why parachutes are not carried on these planes, considering that the parachute (first used for a "free drop" from a plane by Leslie L. Irvin at Dayton, Ohio, in 1919) was the first aeronautical rescue equipment. There are several reasons for this. For one thing statistics show that most accidents in passenger flights occur during the take-off or the landing. If a plane gets into trouble during the actual flight, the nature of the accident would make it impossible for the passengers to use parachutes: the plane explodes, collides with another plane, or goes into a tailspin so quickly that even the crew would hardly have a chance to bail out.

But whenever (which is usually the case) the captain can go on flying a seriously damaged plane, an emergency landing or a "ditching" is a hundred times safer than a jump with a parachute. When sixteen U. S. Air Force training planes got lost and ran out of fuel over the Atlantic, fourteen pilots ditched and only two bailed out by parachute: all fourteen "ditchers" were rescued unhurt, but one of the jumpers broke his neck.

One can imagine the chaos and helplessness if eighty or ninety passengers—with old people, women, and children among them—had to jump out of a plane in flight. None would ever have made a jump before, some might even be flying for the first time. Most of them would have to be pushed out of the exits by force. Even then it is uncertain whether they would pull the release cords of their parachutes at the right moment. The plane would be flying on, so the first and last to jump would be several miles apart, with the rest of the passengers scattered along the distance like the beads of a torn necklace. Finding them would be immensely difficult, and their chances of survival very small.

Moreover, a parachute jump in an emergency, even for the experienced, is more dangerous than a forced landing; and that goes for the occupants of military planes too. Parachute jumpers incur dangers which in some cases sound truly impossible. These are exceptional, it is true, but they show what the average pilot has to reckon with if he decides, or is compelled, to go against the rules, and bails out instead of making a forced landing.

Even with the propeller-driven planes of World War II, it became clear that bailing out was a dangerous maneuver. In the U. S. Air Force, for instance, three-quarters of all the accidents connected with parachute jumps have occurred because the jumper, hanging from a parachute, was injured by his own spinning plane.

For instance, the pilot of a P-38 fighter first discarded the perspex roof of his cockpit. Then he tired to climb out of the plane, but the air current kept on pressing him back into his seat. So he turned the plane on its back and dropped out of the cockpit. His parachute was opening normally, when he suddenly saw the plane shooting toward him. He tried desperately to close the parachute, so that he would fall a bit: no good. He grasped the cords and pulled himself up on them, but not enough. The plane hurtled past very close to him, and the propeller tore off his right leg, just above the knee. Almost fainting from pain and loss of blood, he landed in a wood, and was left hanging in his straps a few feet above the ground. While dangling to and fro for almost an hour, he managed to bandage his stump with a piece of cloth from his uniform. Eventually a native who happened to be passing cut him down and put a tourniquet on the stump.

Many pilots and air crew have in bailing out been hurled against the plane's controls, and suffered severe injuries or even been killed before they could open their parachute. Others, wanting to prepare carefully for the jump and afterward, slung extra pieces of equipment round them like a haversack, water bottle, bush knife, etc. What happened then is described by one of many who tried this sort of thing:

"When I stood up in the cockpit (of a P-38), the air current at once tore my goggles off and pressed me back into the seat. I tried again to climb out of the cockpit, this time feet first. The wind did in fact pull me out of the plane, but I smashed my right arm on the controls. That was only the beginning of my troubles. The heavy equipment I had hung about me pummeled me during the 'free drop.' A bush knife banged against my chin, knocked three of my teeth out and dislocated my jaw. Half-unconscious I eventually landed in the Pacific. There I had to throw away all the 'extras' so as not to sink."

While parachutists normally jump only in favorable weather conditions and onto terrain more or less suitable for a landing, pilots often have to jump "into the blue"—which is safest over sandy ground, as in deserts. In all other climatic zones the chances of a successful landing are much smaller. In the Arctic and Antarctic to jump at night or through clouds is extremely dangerous; the number of pilots reported missing or fatally injured after jumps over those regions is far higher than anywhere else. Many were dragged to death by the wind after landing. Others got entangled in the cords of their parachute and were suffocated. There are also many pilots who came down in the water, were covered over by the parachute, and drowned beneath it. To avoid this fate, a lot of them tried to get clear of their harness when a few feet above the water; but they would often underrate the distance, and so perish by crashing onto the surface of the water, which hit them like glass.

Pilots who landed with a parachute in the jungle often got caught in trees two hundred feet or more above the ground, and sometimes could not get down. They would be found weeks later, "starved in the air." Others, landing by night, though lucky enough to reach the lowest branches of a tree, made the mistake of jumping to the ground in the dark. Most of them injured themselves, and one slipped, rolled down a slope and broke his neck.

Pilots sometimes have to bail out over walls of stormclouds, as happened to Wing-Commander William H. Rankin, flying an F-8U jet plane across South Carolina in 1959. At 45,000 feet he had a "flame-out"—that is, the engine stopped. Everything broke down, gauges, radio, even steering; and there was nothing to do but to bail out. Rankin discarded his cockpit top and used the ejector seat. He had to get through the layers of thin air in a free drop, or he would have frozen to death. There was a built-in air-pressure meter in his parachute set to open it automatically at 10,000 feet. "But at 40,000 feet," Rankin said afterward, "everything suddenly became black around me. I couldn't see anything. I was in a thunderstorm. I dropped and dropped without seeing a thing. Because the air pressure was apparently higher owing to the storm, my parachute opened already at 20,000 feet. The same moment I was caught by the turbulent masses of air in the center of the storm. Instead of falling I was carried up. Hail, rain, and lightning surrounded me, and there was also deafening thunder and the dangerous upward current. I kept checking the straps to make sure the parachute was still open. Sometimes it collapsed, and that was a horrible feeling. But it would always fill out again after a few moments. I was blown to and fro in the storm, up and down, sometimes up to 60,000 feet. I felt as if I were in a lift that was rising very fast, with compressed air all round. Sometimes I was afraid I should lose consciousness, but luckily this did not happen. Even when I shut my eyes, the lightning was so bright that I thought an atomic bomb had gone off in front of me."

Then he came into hail, which might easily have torn his

parachute. He got a black eye, and bad bruises all over his body. His left hand was broken. Even breathing gave him trouble, not because of lack of oxygen (he had already sunk into lower layers of air), but "there was so much water in the air that I felt as if I were at the bottom of a swimming pool."

At last it grew warmer round him. At about 300 feet he could make out the tops of trees in a wood. A strong wind swept him over them, and his parachute caught in a tall tree. His head was banged against the trunk, but his helmet stopped him fracturing his skull. He undid his straps, fell to the ground—and set out to find a road. When he eventually reached a highway and took up his stand there, the drivers of the first dozen cars were so scared of his horrifying appearance that they drove past without stopping. Then a small boy recognized Rankin's flying helmet and made his father stop. Rankin learned from the father that during his forty-minute drop he had been carried twenty-five miles from where he had jumped. The doctors who examined him afterward said that only his excellent physical condition had kept him from "death by parachute."

Even trained parachutists cannot protect themselves against the dangers of a sudden squall. In April 1959, for instance, 1,300 American paratroopers jumped out of eighty-six transport planes over Fort Campbell, Kentucky, at about 1,350 feet. Conditions were extremely favorable, with fine weather and no ground wind. But seconds before the first men touched the ground, the landing strip was swept by a squall, which took hold of the parachutes and made many of the jumpers fall. They lay helpless on their backs like beetles, and were dragged over the ground at frantic speed. Reporters, cameramen, and staff officers rushed up to help them but came too late for many, who were dashed against rocks and tree stumps. One man got his neck caught in the cords of his parachute and would have been strangled if an officer hadn't cut him loose at the last moment. The brief squall cost five dead and 137 seriously injured.

For curiosity's sake I would mention a few cases where parachutes refused to open or pilots have dropped without them—and yet survived. These cases are authentic, incredible as they may sound.

One of them is the story of Captain George E. Day, pilot of an

American jet fighter. In June 1959 he had to jump from 400 feet up. His parachute did not open. Day ricocheted off the branches of a pine and fell underneath the tree, having broken a few bones. He was soon flying again.

During World War II a U. S. Marine pilot fell into the water from 2,300 feet with his parachute only partially opened. He ruptured his navel when hitting the water, lost consciousness and sank. The cold water brought him round, and twenty feet below the surface he released the automatic inflator of his life jacket and shot up to the surface again. Besides the ruptured navel, he had bruises and cuts and both ankles sprained. He swam fifteen hours to reach the nearest island.

In August 1960 a man on a Soviet geological expedition in the republic of Komi (in the Urals) was careless enough to fall out of a helicopter. He fell nearly 1,100 feet, and landed in a snowdrift unscathed. The same goes for a Swedish fighter pilot who fell from a height of 2,000 feet and landed on a haystack.

In the summer of 1962 a girl on Cape Cod was making her first jump, from a height of 2,600 feet, and her parachute failed to open. She plunged past her fiancé into a lake—and only broke her nose.

Probably the most amazing "free drop" occurred during the war when Nicholas Alkemade, a British rear-gunner (aged twenty-one) in a Lancaster bomber, fell 20,000 feet—one and a third times the height of the Matterhorn—and survived. His plane was shot down in flames over the Ruhr (on a night in March 1944). The commander gave the order to bail out. Alkemade crawled out of the narrow gun turret to put on his parachute, which was stowed in the rear of the plane to save space. To his horror the parachute was blazing. His only alternatives were to stay in the plane and be burned to death, or to jump without a parachute and be shattered on the ground. "Because of the fresh air outside I opted for the latter form of death," he said afterward. He crawled out of the plane and hurtled head first toward the ground at about 110 miles an hour. It was just after midnight.

About 3 A.M. he regained consciousness. He was lying on a cluster of stunted pines. It was covered by a snowdrift, and surrounded by tall pines all round, the springy branches of which had cushioned his fall. He was not too badly injured. He was taken to a German prisoner-of-war camp, where the German officers heard his story incredulously. They did not believe him until they found the remains of his burned parachute in the wreck of the Lancaster, and checked that the shoulder straps Alkemade wore showed no signs of pull. Long after the war he was still proudly showing skeptics a proper attestation of the story by the German camp commander and an officer of the German antiaircraft defense.

All these jumpers who survived their terrible falls from various heights owe their lives to immense luck, of course, including two important circumstances: they nearly all fell on soft matter which absorbed the shock (pine branches, haystacks, snowdrifts, etc.); they all lost consciousness, so that their bodies were completely relaxed, thus reducing the impact still further.

But the high number of accidents from parachute jumps in unfavorable conditions is understandable when you realize the following facts. A jumper landing on the ground with a parachute which opens normally has as much impact as if he were jumping onto the ground from the radiator hood of a car. With an increase in ground wind the speed of landing also increases. In a wind or gale of forty miles an hour the shock of landing is as great as if the car in the above example were driving over a bumpy road at that speed. With amateur parachute-jumping, a sport which is enjoying growing popularity in all countries, the ground wind should therefore never exceed ten miles an hour—when casualties will be correspondingly low. In one of the largest centers for this sport in America (in Orange, Massachusetts) 23,505 jumps had been made up to August 1, 1962; the number of accidents (including scratches, bruises, sprains, and minor fractures) was only .194 percent.

To return, then, to the reasons for not carrying parachutes on passenger planes, this is really the main one: the occupants of such a plane hurtling through the air with engine trouble or a burning wing could not choose the best time for a jump, nor the best weather for it, nor a good place to land. For passenger planes in difficulties an emergency landing is a much less dangerous business.

We have also the comfort of knowing that, at present anyhow, the airplane is the safest means of transport in the world. According to a survey in 1956, in 100 million passenger miles there are 2.7 deaths on the roads, 1.9 on rail, and 1.6 by air. Unfortunately, however, the chances of passengers surviving an emergency landing may decline very rapidly in the future: because there is an urge to fly long distances even faster, at greater altitudes and with still bigger planes.

While few would deny that supersonic planes may be necessary for national defense, it is hard to see why a passenger plane needs to fly, say, from London to New York in two hours instead of six. Instead of spending millions on the development of supersonic aircraft we should spend the money on modernizing air safety arrangements. These are hopelessly outmoded in relation to the ever-increasing density of air traffic and above all the rising speed of flights.

Military flying, with its slogan of "higher—farther—faster," shows with terrifying clarity (as in road traffic) that the number of dead and injured in an accident increases when the plane (or car) is traveling faster. The chances of a jet pilot surviving a breakdown of his fast plane are 50 percent smaller than those of a pilot who has to bail out of a propeller-driven plane, or make a forced landing with it.

Whereas the old propeller-driven planes were extremely reliable because of their relatively simple construction, the modern jets are as sensitive as a watch. If a bird gets into the controls, it can cause a jet to crash; the plane, designed for high speeds, often becomes uncontrollable if there is a flame-out. Because of its swept wings, it has too little lift without thrust, so it drops to the ground like a rock. During the war a B-26 bomber could still fly with two to three engines shot to pieces and its fuselage ripped open; but a jet often ceases to be airworthy if there is only a small hole in the cockpit. Jets are also exposed to many other dangers, such as sudden lack of oxygen, a drop in pressure, acceleration troubles, and air resistance (to name only a few).

So in an emergency the pilot of a modern jet often has no chance to make a forced landing, and has to bail out. To do that successfully is hard enough from a propeller-driven plane; from a high- and fast-flying jet it is an "exact science," and one which for years has formed the most important part of pre-flying training in all the world's air forces.

Even with the first jets it became clear that the pilot could not simply turn his plane on its back so that in an emergency he could drop out. Compared to the high speed with which the plane was traveling, his drop would be so slow that it would "catch him up" and smash him to bits. After many casualties the problem was solved through the ejector seat—which shoots the pilot out of the cockpit in his seat like a cannon ball. But air speeds go on increasing. When the first planes broke through the sound barrier, the ejector seats which had been developed till then soon proved to be not much use: they merely served to take the pilot away from a crashing plane. But the air pressure above the sound barrier is so great that you might as well bang an unprotected pilot against a brick wall to "rescue" him.

The American George Smith was the first person who could report what it is like to have to bail out beyond the sound barrier. On February 26, 1955, he was flying a Super-Sabre F-100 close to 800 mph eight miles above the town of Laguna Beach on the coast of California. Suddenly the plane nose-dived and plunged toward the sea. He tugged desperately at the joy stick, but nothing happened. The elevator did not react, the plane went on falling.

He had only two alternatives: at the stage of rescue technique then reached, both seemed equivalent to suicide. He could stay in the plane and try to right it within fifteen seconds, or else work his ejector mechanism and simply hope to be the first man to survive a "bounce" on the sound barrier. He chose the latter.

At 7,200 feet, traveling at a supersonic speed, he shot out of his cockpit. The moment he hit the outside air the supersonic speed at which his body, too, had been traveling was brought down to less than 200 miles per hour within seconds. Because of the deceleration he was exposed during these moments to forty times the normal gravity, which meant that his normal weight of 224 pounds went up to 8,960 pounds. Then Smith lost consciousness.

Meanwhile, blood vessels burst in his eyeballs, round their sockets and at twenty other places on his body. The wind performed a cruel strip-tease with him, tearing oxygen mask and helmet from his head; the blast hit his unprotected face, tore off his nose and found its way into his stomach, which became inflated like a medicine ball. He also lost his boots, stockings, and gloves, even his watch and the rings off his fingers. His arms and legs were whirled around, dislocated, broken, bruised, and crushed. The parachute eventually opened, and he landed in the water still unconscious. He did not sink, for the air in his inflated stomach kept him on the surface till a rescue boat dashed to the scene. He did not regain consciousness till five days later in a hospital; and after another three months he was discharged.

Smith's injuries are not surprising. Jumping at the speed of sound is like falling on a concrete floor. It will break all the bones in the body of a pilot who bails out unprotected.

In the last few years, especially in the United States, ejector seats have been developed. In them the pilot's face is protected against the air blast outside his plane through a sort of visor, or curtain. Also his arms and legs are fixed in special rests so that they are not broken or dislocated by the enormous impact of the air, which in the first moments reaches many thousand pounds of pressure per square inch. These seats are not suitable, however, for bailing out from beyond the sound barrier.

The earlier seats were only half automatic, eight manual operations being necessary before the pilot could get clear of his plane. The latest models, for particularly fast and high-flying aircraft, are completely automatic: that is, one pull is enough, and the pilot is shot into space with his seat by a cartridge with a firing power equivalent to a 35-millimeter grenade. The violence of this is so great that for a second he is exposed to twenty times the normal force of gravity. His vertebral column is contracted by about half an inch. After two seconds he is automatically extracted from his seat, and falls into thicker air layers in a free drop. Meanwhile he is breathing from a small steel cylinder which contains enough oxygen to last for about eight to ten minutes. He must keep his body in a particular position so as to "steer" his flight, or he would go into a tailspin, and the centrifugal forces might make him lose consciousness.

At a height of 12,000 feet, when the speed of his fall has been slowed a bit, the parachute is automatically pulled out of its case. There is a jerk, and the parachute is out. Two seconds later there is another violent jerk (caused by deceleration) of about eight times the force of gravity; the parachute has opened, the pilot floats toward the ground.

Although with increasing height the danger of excessive air blast at supersonic speed declines, two other dangers are increased: lack of oxygen (hypoxia) and the symptoms caused by very low pressure.

The former has been known about since the days of the first balloonists, although they did not then quite understand it or recognize it for what it was. In 1875 the aeronauts Sivel and Groce-Spinelli became its victims. On April 15 that year they went up in the balloon *Zenith* on an altitude flight with the French scientist Gaston Tissandier, to test some oxygen apparatus for the first time in the history of air travel. They never made their tests, not realizing when they needed oxygen; for one of the symptoms of too little oxygen at great altitudes is that a man becomes more and more elated as his physical danger increases.

While the *Zenith* was still climbing into thinner and thinner air layers, so that the men were taking in less and less oxygen, Spinelli and Sivel were increasingly carefree and happy. They were so elated that they kept on laughing and joking all the time. Rolf Strehl, in his book *Der Himmel hat keine Grenzen* (*The Sky Knows No Limits*), has an impressive description of what happened then, at 23,000 feet, inside the *Zenith:*

"Only Tissandier was strangely quiet. Laboriously and with rattling breath, he absorbed the thin air. He was fighting for air, feeling more and more constricted. 'The oxygen apparatus,' he had time to think. 'My God, we were going to try out the oxygen apparatus!' Then he lost consciousness.

"When he came to again, there was darkness round him, pitch-black night. His optic nerve failed him. He felt the balloon falling with terrible speed. 'Sivel—Spinelli,' he called, but only the hiss of the biting wind answered him. He broke the glass of his watch with trembling fingers and felt for the hands: he had been unconscious for only half an hour. The next second he grasped the full horror of the situation. His companions lay unconscious on the floor, and the balloon was falling from a crazy height . . ."

With his last strength Tissandier managed to drop ballast, then he lost consciousness again. The balloon went on falling. "When he came to for the second time a few minutes later, his optic nerve was working again, though not perfectly. Then he dimly saw the figures of Sivel and Spinelli lying huddled in a corner, blankets pulled over their heads, as if they couldn't bear the sight of the earth rushing toward them. He tried shaking them awake. Horror seized him as he pulled back the blankets. Sivel was black in the face, there was bloody froth at his mouth, his eyes were wide and staring. He was dead. Spinelli too never moved again." Tissandier threw out the last ballast. Even so, the balloon's fall was so violent that he was seriously injured in the landing.

It was probably for the same reason that the American Thomas Gatch perished in February 1974, when he tried to cross the Atlantic with a set of high-altitude balloons. Although neither Gatch nor his gondola was ever found, experts believe this is what happened: suffering from lack of oxygen, Gatch became unconscious during his flight. Uncontrolled, his balloons burst and he crashed into the sea.

Modern military planes protect their crews from hypoxia by carrying oxygen apparatus. But since even the best apparatus can fail, future air crews learn how to recognize the first symptoms of this in low-pressure chambers during their pre-flight physiological training. At 10,000 feet there may be headaches and feelings of tiredness. At 15,000 feet the pilot "just wants to go to sleep," and feels uncomfortably hot. At 18,000 feet his optic nerve and powers of judgment are affected; he can make mistakes without being aware of them, and may even think he has done the right thing. This over-confidence has already proved fatal to many jet pilots: they took no notice of ground control or of their instruments, and behaved like drunks at the wheel.

A pilot who recognizes the early symptoms of hypoxia must at once go down into thicker air layers. But the time he has to do this decreases, the higher he is when his oxygen apparatus fails. At 25,000 feet he can remain conscious for five minutes. At 40,000 feet he has only twelve seconds to save himself, but from there up to the stratosphere the time remains constant. The blood in the lungs, which does not contain enough oxygen, takes twelve seconds to reach the brain via the heart. As soon as it gets there, the pilot loses consciousness from lack of oxygen. If he does not succeed in taking the plane lower within twelve seconds, he can only bail out. He may lose consciousness afterward, but his parachute will open automatically in thicker air layers, and he will regain consciousness when he gets oxygen again.

So much for hypoxia; extreme cold, especially the low pressure at great heights, represents just as serious a danger. Any pilot who climbs and descends over long distances can become a victim of lowered pressure. With increasing height there is an expansion of the air enclosed in various cavities of his body, such as the aural, the abdominal and intestinal tracts. This can be very painful. So pilots flying at great heights should eat only light food, for the expansion of gases in the intestines can not only cause flatulence pains but also affect the breathing. This disturbs the supply of blood to the heart, and sometimes even causes unconsciousness.

Other, more dangerous symptoms occurring through changes of height are "the bends": the nitrogen in the blood is transformed into a gaseous state and causes frightful pains, especially in the joints. Divers who rise too fast from great depths to the surface, are also attacked by it, and may be partially paralyzed for life. In a condition known as the "chokes" the same nitrogen bubbles cause a painful itch between the layers of skin. If nitrogen gets into the venous blood passage of the lungs, this leads to a terrible choking fit.

Volunteers have repeatedly been exposed in pressure chambers to sudden though not extreme drops in pressure, in order to investigate their reactions. When the pressure at sea level was lowered, for instance, to the same pressure as prevails at 25,000 feet, the air went abruptly out of the lungs of the "guinea pigs," and within seconds their stomachs became painfully dilated.

At heights of 50,000 feet and upward the body of an unprotected pilot would actually explode. The blood would be transformed into a gaseous state, bodily cavities and tissues would burst. The only man who has so far survived a sudden drop in pressure, unprotected, at a height of 40,000 feet is the above-mentioned Wing-Commander Rankin, when he jumped from his plunging plane and before he came into the storm zone. Wearing only a light Air Force uniform, he was exposed for several minutes to the biting cold and the low atmospheric pressure of the great height.

"The first thing I felt," he recalled, "was a terrific distension.

The air shot out of my lungs and tore the oxygen mask from my face, which bounced back at once, however. The air in all the body cavities expanded. I felt as if my body had swollen to many times its size. Then I suddenly felt this great cold. The temperature was minus 76° F., and inside my plane it had been plus 82°. The sudden 'refrigeration' acted on my body like a violent shock. My ankles and wrists began to burn as if someone had put dry ice on my skin. My left hand became numb, for in bailing out I had lost my gloves.

"I had to make a free drop. It was a tremendous temptation to open my parachute by hand, but I knew this would mean certain death. I should have been frozen stiff at once."

Rankin was not wearing a pressure suit, that "second skin" with which modern pilots flying at high altitudes protect themselves against sudden decompression. There is, for instance, a "partial pressure suit," with many pockets and tubes, which is strapped tightly round the body and limbs—it is, in fact, uncomfortably close-fitting. As soon as the pressurizer in a cockpit fails, or the pilot discards his cockpit roof, the pockets of the pressure suit expand, clinging still more tightly to the pilot's body. This produces a sort of artificial pressure which allows him to stay safely for some minutes at heights of up to 100,000 feet. The complete pressure suit, such as is worn by astronauts, encloses the whole body, including head and hands, with a protective skin, which also expands automatically in an emergency.

But with the ever-increasing speeds and ever-increasing heights of modern planes, even the most modern rescue apparatus will scarcely be enough to protect a pilot who is bailing out. Nobody has such a "solid" constitution that he can stand up to the air pressure of a speed two or three times as fast as sound.

One of the latest projects, therefore, envisages the crew of a plane in distress being "blown off" with the front of the plane, i.e. the actual cockpit, from the rest of the fuselage. The cockpit would thus be preserved as an "artificial environment." It contains all the equipment the pilot needs for his drop: oxygen apparatus, pressurizer, air-conditioning, and also radio. Immune to the dangers of space, he falls with it into thicker air layers. At 10,000 feet a parachute opens at the rear of the capsule, to cushion the fall. The pilot can then come down on land or sea. Since the capsule will float, he need not transfer into a lifeboat. It is also planned to give him the same survival equipment as the Mercury, Gemini, and Apollo astronauts carried aboard their space capsules for emergency landings on our planet.

Chapter 8
Today's Rescue Equipment—
Good and Bad

The rescue equipment in use today is essentially the same as a hundred years ago. *The shipping journal* Hansa, *1961*

In April 1961, when Alan Shepard, the American astronaut, was shot into space in a small bullet-shaped Mercury capsule, he was better equipped than anyone ever had been before for a pioneer feat of similar importance. "In theory nothing could go wrong," said one of his trainers, "even if the carrier rocket or individual systems in the capsule failed."

All the important instruments, separate systems, switches, knobs, and signal lights in the space-capsule were duplicated or even triplicated. Switching over from one circuit to another would follow automatically. But in case the automatic system failed, Shepard could switch over to manual, just as all the automatic devices on board could be operated by hand. In case both automatic and manual systems should fail, each operation inside the capsule could be triggered by radio through ground control.

But that was not all. In the narrow capsule, crammed with instruments, fittings, film cameras, radio equipment, tape recorders, and steering apparatus, the engineers had also packed a comprehensive kit for distress at sea; to make sure that after his parachute landing the astronaut could keep alive on the open sea until the first rescue ships arrived. This kit included an inflatable dinghy; an apparatus for desalinating sea water; shark-repellent; a strong dye to color a patch of water so that it would be noticed from a distance; a first-aid kit; an alarm whistle; distress signals; a portable radio that would float; iron rations; matches; ten feet of nylon cord; and a knife of special alloy hard enough to cut through a steel bar the thickness of a finger, without the blade becoming jagged. If the need arose, Shepard was to use this to cut a hole in the capsule's side and bail out.

The capsule also had a reserve parachute and a lot of signaling apparatus fully or partly automatic: radio beacon, flashlights and an alarm bomb. The last worked on the so-called *Sofar* process, developed by the U. S. Navy for locating castaways. The bomb only explodes at a certain depth with layers of water which carry the detonation waves over a wide distance, sometimes thousands of miles. When several search ships receive this underwater alarm, the center of the explosion can be more or less precisely located, after which search planes can comb the area for the missing man.

Such care for the life and success of an astronaut is understandable, since his training costs several million dollars. Training even an "ordinary" pilot costs hundreds of thousands. The authorities cannot afford, if he crashes, just to "write him off" as a loss. Thousands of anonymous castaways, however, fare much worse. True, a search is made for them as well, and often a very thorough one; but right from the start, they have very little chance of being found. For these are only "ordinary mortals," their equipment for distress at sea is as a rule completely inadequate or obsolete, and their lifeboats often turn into regular death traps.

About three thousand ships (with a tonnage of over three and a half million) sank on the world's seas between 1958 and 1961. For the past years the annual average was around 370, or, to be exact, 377 ships sank in 1971, 371 sank in 1972, and 363 sank in 1973, according to Lloyd's of London. The experts are agreed that far more could have been done to rescue their crews and passengers. According to *Hansa* (as quoted at the head of this chapter) "The rescue equipment in use today is essentially the same as a hundred years ago." This is saying something—for a hundred years ago the castaway had practically no rescue equipment except rowboats and cork belts.

Inflatable life jackets were first developed in 1927, and were first used by the pilots of hydroplanes which were catapulted with

mail off the German steamer *Bremen* on the high seas. The same
year Admiral Byrd tried out one of the first two-man dinghies off
the coast of New Britain. It had to be inflated in a complicated
manner through compressed air stored on the plane in a special
tank. The disadvantage of this method was obvious: if the tank
sprang a leak in a "ditching," or the plane sank too quickly, the
dinghy was not much use.

It was eight years before the Americans, in the summer of 1953,
first used CO_2 (carbon dioxide) to inflate a raft. The gas was kept
in a small flask attached to the raft itself. The method proved
successful a few months later when the American airship *Macon*
broke up off the coast of California: all but two of the crew of
eighty-one climbed out of the ice-cold water into the new quickly
inflatable rafts, and were rescued.

The introduction of CO_2 for inflating rafts was a great step forward; but even this has not been adopted widely enough for rescue
equipment in the civil sector. Most shipping still carries cork life
jackets chiefly because they are less expensive, and also need no
maintenance. For the same reasons most shipping is still fitted
with open wooden lifeboats instead of rafts. Even the portable
transmitters, developed about 1939, can be found today in relatively few lifeboats; and anyhow they are already outdated.

Such false economies were little modified by the bitter experiences of the war. On the Allied side a fifth of all military planes
which made forced landings were found to be carrying inadequate
emergency equipment. Their crews not only had little or no idea
of the art of survival; they were also ill prepared for possible
hardships after the landing. Many planes had maps with simply
the flight route and the destination area, and no ground maps for
use after a forced landing. In some cases even the rescue planes
were not properly equipped, and if they broke down during sal-
vage operations, their pilots too had to rely on the help of further
rescue planes instead of being able to help themselves.

But where rescue equipment was available, it proved as a rule
not to have been thoroughly tested and perfected. Pilots who came
down in the sea and castaway sailors were continually complaining
of such deficiencies after their rescue. Here are a few extracts from
an American collection of such complaints:

"Our plane carried no K rations—only dog biscuits for the crew's dog."

"There were no tracer bullets for the signal pistols in our raft."

"The one rubber water bottle in the raft was less than half full and contained a muddy fluid which tasted revolting."

"The frostbite ointment in the first-aid kit became hard as stone in the low Arctic temperatures."

"The zippers jammed on the case of my raft. My fingers were so stiff with cold that I couldn't undo the patent fasteners either!"

"All our bandages were frozen and couldn't be put on. Ointments and frostbite remedies started crumbling, the tubes burst in the cold."

Many castaways complained that the containers with supplies dropped for them burst on hitting the water. On land the same sort of thing happened.

"The container broke through a six-inch layer of ice and froze in at once."

"It was so heavy that in our hunger-weakened state we couldn't drag it to our camp."

"We sat under a tree (in Ethiopia) in agonies of thirst, and were already much too weak to stand or walk. A plane dropped five water containers for us. They all burst when they hit the ground. We could save only a quart of water."

The food containers were also an inconspicuous gray instead of a bright color. In the Libyan Desert one party searched two days for nine containers which had been dropped for them (without parachute). "We found only one, and all that had in it was hard bread."

There were also complaints about the arms and ammunition: "The rifles in our emergency equipment were so light and low-powered that the bullets bounced off the thick feathers of the Arctic wild geese. Either they did not even deign to stir off the ice or they slowly flew off cackling loudly." "Rifles were too high calibre for hunting small game. The bullets tore the prey into hopelessly small pieces like a grenade."

The same deficiencies existed on board many convoy ships in the middle of the war. In his *History of U. S. Naval Operations in World War II*, the American naval historian Samuel Eliot Morison described what happened when an Atlantic convoy was torpedoed in 1943: "There was the same negligence and lack of discipline on board the merchant ships as had already cost the lives of far too many men in the last four years. Lifeboats capsized or got jammed because they were lowered the wrong way: boats and rafts were put to sea before the ship had fully come to rest; oars were missing, there were too few ropes. The lifeboats were not fitted with stream cables to throw to drifting sailors. Life jackets were without belts and straps . . ."

The Robertsons of England, adrift for thirty-eight days in the Pacific, soon found out that some of the air chambers of their rescue-island had become leaky. They had to be inflated orally every fifteen minutes, a tiring job even for a strong person. A repair was impossible, for the liquid rubber solution in the repair kit had long since dried up. Finally, all six of them spent almost half of their trip in their small dinghy, barely nine feet long. With it, they managed to cover a distance of seven hundred miles until they were picked up at last.

In the Hamburg floods most of the rescue equipment proved equally defective. As has been mentioned, even the warnings issued to the population left much to be desired. Many people who had their radios tuned to South German stations heard dance music instead of alerts. Others, who had switched off their radios and TV sets, did not grasp the significance of ringing church bells and howling sirens. When the dikes broke, the complicated machinery of a great city came to a grinding halt: the lack of foresight and organization led to further avoidable losses. First of all, four of the five Hamburg power stations were put out of action by flooding: Hamburg's output of power dropped from 1,156 to 110 megawatts. All the trains and streetcars suddenly stopped, the city was paralyzed. The roads sank into darkness, and the city was blind. Telephone, radio, television, teleprinters, were not working, the city was deaf and dumb. It was now quite impossible to warn the population effectively.

With the power failing, the gasworks also went out of action. There was still enough gas in the tanks, but the biggest main was broken in two places by the water. Since gas is still poisonous, it had to be lit.

In the flooded areas the water supply was also interrupted. In the rest of the city the population were told to boil the water because of the danger of epidemics. But the higher stories of buildings could no longer be supplied owing to the falling pressure. Out of twenty-one waterworks the five most important went out of action. Hamburg did not even have sufficient stocks of food; the retail trade could have supplied the population with food for ten days at most. The day after the night of the floods, food shops were already being burglarized.

The effects of the "Big Blackout," as mentioned in the beginning of this book, were similar. A flabbergasted Congressman Richard McCarthy, Democrat from Niagara, declared: "Four or five people could probably push the entire United States into total darkness, making the country vulnerable for a surprise attack. . . ." And Senator Warren Magnuson of the state of Washington declared: "The safety, the well-being, and the protection of the population were endangered. Without electricity most rescue and first-aid stations could have done very little (to help). Most emergency plans would have failed or would have, at least, severely suffered."

Since the war all the larger countries have equipped the members of their armed forces with the most modern equipment, which is continually being supplemented, tested, and improved. But very little seems to be done about this in the civilian sphere. Anything new and good takes years to be adopted, for everything old and bad is generally retained until it breaks down in an emergency.

After the sinking of the *Titanic* in 1912, a regulation was made that no ship should again go to sea without sufficient lifeboats. From then on, every seafaring vessel, from the smallest freighter to the largest ocean liner, carried boats for all passengers and crew members. But these boats were (and are) almost invariably suspended and lowered from a pair of cranes, the davits, which swing out from the ship's side; and these davits have been repeatedly proved of little use when the ship had more than a slight list.

The luxury liner *Andrea Doria*, for instance, after her collision with the passenger ship *Stockholm* in 1956, had such a violent list after a few hours that the lifeboats on the side which was rising higher and higher got stuck in the davits. Only the boats on the heeling side could be launched. The passengers had to be put on the boats of the *Stockholm* and other ships which raced to the scene; and that, too, was only possible because the sea was completely smooth.

After the fire aboard the *Yarmouth Castle* many of the rescued passengers complained that "there had been no life belts in the cabins" and "no life preservers on deck." Or: "The ropes for the lifeboats could not be moved because they had been painted over with white 'cruise-liner paint.' The davits were rusted through—the crew did not manage to lower all the boats." Or: "The fire-extinguishers and related equipment, such as the sprinklers under the cabin ceilings, did not work." Or: "Fire hoses were lying limp on deck—without water." Or: "Some lifeboats had no rowlocks, so we had to use the heavy oars like paddles."

After the *Pamir* disaster, there was a general impression that she had not carried enough lifeboats; but this was wrong. There were five rowboats, one motorboat, and three dinghies. Together they could (in theory) take 210 men. According to Hasselbach, one of the cadets rescued, the reason why very few of the crew of eighty-six found room in them was because "it was impossible to get the boats out before the ship capsized. On one side they were in the water, on the other was the steep ship's side. My boat sank with the ship. But under water it apparently broke clear and drifted to the surface again. It had four big holes." Two of the three dinghies were also dragged under water by the sinking ship. The third, which the cadets had managed to get clear, was packed tight with twenty men.

Subsequent inquiries have proved that if a ship has over a 15° list, only the boats on the heeling side can be put to sea with conventional davits. If the wind force is higher than seven, even with the most modern davits it is only on the leeward side at best that the boats—mostly still of wood—can be put to sea undamaged. Even these are generally smashed to pieces against the side of the ship by the raging sea. After the *Pamir* sinking, it was stated at the inquiry before the Lübeck Court of Admiralty: "None of the six wooden lifeboats"—one had already been washed off the deck by the breakers—"got into the water in even reasonably undamaged condition." Heavy seas also smashed the dinghies on board the 4,000-ton steamer *Mercury,* which got into difficulties in 1959; as a result seven seamen were drowned.

Cork life jackets are equally old-fashioned. They keep a castaway above water, it is true, but support neither his chin nor his neck. Folkert Anders, after rescue from the *Pamir,* showed what this can lead to: "There certainly weren't many who were drowned directly the *Pamir* went down, but ten minutes later things looked very different. Their heads dropped. That's how it is with the old life jackets the *Pamir* had. New life jackets stop the head dropping, which means that those who are temporarily unconscious do not drown. But with our old life jackets many slumped forward, swallowed water and were drowned."

In September 1955 the crew of a ditched DC-4 drifted for over forty-four hours in their inflatable Mae Wests. They said they couldn't relax for a moment, for the Mae Wests wouldn't have automatically kept their heads above water.

There are similar deficiencies in the equipment of lifeboats. The *Pamir* life jackets, for instance, were painted gray and so were extremely hard to spot. In the boat into which Dummer and his companions had scrambled, there was only one water barrel and two sacks of food. Everything had been swept out, the air tanks were destroyed. Much the same happened with the other *Pamir* survivors. Hasselbach: "The water barrels were gone. So I had only canned bread, biscuits and canned milk. Eating canned bread without water is horrid." Wirth: "The bread fitted so tightly into the cans that we cut our numb fingers opening them. There were no can openers. The very sweet condensed milk was so viscous that it wouldn't pour out, and it only made us feel madly thirsty."

In that boat there were five pints of water per man, two pounds of bread and a pound of condensed milk, a medicine chest, rowing and sailing equipment, and also distress signals. But as Hasselbach said at the court of inquiry: "I couldn't get either a red flare or a smoke buoy going. The red flares were sodden, the smoke buoy didn't work." He couldn't find a hurricane lamp, for the boat was full of water. "If you wanted to find anything, you had to put your head into the water. I had to undo the fastener of the smoke buoy with a chopper."

None of the *Pamir* boats had a proper transmitter. But if there had been any, these would presumably have been little use, seeing that even the emergency transmitters carried today by most merchant and passenger ships are quite obsolete. Admittedly, the Shipping Safety Convention of 1948 said that every ship (not "every lifeboat," however) should have "a transmitter for life-boats" on board. It should be "easily portable," and "able to float in the water." There is also the regulation that the transmitter has to work on the International Ship Disaster frequency of 500 megacycles (which is continually monitored by all shipping) and also on the short-wave (8,364 megacycles), which has a wider range. It automatically transmits SOS signals which are then located by search ships.

But the transmitters which have since been developed for general shipping, though they may well have done all right in the ship-builder's water tank, will very rarely work in a tossing lifeboat, if only because they are too complicated for all but experts and generally too much of a strain for a weakened castaway to rig up and use. Their disadvantages in a real emergency are apparent at once: you have to drag the heavy transmitter aft on leaving the ship, throw it overboard, and then fish it out again—which is very difficult in heavy seas or a storm, and almost impossible in the dark. If you do manage to get it into a boat, then according to the instructions attached, you have to bore a hole in a bench of the lifeboat with a drill (also attached). The radio has a bolt welded to it, which you have to stick through this hole and fasten with a thumb screw. This sounds all right on paper, but how are castaways to do it, when they can't even crook their fingers in the cold water?

Further complicated procedure is needed to get the transmitter actually working. First you have to drop a plummet which acts as earth. Then you have to send up an "effectively high" aerial by means of a balloon or a kite. Not too easy to get a kite in the air during a storm; and in any case, what is "effectively high"? (You would only know your aerial was high enough if you got a reply.) With an American transmitter which was used almost exclusively during the war, search planes often sighted the balloon before they heard the castaways' signals.

To transmit distress signals, the crew of a lifeboat do not simply have to press a button. They must turn a crank by strenuous manual labor in order to work a dynamo which provides the transmission energy needed. Rudolf Förster, radio director of the Bremen sea-school, wrote to me on these problems as follows: " 'Easily transportable' means that the set can be carried by a weak man, a boy or a woman (female radio operators, nurses, stewardesses). The set now used in many merchant ships, for instance, is so heavy that a strong and well-built girl, serving as radio officer on a big freighter, can only just drag it over the ground but never carry it. In an emergency, therefore, she will never be able to throw it overboard or get it into a lifeboat, although she will probably be the only person to think of the set when the ship is being abandoned.

" 'Easy to use' should above all mean that no great physical strength is needed to produce the transmission energy, such as is still required for the hand-operated generators of lifeboat radios. Turning the crank takes so much strength that a healthy average woman could not get the generator going by herself at all and only for three minutes at most with the help of another member of the crew. Experiments have been reported to me which were made on deck in calm weather. In a lifeboat, of course, with far stronger motion from the sea, the results would very probably be far worse."

Even the American distress transmitter developed during the war, AN/CRT-3 (known as *Gibson Girl* for its sinuous curves) shows similar disadvantages. Castaways were always saying they found it very hard to use "the girl." The generator crank had to be turned eighty times a minute—and in an open boat castaways would be too weak to do this for more than an hour or two. In other cases the cranks jammed after several hours' use, or in great cold even after a few minutes. Often, too, the castaways could not blow up a balloon or start the kite which was to pull up the aerial. One survivor commented: "I wished I had been able to climb out and run off with the damned kite to start it."

In such circumstances it is no wonder that ships are continually going down without the crew being able to send out a call for rescue. In 1959, for instance, the "unsinkable" Danish steamer *Hans Hedhoft* had left for Greenland on a maiden voyage in winter despite many warnings. Soon afterward the call came over the International Ship Disaster frequency: "Collision with an iceberg." Four hours and five minutes later there was a new message: "We are now sinking." After that there was silence. The transmitters could presumably no longer be worked because of the cold. There were fifty-five passengers and forty crew members: none was ever seen again.

"It would be a trifle for industry to build tough emergency radios," one German radio journal remarks, and goes on to demand that there should be a small transmitter built into every life jacket. "The price of several such transmitters shouldn't be much higher than that of one of the present lifeboat transmitters . . . considering that today miniature transmitters are already turned out by the toy industry."

Such excellent equipment has been designed and built. Unfortunately, much of it is classified and used by the armed forces only. One dramatic example that illustrates its effectiveness occurred in January 1959 when the deep-sea motorboat *Atair* caught fire off the coast of Bermuda. The two members of the crew, American amateur fishermen, could not send out a distress call on their radio telephone. They only had time to launch their dinghy and hope for a passing ship. One of the most important pieces of rescue equipment they had with them was a "radar reflector," a big strip of canvas with metal overlay. They hoisted this as high as possible on an improvised mast.

About the same time some NATO forces were on naval maneuvers in West Indian waters. A jet fighter pilot from the Dutch aircraft-carrier *Karel Doorman* on a mock "submarine hunt" was to try to locate "enemy" submarines (represented by American atomic submarines) with a sensitive radar apparatus, over a particular stretch of sea. About three in the afternoon a tiny white dot appeared on the screen in the cockpit of his plane. On the dial he read the distance: 37 miles. Was it an "enemy" submarine? He decided to fly up and see.

In a few minutes the tiny dot was caught in the ring-shaped center of the screen: the plane was right above its target. But instead of the lines of a submarine the pilot saw a raft with two waving men—it was the men from the *Atair*. Within seconds he was sending a message to the control room of the *Karel Doorman*. A helicopter took off from the deck, and barely half an hour later the two fishermen were safely on board the aircraft-carrier.

They could attribute their rescue through the radar reflector chiefly to chance. Nobody was searching for them, hardly anybody had missed them, yet they were found because maneuvers hap-

pened to be going on near them at the right time. Even so, their
being found proves how successfully military rescue equipment
could be used in the nonmilitary sphere—which it rarely is. The
radar reflector they had made fast in their raft is today a standard
fitting for all rafts of the U. S. Air Force; but is carried by few rescue vessels in the merchant navy. The sensitive radar apparatus in
the plane, having been specially developed to spot submarines, is a
secret device and so cannot be used by nonmilitary rescue planes.

It is the same with a great many other lifesaving devices. The
armed forces possess them, in the most modern form, so that their
members have the maximum chance of survival in an emergency;
and also have the most modern methods of locating these survivors. But both equipment and methods have spread very slowly
indeed to nonmilitary sectors of shipping and air travel and to the
mountain rescue service. This is partly because much of the equipment is kept exclusively for military use; and the rest is often too
expensive for those it is meant to serve. For reasons of economy,
airlines and shipping lines merely obey to the letter safety precautions which are partly obsolete, and provide only the bare
minimum of regulation lifesaving equipment.

A typical example is the continued use of open wooden lifeboats. Although they fulfill the regulations for size and number per
ship, they are patently and hopelessly obsolete compared with
recent models. For instance, there is the plastic boat which was
tested in New York harbor in September 1960 by American coast
guard. It was packed with five tons of concrete blocks (equivalent
to the weight of seventy-eight passengers), and then thrown into
the water without damage from a height of ten feet. Built-in air
tanks kept it afloat, even when it had been pumped full right to the
top. A wooden lifeboat cannot sink, of course, even without air
tanks; but what good is that if it is smashed to pieces by the sea?
The designers of the plastic boat crashed it several times against
the sides of the ship, and it always bounced off like a rubber ball.
According to some shipping lines, however, it is too expensive,
considering the fact that it might never have to be used.

An aluminum boat designed by Ernst Nicol, a German, has the
special feature that it is not open like a wooden rowboat of the
standard type, but can be closed by a sliding roof, thus protecting
the occupants from wind and weather. They can look outside

through perspex windows. Instead of oars, it has a hand-operated screw turned by a crankshaft in the boat. By the end of 1962 of all the German lines only two were using such boats in their ships.

Another German, Gustav Kuhr, has designed a plastic lifeboat, also closed, like a deformed submarine with two domes. He says it will right itself like a jack-in-the-box even after the heaviest breakers. Forty people can board it in an emergency through large hatches, which are then closed from inside. Its screw is also worked by a crankshaft.

Rescue experts today, however, think that means of locomotion like hand-operated screws or a dozen oars are no longer necessary, for a simple reason: in the old days, before the invention of telegraphy, the survivors of a shipwreck had little hope of being saved unless they reached the nearest land by rowing (one reason why lifeboats had to be open). But today, when any ship's radio operator generally manages to transmit an SOS giving position before his ship goes down, the survivors would actually reduce their chances of being rescued by moving away from the scene of a sinking ship. From 1948 onward there was a ban on inflatable life rafts, which are not designed primarily for locomotion. But the International Shipping Safety Conference, held in London in July 1960, agreed to lift this ban, and they now may be carried aboard larger ships in addition to the regular lifeboats.

At the official inquiry on the sinking of the *Pamir* the Lübeck Court of Admiralty had already said in its verdict: "The maximum attention will have to be given to the development and use of modern dinghies, 'life rafts,' etc. . . . It is well-known that such modern vessels have stood the test admirably in other naval accidents even with very heavy seas . . . Lifeboats of this sort have still most chance of being put to sea undamaged." It would indeed be welcome if the permissive clause approved by the above conference were to become a compulsory regulation: that inflatable rafts not *may* but *must* be carried, in addition to rowboats. For they have all the advantages men in a shipwreck could desire.

They too are a result of improvements in rescue equipment for the armed forces. Whereas pilots in the war who came down in the water usually had to make do with tiny open rafts, the so-called "Elliot island" was introduced after 1945 by the British Navy. When folded this makes a package about three feet long. As soon as it is thrown into the water, it inflates automatically and then forms into two taut rubber rings, each consisting of several sections and both totally encased in rubber sheeting. Because of its bright coloring it looks like a huge orange drifting on the water, and accommodates thirty men, whom it protects from wind, cold, and damp, the castaway's greatest enemies.

Moreover, the Elliot island will not capsize. But if for any reason it inflates in such a way that the top is in the water, its hemispheric shape will allow castaways swimming alongside to right it easily by means of ropes strung along its bottom. Here there are also four rubber sacks which will then automatically fill up with four gallons of sea water each, thus giving the "island" the stability needed. Even when fully occupied, it is buoyant enough for any water to be bailed out, which is impossible in simple one-man boats. It also has a second deck, which can be inflated by hand, so as to serve as insulating layer in cold weather. In warm weather the air is let out and the water can cool the deck. Since it has two openings, a cooling air current can be provided in southern latitudes.

Then again, the signaling apparatus on board is excellent. There are hand torches and parachute rockets in watertight boxes. There is a battery-powered flashlight on top of the dome (which reflects radar rays), and directly after the "island" hits the water, a completely automatic radio transmitter with a range of nearly a hundred miles starts working on the International Ship Distress frequency. Its batteries provide electric current through the chemical reaction with salt water. Thus, no generator has to be cranked, as was the case with the *Gibson Girl*. Nor is it necessary to send up an antenna with a kite.

The "island" has been fully proved both in many experiments with volunteers and in real emergencies. In a rough sea, bitter cold water and biting wind, British sailors jumped from a cruiser fully clothed into the water, and tried to reach the "island" by swimming. As soon as the rubber "hemisphere" was fully occupied, the hatches were closed. As in an igloo, the temperature inside rose, through the bodily warmth of the occupants, to the comfortable temperature of 68° F. The sailors spent five days in the "island," living on their K rations, and were then taken on board a rescue ship in good physical condition. Admittedly they knew they would be saved, so they were carrying little psychological "load," but even so their good condition says much for these inflatable rescue stations.

In recent years various types of closed dinghies, modeled on the British "Elliot island," have been developed in the United States too, chiefly for the Navy and Air Force, but also for the merchant navy and passenger shipping. The Garret Corporation in Rhode Island has a twenty-five-man raft which inflates within eight seconds through an automatic pump, directly it touches salt water. The U. S. Rubber Company has developed a raft which when folded is stowed on deck in a light metal box. If the ship sinks, the box detaches itself at a depth of thirteen feet at most and drifts to the surface. It can, of course, also be thrown overboard before the sinking, when the metal container opens automatically, and the lifeboat inflates while still attached to the ship by a rope.

Since women and children cannot be expected to jump into cold water in high seas in order to swim to a "rescue island," some of the newer inflatable lifeboats have an open platform, forward of the enclosed space, consisting of a simple air-filled rubber ring, into which people can jump from heights of up to twenty-five feet without tearing the bottom of the ring. But special davits too have already been developed, to put to sea inflated and fully occupied dinghies from the deck of a ship.

The "Elliot islands" are now carried by all British Navy ships, and also on vessels of Britain's fishing fleet. Variations of these "islands" are now even offered for sale by stores for yachting supplies. As a result the number of fatal casualties from ships going down has apparently dropped a good deal. But it will be years before the bigger shipping lines decide to carry "rescue islands" on all their ships, or this is made compulsory in another international congress on maritime safety.

In contrast again to the equipment on a normal nonmilitary lifeboat, the quantity and variety of equipment today in rafts for military use is quite satisfactory. The survival experts of the U. S. Air Force have designed a number of different survival kits for particular climatic zones (a different sort of kit is needed if you are flying over Polar regions or over the Pacific).

All these kits are masterpieces of packing. The E-1 kit (in a can) is no bigger than a briefcase, but when a pilot who has come down in the water gets it out of the raft, he will find in it the following: a mirror to flash distress signals; waterproof matches; sunglasses which can also be used as snowglasses; several cheap watches for bartering with natives; a compass; a knife; a dagger; a razor blade; a whetstone; a file; salt tablets; a bush knife which can also be used as a saw; a first-aid kit; fishing gear; a fishing net; an ax; a water flask; a face cloth; wire, to make traps with; a small-caliber rifle; ammunition; needles; thread; soup cubes; dried meat; a bag for the desalination of sea water—and various other things. This outfit, though not quite as extensive as that carried by America's astronauts, is enough to give the maximum chance of survival to anyone who has it. But in most merchant navy lifeboats even important articles like the water-desalinater are missing.

The U. S. Armed Forces have several methods for the desalination of sea water. The simplest requires a small plastic bag and half a dozen cubes of a particular chemical. The castaway fills the bag with about a pint of water, adds one of the cubes and starts kneading the container. The cube gradually absorbs all the salt in the water. After an hour of patient work the castaway can draw from the bag, through a filter, the same quantity of fresh water as the sea water he has put in. The sole disadvantage is that each cube can be used only once. A castaway who used it several times was found after a week at sea with all the symptoms of salt-water poisoning.

So in 1943 rigid as well as inflatable distilling apparatus was produced, which provides fresh water from the sea for any length of time, on condition that the sun is shining. It looks like a large bladder and works like this: it has a black cloth stretched flat inside it, onto which salt water drips continually from a small container; the black cloth is warmed by the sun, and the drops of water evaporate; the salt remains in the cloth, while the salt-free moisture condenses on the sides of the rubber balloon, runs down to the bottom of it, and from there into a bag for fresh water. With the American LL-2 apparatus you can get up to a quart of fresh water a day from the sea.

Portable desalinating apparatus, which is also simple and cheap, is carried on the dinghies of American military planes as standard equipment, but can otherwise be found only in the emergency equipment of some big airlines. The rescue experts of the U. S. Army have also produced filters to make brackish and marsh water drinkable. The filters are the size of a handkerchief, and with the help of some chemicals they will clear a liquid of all bacteria, dirt, poisons, and even smells.

When during the war there were repeated reports of sharks attacking castaways, the American survival experts revised their old idea that it was enough "to yell at a shark or chase him off by a punch on his sensitive nose." They immediately began to develop a shark-repellent, and eventually came up with an effective one, a bag containing a particular chemical substance; if a castaway throws this into the water, all sharks in the immediate vicinity clear off, leaving him unmolested for a good while.

Shark-repellent is today part of all military emergency equipment at sea, but it was not produced without patient and laborious efforts, for a long time unsuccessful. A substance had to be found which would put off even the greediest sharks. Poison seemed the most obvious choice; so in the aquariums of the famous Marineland Studios (Florida), and the Woods Hole Oceanographic Institution (Massachusetts), marine biologists saturated tasty chunks of meat with every sort of poison—and the sharks promptly swallowed them. Admittedly they died a little later, but it would be small consolation for a castaway to lose a leg (covered with poisonous ointment) to a shark which afterward expired. New experiments followed, this time with supersonic waves, and again without success. Dyes and ink were poured among the sharks, but they found their prey unerringly, their sense of smell not being affected by the chemicals. Even poison gases produced the same negative result.

Then one of the biologists heard of a strange observation made by some fishermen off the coast of Florida: whenever a shark was decomposing in their nets, the waters remained free of sharks for miles around. New experiments were made and surpassed all expectations: a piece of rotting shark's flesh in the water was enough to make all sharks give it a wide berth, although they would otherwise fall like cannibals on the flesh of another shark which was fatally wounded.

The mysterious substance in this rotting flesh was analyzed as ammonia acetate, which in water turns into acetic acid. It was fairly simple to find other related substances, and copper acetate was eventually decided on. In dramatic experiments off the coast of Florida it did indeed prove a highly effective repellent. The biologists threw several basketloads of small fish into the water, thereby enticing dozens of sharks, which started to gorge themselves. But the next basketful thrown into the water was mixed with copper acetate, and within a few seconds the sharks beat a retreat. They circled round the infested patch of water at a considerable distance, and not even an appetizing steak could lure them back.

These experiments, and others successfully undertaken off the coast of Australia, led to the Allied forces commissioning the mass production of small bags filled with copper acetate. This trickles very slowly through the canvas of the bag and can protect a swimmer from sharks for hours, and even days. Very few lifeboats of merchant ships have these bags, although they are urgently needed. Some of the cadets in the *Pamir* for instance, who wanted to warm themselves in the water when it was too cold in their windy boats, had to give up the plan when they spotted sharks in the vicinity. Conversely, castaways in southern latitudes who might have got cool by getting into the water, did not do it either for fear of sharks.

Lately, scientists are tending to believe again that sound of a certain frequency may still be the best shark-repellent possible. In tests conducted between 1970 and 1974 off the Florida coast, Dr. Arthur Myrberg of the University of Miami has found that certain staccato sounds, as emitted by speared fish, swimmers in panic, or helicopters (some ironically approaching to rescue a swimmer!) attract sharks like magic. Other sounds of a different frequency however tend to chase sharks away. They leave the area of emission immediately. Myrberg's hope is to develop a small, portable sound transmitter that will help to keep the area around a survivor free of sharks. Until then, Myrberg advises, "don't panic and thrash around if you fall into shark-infested waters. And don't run away immediately. Face him (the shark) and then slowly move away, using a smooth breast stroke—a sound that sharks don't find particularly interesting."

Shark-repellent, of course, was (and still is) only one among many forms of lifesaving equipment on which much time and money was spent during the war. In America, several commissions were set up to test suggestions from rescued sailors and airmen for improving such equipment. In England there was a special branch of the War Ministry which (under Captain Clayton Hutton) during World War II produced a comprehensive livesaving arsenal. Part of this equipment is still a military secret today, and much of it, being designed only for prisoners-of-war trying to escape, would be no use for the "normal" castaway. But I think it is worth describing a few of these ingenious devices to show the remarkable achievements possible through long and concentrated work, and also how little space is taken up by well-designed lifesaving equipment.

With the aid of a "chain" saw, for instance, which was concealed in the lacing of their boots, R.A.F. prisoners could saw through iron bars half an inch thick. An ordinary fountain pen contained not only ink but a compass, pep pills, a colored map of the whole of Europe on crease-resisting rice paper, and two bags of dye with which the prisoners could turn their uniforms into civilian clothes, after taking out the lining and turning them inside out.

Clayton Hutton had magnetized strips of metal put in pencils, so that if you hung the pencils from a thread, they would point north. Flying boots were so designed that some parts could easily be detached, to turn them into ordinary walking shoes; the detached parts, buttoned up the right way, provided a warm civilian jacket. In the heel of the boot there were also maps, and the buttons had a small compass built into them. With these and similar aids three thousand R.A.F. prisoners made successful escapes from German camps.

Hutton also designed cans with a built-in "stove"; when the cans were opened, the reaction from two chemicals meeting in their extra bottom produced enough warmth to heat the contents of the cans. For their soldiers stationed in the Arctic and Antarctic, the U. S. Army devised a boiler the size of a briefcase, which could supply ten pints of hot water within ten minutes through compressed propane gas, even in an outside temperature of minus 4° F. When it was realized during the war that the batteries of radio transmitters and torches gave out quickly in Arctic cold, an American firm (commissioned by the army) produced a "battery belt" built into a life jacket; a survivor's body warmth ensures that batteries last ten times as long in temperatures of down to minus 58° F. He can attach the batteries to flashlights, radios, etc., with a wire.

A "heat pill" for internal use seems possible, to increase the survivor's powers of resistance to great cold. It would contain a particular amino-acid, which by accelerating the metabolism makes the body produce more warmth. Even better protection is given by the "climate suits" (also designed during the war for airmen and sailors in Arctic regions).

Many of these can carry a man on the water like a raft and enable him to stay several hours in near-freezing water. On dry land the same suits can easily be turned into sleeping bags. Some of them can be stowed in a tiny space: a suit consisting of down-lined nylon trousers with matching boots, down-lined greatcoat, hood and gloves, fits into a bag the size of a thermos bottle. Many of the suits are heated by batteries, and through the new semiconductor technique the same suit can also be cooled down by simply reversing the flow of current through the heating elements. The suit can then be worn also in the tropics at temperatures of up to 130° F., without the temperature inside rising above 77°. There is also a "heat suit" with no battery, so designed that it keeps about an inch clear of the body in almost all places, especially the wearer's sweat glands; this causes a current of air from trouser legs to collar, which cools him off. On the same principle the U. S. Army has developed a tent for their desert troops in which it is cooler than outside.

It would be futile, of course, to try to pack all these things into a lifeboat or get every mountain climber to take them along. But many lifeboats and sports planes, for instance, are woefully short even of signaling equipment. Yet this is the most important thing after a shipwreck or forced landing, the chief means by which a

missing man can hope to get himself found by his rescuers.
Without signals, as General Nathan Twining said from his own experience, "the chance of seeing a small boat in the hills and valleys
of the sea is as hopeless as finding a collar button in a plowed field
—even if a search plane is cruising directly above the boat."

As early as 1937 the Frenchman Georges Claude proposed to
the French Air Force that their men be given a bag with a special
dye to spread on the waves if they had to come down in the water.
He had observed that the dye produced a phosphorescent and
persistent splash of color which could easily be spotted from the
air. The French Air Force was not interested, and the Allies only
started producing dye cartridges after the German *Luftwaffe* had
successfully put Claude's idea into practice and very quickly
located, sometimes from great heights, the spots where many of
their men had crashed in the North Sea. But even today these cartridges are still not part of standard equipment for civilian lifeboats; nor are "smoke torches."

Smoke torches have proved their worth particularly on land. In
August 1959 near Juneau, Alaska, a smoke torch saved the lives
of two airmen just in time. Robert Sheldon and Melvin Guerrera
were in a helicopter which crashed on a glacier. They spent seven
days and seven nights near the helicopter in extreme cold, sleeping
by turns in a sleeping bag. They lived on their K rations and
waited for the search planes to come. They were confident these
would come, having informed all bases of their flight beforehand.

"Once a plane came flying over our glacier," said Guerrera afterward. "But it was too high. We had only one torch and
couldn't risk wasting it. It was a terrific test of willpower not to
light it. But the result was worth it. Two days later a second plane
flew past us pretty low and we lit the torch." The colored smoke at
once attracted the pilot's attention, and soon the two missing men
were rescued.

One of the simplest, most effective and cheapest articles of lifesaving equipment is the signaling mirror. It is quite like a pocket
mirror, but has besides a small sighthole through which the missing men can sight any plane or ship so as to flash at it with the
help of the sun. Such mirrors have saved the lives of countless sailors and airmen who either carried them or improvised them from

polished metal parts. So effective is the flash method that the pilot of a search plane said: "I noticed at once the bright patch of light someone had flashed at me. Then I saw the castaways far below on the water. I looped the loop twice to show that I had located them, but then I suddenly couldn't see a thing. They went on flashing, so that the sun blinded me, and in the end I made off for a while in despair."

While flash mirrors are designed chiefly for signaling to planes, British shipwrecked sailors and airmen who have come down in the water use alarm whistles to attract the attention of a lookout on a passing ship. This method of signaling first proved its worth at the sinking of the *Titanic,* although at that time only the officers had such whistles with which to give their orders; their sound carried clearly over the water. It did so even in night and cloud, and soon became part of the standard equipment for men in the British forces. But none of the cadets on the *Pamir* had whistles or anything with which they could have signaled to the rescue ships —and the ships in fact passed near them several times.

Many jet pilots have a small flashlight fitted on to their life jackets, so that if they come down in the water, they can be seen on the waves during the night even from a considerable distance. But very few airlines have fitted their life jackets with flashlights; when the Superconstellation mentioned earlier had to come down in the Atlantic by night in autumn 1962, some of the passengers would certainly not have drifted off unnoticed, if they had had these flashlights on their life jackets.

But the most important signaling equipment for survivors is still the radio transmitter, and here above all the position is most unsatisfactory. In autumn 1962, for instance, an American firm announced the development of a transmitter for distress at sea as "the most important step forward in life-saving since the invention of dinghy and inflatable life jacket." This battery-operated transmitter, the size of a cigar box, has only a small telescopic steel aerial to be pulled out by hand. Any castaway can use it— provided he is a member of the U. S. Armed Forces! When I was collecting material for this book and asked the firm in question for further information, I was told the equipment had been developed for the U. S. Air Force and was "classified."

Six months later another electrical firm produced, also for the U. S. Air Force, a transmitter for distress at sea which was only the size of a pack of cigarettes, with batteries and aerial built in. Apparently it can not only transmit a direction signal but will also allow for two-way communication. This too is a military secret. The same applies to other transmitters developed by industry during recent years: they are only for use by each country's armed forces. Or else they cannot be used in nonmilitary lifeboats because they operate on a frequency not monitored by merchant shipping.

These new transmitters comply exactly with the requirements stated earlier in this chapter: they are light, stable, and above all extremely easy to use, with no crank to be turned—they are completely automatic. They send out direction signals or they are used as a radio telephone—the castaway calls for help. If he is heard, he will receive an answer, a factor of great psychological importance for the will to survive.

The production of such sets for military use was already beginning in some countries during the war. In America the *Gibson Girl* was supplemented in 1945 by a radio telephone called AN/URC-4, which is no bigger than a loaf of bread and operates in the VHF band on Ship Distress frequencies 121.5 and 243 megacycles.

The British VHF set *Sarah* was tried out in the summer of 1962 in the Caribbean. British and Canadian forces were on maneuvers there which involved finding a castaway on a raft fitted with the new emergency transmitter, which is the size of a cigar box and can also be attached to a life jacket. The volunteer castaway switched on the set at the time fixed (it works continuously for twenty hours) and started repeating his "Mayday" call into the microphone, with short pauses in between to wait for an answer.

After ten or fifteen minutes the words suddenly crackled out of the loudspeaker: "We are receiving you. Send some Morse signals now so that we can locate you." A plane ten thousand feet up and a hundred miles away had picked up his distress call. Half an hour later the "castaway" saw it appear in the sky and "talked" the pilot down to him until he was sighted. The set cost about £100 then and was soon put into mass production for the R.A.F.

An American walkie-talkie for the army is so small that the receiver can be attached to the helmet, while the transmitter is put in a trouser pocket. In flat country and at sea its range is a hundred miles. It also operates in the VHF band. For the war in the jungle the Americans even produced a two-band transmitter only about forty pounds in weight. It operates in both the short-wave and VHF bands and is equipped for both speech and Morse transmission. According to which band is used, the range is between sixty and five hundred miles—enough to attract the attention of search planes or ships. Earlier sets with this performance weighed over three hundred pounds.

As will be clear from these few examples, none of the above sets operates in the medium wave band. They are therefore—at the moment—unsuitable for use in civilian lifeboats: searcher and missing men would literally be "talking on different wave-lengths." After the *Titanic* disaster the medium-wave frequency of 500 megacycles became agreed on as the "International Ship Disaster" frequency. All transmitters for civilian use, including the *Gibson Girl,* are so designed that they transmit their distress call on this frequency. The radios of all coast stations and all ships are obliged to monitor this frequency continuously either by personnel or through a kind of burglar alarm: this makes it almost certain that every call for help transmitted will be heard at once and located.

But when this frequency was fixed, air transport was still in its infancy. Radio telegraphy from aircraft in the medium-wave band soon proved unsatisfactory, for long trailing aerials had to be used, which brought new problems with the growing speeds. So air transport changed over to short-wave and VHF, which also made possible radio telephony. But of course the International Ship Disaster frequency was now no good for aircraft, since they could neither receive nor transmit by medium or long wave. A new international frequency was needed for air transport, and 121.5 megacycles was agreed on (for short-wave). Military planes, however, use 243 megacycles in the VHF band for distress calls. And an international frequency of 8,364 megacycles was agreed upon for communication between rescue planes and lifeboats (i.e. rafts).

The disadvantages of this confused situation are apparent today with every big naval rescue operation: only weather ships and a few warships and coast guard ships are fitted with short-wave and VHF sets; so there is no possibility of direct radio communication between planes, ships at sea and castaways. The Superconstellation I have quoted so often will again serve as an illustration.

When it came down off the coast of Ireland, the navigation officer could not send out a direct SOS to any shipping which might be in the vicinity. It had to inform Prestwick Airport, five hundred miles away, of what had happened. From there his message was passed on to a coast station on the Irish Sea, which could finally transmit the distress call on the medium-wave frequency of 500 megacycles to all shipping.

Although this relay may only take a few minutes, the disadvantages of not being able to communicate direct is much clearer in a rescue operation where the missing men have only an ordinary SOS transmitter. They can't reach any plane directly even if they can see it, but have always to transmit to another ship or the nearest coast station. The plane is then guided by the coast station, more or less "blind," to the spot where the castaways are presumed to be.

For instance, sixty-seven ships from thirteen countries and a large number of planes were searching for the survivors of the *Pamir*. But direct communication between the helpers at sea and in the air was not possible: they had to communicate by relay stations on land. After the disaster, experts stated that all the survivors in the Atlantic could probably have been found had the lifeboats been fitted with modern radio telephones instead of the ordinary SOS transmitters. They could then have called direct to the search planes, which could of course search an extensive area much faster than a ship.

Besides the miniature transmitters with their amazing performance, some other articles of rescue equipment have come out in recent years, which should be mentioned, if only for curiosity's sake: they are scarcely for the "normal" castaway, because to use them you need practice, and therefore training.

The U. S. Navy, for instance, produced a miniature plane made of rubber. Folded up into a small packet, it is dropped by parachute to a stranded pilot. He can quickly inflate it by hand, fit in the engine, which is separate, and leave the scene of his crash heading for the nearest human settlement. Its range is two hundred miles.

But since it was soon realized that not all castaways were also pilots, the U. S. Navy worked out other possibilities for getting a man rapidly out of a region where search planes couldn't land. Their technicians built the "sky-hook," with which a fast-flying plane can literally pull a man off the ground or out of a stormy sea. It works as follows:

As soon as the castaway is located, a package weighing about a hundred pounds, which contains a sort of rucksack, is dropped to him. He slips both arms into the harness and then operates a release cord, which sends helium from a steel cylinder into an air balloon. The balloon soars, pulling up a plaited nylon rope five hundred feet long. The pilot of the rescue plane, usually a transport plane with open rear, must then try to catch the rope with a special appliance. As soon as he manages this, the balloon will burst, and the rope, which has been pulled taut, now contracts like an elastic band, and the castaway is lifted almost sheer into the air, abruptly at first but then very gently. At a hundred feet his flight becomes horizontal, a hood protecting him from the strong air current. A winch pulls him slowly into the rescue plane. During the Vietnam War the "sky-hook" was used quite successfully to rescue pilots out of jungle clearings.

The idea of having floating rescue stations has been repeatedly canvassed and then dropped again. German spokesmen during the war called for such stations to be built in the North Sea, which should then be under the International Red Cross. With a field dressing station and one orderly on board they were to save airmen forced down in the water. An American firm, which in 1963 was working out plans for space stations to observe manned satellites, also envisaged a hospital for these floating platforms. Damaged planes, and also castaways, could often reach such stations sooner in an emergency than they would be found by search parties.

A team of American doctors and physicists have worked on plans for a pre-fabricated hospital to deal with major disasters. It is round like a tart, put together from twelve large "slices." Each slice (or segment) will float and is so light that it can be flown by helicopter to where it is needed. Inside it there are several hospital beds and parts of an operating room. Batteries, water-desalinating apparatus, and administration are in an extra partition below the bottom. As soon as all segments are put together, a process which takes only a few hours, the hospital is ready for work.

But all that is perhaps far in the future, and anyhow, as I have said, of no immediate relevance for civilians who become castaways or get into difficulties where they are exposed to the elements. But if *they* still have to put up with very inadequate rescue equipment, this makes all the more admirable the devotion shown by many voluntary and state organizations in all countries toward saving civilian lives. As a German, I think of the splendid heroism of soldiers in the Federal German Army helping the population of Hamburg during the floods, and of the Bavarian Mountain Watch, whose volunteer members are constantly risking their lives for foolhardy amateur climbers. Day and night, summer and winter, they are always ready for action, and their men in one area (Garmisch-Partenkirchen) saved 317 people in 1962 alone, also bringing nine dead bodies down to the valley.

Then there is the National Ski Patrol of America, and in a different "element" the Surf Life Saving Association of Australia —for as well as climbers in the mountains there are foolhardy swimmers (and even non-swimmers!) in the sea. Since this Association was founded in 1910, it has saved over 100,000 lives. A great many missing people have been found by the American Civil Air Patrol, financed exclusively by contributions from its 40,000 members. For Britain, the Royal National Lifeboat Association (to name one among very many organizations) saved 364 people in 1963, and from its foundation in March 1824 to December 1963 has saved 84,600 people in all.

Nowadays, of course, volunteer lifesavers not only dash to the aid of castaways or stranded people in boats or planes; they jump down to them in parachutes, with surgical equipment, dressings, and food. Since the American Air-Sea Rescue Service was started in 1947, its men have flown in over 45,000 operations, rescuing 8,000 civilians of all races and nationalities and bringing first aid to 52,000.

Their motto is "That others may live," and their devotion is gratefully remembered today in countless homes. Not, of course, that they do it to win gratitude. As one of the jumpers said after an action, "Our best reward would be if everybody showed a bit more care and sense in the way they lived. Then we shouldn't need to be sent into action at all."

Chapter 9
What Man Can Stand

We shall succeed in so changing Man that he can survive even in
the most unusual situations.
An American survival expert

"First they put me in a bath with water at 60° F. The experiment
was under careful supervision; my pulse, respiration, and blood
pressure were being continually checked. After two hours my body
temperature had dropped by 1.8° F. I was cold, and felt quite
fuddled. The doctors got me out of the bath and led me into a hot-
air chamber. Directly the door had closed behind me, the temperature shot up to 160° F. That is a heat at which in normal circumstances the senses would very quickly be dulled. But at first it
didn't affect me at all. For two hours I stood it almost as easily as
if it were a mild spring day. Then I began pouring with sweat, but
soon after that the experiment ended."

This is how a volunteer describes a test carried out in the late
fifties in an American research institute for aeronautical medicine. What was the purpose of the test?

In the previous chapters some of the ingenious equipment was
mentioned which safety engineers have developed for the members
of the armed forces in various countries. But after the end of the
war, survival experts came to the conclusion that this alone was
not enough; man himself must be turned into "superman," so that
he survives even dangers and privations which would finish off a
"normal member" of the species Homo sapiens.

Medically speaking, man is a frail creature. His body "functions," for instance, only at a temperature range of five degrees (between 97° and 102° F.). Could nature's "faulty design" be corrected in this respect? Physiologists thought so: they said the human body could be adapted to the hardest environmental conditions by appropriate training and also by artificially influencing the activity of certain glands. Psychologists were equally convinced that they could toughen Man's mind, also partly by appropriate training, but partly too through the influence of tablets, the magic charm of our day.

Experiments in both directions have already been proceeding for a long time, among them the heat test described above. One of the most urgent aims of these experiments is to determine the scientific prerequisites for methods of training picked men, whether to become astronauts, jungle warriors, or members of Arctic battle units. For instance, the scientists needed to find the maximum in physical and psychological privations which a man can actually stand, i.e. his so-called "stress tolerance." There is, of course, no universal maximum: one test subject may "go under" at 82° F. in the shade, another not till 95°. But this does not necessarily mean that both could not potentially survive temperatures a good deal higher. Besides, the true "maximum" could only be found if such a test were continued literally "to the death"—for you cannot really say that someone has gone beyond his capacity to survive unless or until he has died. So the ordeals to which the test subjects are exposed are brought to an end as soon as they feel they could not possibly stand any more.

In the University of Washington a volunteer was put in a hot-air chamber wearing a cloth suit a third of an inch thick. He stood a heat of 950° F. for a minute and a half before collapsing. The temperature he could stand for the same time without protective clothing was only 300°.

At a slightly lower temperature the "survival time" goes up, as is shown by the present record holder, Dr. Craigh Taylor, of the University of California's Engineering Department. In order to investigate the effects of great frictional heat on astronauts, he exposed himself, completely unprotected, to a heat of 250° F., at which even acetic acid boils. He at once began pouring with sweat, followed by nausea and dizziness. Almost unconscious, he pressed the panic button after a quarter of an hour, and was let out. His pulse beat was twice the normal rate, and for several hours afterward he suffered from defective vision and hearing.

To carry out any work in extremely high temperatures is impossible. A pilot wearing a light flying suit, who was to work some controls at 240° F., found it impossible to concentrate at all: his hands repeatedly missed the levers, and he gave up, also after a quarter of an hour.

But when test subjects had first been made very cold, they afterward stood temperatures of up to 212° F. for one to two hours, without being much affected. The practical aim of these experiments was to create a new survival technique for astronauts.

Normal earth dwellers would never be exposed to such extremes of heat, but in lower temperature ranges too there have been records. In 1905 Pablo Valencia, a Mexican trapper, was stranded in the southwest of the Arizona Desert. With only a day's ration of water, he first rode on horseback for over thirty miles. Then he dismounted and continued on foot for eight days, without water, covering 150 miles altogether in 160 hours at 90° F. in the shade. He stumbled over rocks, fell against prickly cactuses which scratched his arms and legs. The loss of water had already made his blood so thick that it did not flow from the wounds: he lost a quarter of his body weight in water. When he was eventually found and given something to drink, he recovered within a few hours.

As in his case, there are conditions where people exposed to very great heat carry out strenuous physical work for six to eight hours a day without suffering from it. They stand up to temperatures of 122° F.—not only because they have enough drinking water but because they are used to it. One need only think of the men working in a steel mill or the stokers of a ship's boilers.

In 1960 American survival experts did tests with some volunteers in the Arizona Desert to find out more about the process of getting used to such conditions. All those taking part were flown up from moderate latitudes, so that they were exposed quite suddenly to a desert temperature of 120° F. in the shade. In this heat the first group were put to work on treadmills. At the equivalent to a walking speed of six miles an hour, even the strongest man collapsed after six minutes. His pulse rate had shot up from 115 to 185, his sweat secretion was forty-eight times the normal amount.

Group tests on the first day produced other interesting phenomena accompanying sudden changes in climate. All the subjects were more irritable than usual. In their hours off duty they slept badly or not at all. Things which would scarcely have worried them under normal conditions suddenly turned into a quite intolerable burden. They groused about grains of sand in their shoes, about the flies, and most of all about the food—although it was much the same as usual. In the great heat, even the slightest work tired them out. They were terribly thirsty, although they had enough to drink, and suffered from headaches, shortness of breath, dizziness, and nausea. Many were sick and lost any desire for food. In the end they became completely apathetic and indifferent over the smallest tasks or duties. Obviously they would not have shown any will to survive in an emergency.

The following processes (described in simplified form) had taken place in the organism of each volunteer. The blood vessels on the surface of the body had expanded in the great heat. More blood flowed through them, and more warmth could thus be given off to keep the body at its normal temperature. But the total amount of blood had remained the same. Since the body was working at full pressure, however, the muscles needed more blood than in a resting position (or in a mild climate). This blood was drawn from the peripheral vessels (the blood vessels under the skin), the intestines, and the brain. Thus the amount of blood which the heart pumped through the body at every beat became smaller and smaller. The consequences were an increased pulse rate, rising body temperature, dizziness, and finally unconsciousness.

The trainers treated the second group of volunteers in quite a different way. Instead of putting them directly on the treadmills, they set them to only light work the first day. After a week this second group could do as heavy physical work at 122° F. as in normal latitudes, without experiencing any of the symptoms which the first group had had, except that pulse rate and body temperature rose a little. The gradual heaviness of work had given the body enough time to produce an increase in the blood supply, which prevented dizziness and fainting.

Medical officers and survival experts drew the conclusion that people can stand even extremes of heat if they learn to adapt themselves to it. All "furious activity" is dangerous. Men in units stationed in hot climates must not go all out in the first two or three days, but only do very short periods of strenuous work with long breaks in between. If they do light work only in these periods, getting used to the great heat will take them about a week. If they did no work at all, it would take ages for them to become acclimatized. In Russia there are apparently experiments to make a man's blood production rise very rapidly, so that in great heat he doesn't need to acclimatize himself by such short bursts of work.

America's physiologists are investigating various animal species to find out how these stay alive despite the great heat of their environment. Dr. Austin Phelps of the University of Texas, for instance, has studied a species of snail inhabiting certain desert springs in New Mexico where the water is 113° F. Such temperatures make the proteins clot in most creatures, and Phelps is hoping to track down the secret of the snails so as to exploit it practically for survival technique.

Dr. Schmidt Nielsen, of what used to be the University College of Rhodesia and Nyasaland, has been studying the "survival mechanism" of the camel. As mentioned in Chapter 2, it can sweat out water to an amount of about a quarter of its weight, whereas man can normally lose only 13 to 15 percent. This is because with man the moisture is first taken from the blood (making it thicker and its circulation therefore more difficult), while with the camel the moisture is taken exclusively from the tissues. So survival experts have had the idea of producing a tablet which will prevent a thirsty man's blood thickening, and will cause the moisture to be drawn from the tissues instead of the blood. Perhaps Dr. Nielsen's researches will lead to such a tablet being produced.

There are records too, of course, in standing up to great cold; here also physiologists are working very hard—to discover ways and means of acclimatizing people to temperatures below freezing point.

One of the most extraordinary cases of extreme bodily "refrigeration" occurred in the winter of 1961–62 in the mountains of Pennsylvania. Two hunters stalking game in a wood suddenly heard a weird and horrible wailing from a hut in a small clearing. They pulled the door open, and out dropped a stooped half-naked figure, frozen blue. "It fell to the ground with a regular clatter, like a pottery jar," one of the hunters recalled afterward. "It was a man. He lay before us on the ground in a sitting position, as if he had been pushed off a chair, and hadn't moved. Then he mumbled: 'Shut in . . . in there . . . for days.'"

They rushed into the hut, to see a man in an even worse state. He was lying on his back on the floor, his knees drawn up, his arms stretched out in front of him with the fingers bent, as if he had been holding on to something. Mouth and eyes were gaping —but he was still alive.

Days later it gradually became known what had happened inside the hut: the two frozen men were the Americans Bob Wise and Dick Lantsberry. One evening some days before, they lay down in the hut to sleep, with a small paraffin stove to warm the room. But the open flame used up so much oxygen during the night that it went out. Wise and Lantsberry succumbed to the carbon monoxide, which did not kill them but left them too weak to open the hut door and let some fresh air in. Unable to move, they were exposed to appalling cold, and were frozen stiff in exactly the positions in which they had awakened that morning.

The hunters took them, still rigid, to the nearest hospital. No one held out any hopes for them, for it was more than frostbite; they were literally chilled to the bone. One of the nurses said: "They felt like a piece of meat from the deep-freeze." "Their heels felt as hard as bricks," said another. Their body temperatures could not be measured with the hospital thermometers, because these did not go below 95° F. and so did not register at all.

It was a slow business thawing them out. The doctor in charge applied compresses to their limbs, first cold, then gradually increasing in heat. It took five hours to thaw the limbs sufficiently to bend them out of their mummified posture into a normal position, without fear of further damage to the tissues. The thawing process was carried on all night. The skin eventually started reddening slightly, a sign that the blood had begun to pulse into the tissues again. Then the skin began to break into big frost-blisters, which quickly filled with water.

Toward evening the two men's temperatures shot up to 106.5° F. It was several days before they came out of their tetanus-like state and could speak and eat again. They lost their toes, but nothing else. It was never established how low their body temperatures had really sunk, but probably it would be about 50° F.—lower than that of Dorothy Mae Stevens, a young Negro woman from Chicago, whose temperature in a snowstorm went down to 64° F. She had to have both legs amputated.

Both cases are unusual, for the human body will not normally stand up to extreme cold over any length of time. If the external temperature is about 50° F. the body (partly by shivering) will produce enough heat on its own to make up for the loss of heat through the skin. But if the external temperature falls lower than that, even shivering will not help: it stops when the body temperature had dropped to about 93° F. The next thing to go is the ability to concentrate; the mind becomes cloudy, and the freezing person is overcome by apathy. If the body temperature is only 90° F., he loses consciousness. If it drops still further, the blood becomes thicker and more viscous. All bodily functions, heart, breathing, metabolism, slow down and finally cease altogether.

In water that is 41° F. very few people live longer than half an hour. A volunteer in an aeronautical laboratory exposed naked to a temperature of —211° F. collapsed after only a minute and a half. In later experiments the same man wore protective clothing a third of an inch thick, but could stand —418° F. only for the same time. Through such and similar tests American physiologists have found that the degree of cold a man can stand is among other things dependent on his race. In the Korean War seven times as many Negroes as white men suffered from frostbite.

Experiments are going on now to find out how people can get used to low temperatures without artificial protection such as special clothing, etc. Various methods of "toughening" are being studied, first of all in experiments with animals. In the Army Medical Research Laboratory in Fort Knox several rats had been gradually acclimatized to low temperatures, and were then exposed to great cold together with other "untreated" rats. The acclimatized rats survived for thirty-five hours, three times as long as their "pampered" fellow rats. Subsequent investigations showed that the cells on the skin surface of the more resistant rats had expanded during the toughening period. This apparently made them better able to bear the great cold.

It is not yet known whether the same process goes on in the peripheral vessels of a man if he is exposed to gradually increasing cold. But we do know that a man can become used to low temperatures. American volunteers have been hardened to the point where they can sleep naked for several nights in a room only 50° F. If anyone thinks this is easy, let him try it!

Even more amazing is the case quoted by Sir Edmund Hillary, the conqueror of Everest: "In the mountains of Nepal I met a pilgrim called Man Bahadur, who not only went on long wanderings bare-footed through deep snow, but slept in the open, wrapped in only a thin blanket, at temperatures around freezing point." Sir Edmund thinks that Man Bahadur's body temperature could adapt itself to the weather, since he did not even shiver in great cold.

It has been known for a long time that certain mammals in winter can adapt themselves to the hard conditions of their environment. When the cold season comes, they go to sleep in their burrow and, as it were, slowly freeze up. With the increasing cold outside, their body temperature often drops to half its normal level, and even, with marmots and hedgehogs, to near freezing point. They lapse into the unconscious state known as "hibernation." As with someone who is freezing to death, all their bodily functions are slower than normal. The heart does not beat as fast, and even the cells age less rapidly: in short, the life of these creatures is being extended. Scientists are carrying out new research on how these creatures survive in such a state. Dr. Raymond Hool of the American Arctic Institute even creeps into the dens of hibernating bears and takes their rectal temperatures!

No tablet has yet been discovered for inducing a sort of hibernation in men; but if it were, an airman who made a crash landing in the Arctic winter could "sleep through" the cold months and reawaken in the warm summer. Biologists concerned with space travel think it will be possible one day to put astronauts into such a hibernation for flights to the farthest celestial bodies, so that they "age" more slowly—or to put to sleep an incurably ill person till a remedy for the disease has been discovered.

To make men more resistant to great cold, the U. S. Air Force did for a while experiment with a "heat pill": after taking it, a castaway has more chance of surviving in cold water; while a mountain climber who has had an accident could stand a temperature below freezing point for a longer period, by which time he might be rescued.

The history of sport shows that people can achieve better performances by training, which is really getting accustomed to certain conditions; similarly, according to many physiologists, people can get accustomed to increasingly hard environmental conditions —which seems to be confirmed by some of the heat and cold tests I have quoted. In 1961 Sir Edmund Hillary showed by experiment that "normal men" too can get used to breathing in rarefied air and even working in it. Survival experts of the world's air forces have evinced great interest in this, for it means that in an emergency airmen inured to rarefied air could fly without oxygen apparatus.

Sir Edmund started from the fact that various mountain tribes live and work at heights where most "plainsmen" would already need oxygen apparatus: the settlements of some Peruvian Indians, for instance, are 18,000 feet up. (If these people were suddenly made to work at sea level, too much oxygen would get into their blood, and they would show similar symptoms to a pilot suffering from hypoxia.) Sherpa Tensing (of Everest fame) even moved about at heights of 25,000 feet without an oxygen apparatus.

"But you don't need to be Peruvian, Nepalese or mad," Hillary decided, "to get used to similar heights." So in the autumn of 1961 he and some members of his Everest team built a Nissen hut in the Himalayas at a height of about 19,000 feet. Wearing warm clothes, and with an oil stove and plenty of food, they spent the winter in this hut, adapting themselves to the great height with its shortage of oxygen. Even when the oxygen content in their blood gradually dropped by 50 percent, they remained in full possession of their mental powers, and could soon carry out as hard physical work as at lower altitudes. (Whereas a healthy person unused to rarefied air would become a victim of hypoxia when the oxygen content of his blood dropped by even 35 percent.)

A few months after Hillary's experiment the German mountain climber Detlef Hecker and his team scaled Mount Aconcagua in South America (23,000 feet), also without oxygen apparatus, after a thorough "hardening" process. They had been subjected to endurance tests in low-pressure chambers and had their powers of resistance enhanced by cold showers.

Dr. Benno Balke, a specialist in aeronautical medicine in the United States, has achieved even more striking results by simpler means than Hillary. Convinced that airmen could get used to very great heights, he made a party of volunteers perform gymnastic exercises on some mountains in California: they had to do a hundred knee-bends—first at 3,000 feet, then at 5,000, then at 7,000, and eventually on the highest peak in the range, about 12,000 feet. After being thoroughly inured, they were shut up in a low-pressure chamber, where the pressure was abruptly brought down a great deal, so as to correspond to a height of 37,500 feet. Any "normal" airman would at once have got "the bends," but they were unaffected. Balke then had them do several knee-bends every three minutes (physical strain speeds up the onset of "the bends"), but they still felt nothing. He now had the knee-bends done every two minutes, at which some of them at last felt a stabbing pain in the joints, and had to give up.

But Sergeant Sam Karst (aged thirty-four) felt well enough to "climb higher." Even more air was sucked from the chamber, bringing the height up to 50,000 feet; Karst's eyes began to shine, and the veins on his neck stood out like whip cords. At 55,000 feet: "Now at last," Karst stated afterward, "I felt the first symptoms of hypoxia. After a minute and a half at this 'height' I gave up. But the experiment showed that a pilot whose pressure-cabin and oxygen apparatus fail will still have a good chance of surviving, if (like us) he has been inured beforehand to staying at great heights."

One of the most interesting experiments concerning chances of survival for alpinists at high altitudes was conducted in 1969 in the Swiss Alps, with the results published in 1974. The aim of the experiment was to find out why some mountaineering expeditions of the past had failed for apparently inexplicable reasons. One typical symptom of such failures: the team members, usually good friends down in the valley, became hostile toward each other after several days at high altitudes, thus endangering the success of the expedition and, of course, each other's lives.

Six of the most experienced mountain guides from the three countries Switzerland, Austria, and West Germany were found willing to cover a sixteen-mile-long route along the Alps, with elevation differences of between 10,500 feet (up) and 15,000 feet (down).

The results were astounding. The scientists discovered three main reasons why many expeditions, although conducted by experienced mountaineers, may have failed.

Reason Number One: There were not enough variations in the daily menus. Result: the team members ate without appetite. And although they had enough supplies, they cut down on the tasteless, uniform meals of crackers, tea, corned beef, and vitamin pills. This, in turn, soon led to a calorie-deficiency.

Reason Number Two: In the cold altitude, the expedition members drank too little water, consuming on the average only 1.5 to 2 quarts of water per day, whereas their bodies, because of the hard work, would have needed four to seven quarts. However, because of the cold they had not felt the need for it.

Reason Number Three: None of the expedition members got enough sleep.

These three reasons, combined, resulted in a vicious circle: the longer each of those three deficiencies lasted, the more the members lost in strength, fitness, and alertness. Periods of tiredness became more frequent. At the same time, mental stress increased and so did nervousness—in three typical stages.

Stage One: "Why is it me who feels so tired, worn out, with aching feet, etc.? Why not the others?"

Stage Two: Swearing begins, for little reasons. First an expedition member is swearing at himself, then at the others. Finally, friendships begin to crumble because the others swear back.

Stage Three: Lethargy sets in. This is the most dangerous stage, of course. Necessary things are not being done any more, or are being postponed. Each member of the expedition starts to find or invent excuses why this or that thing does not have to be done, or should be postponed for the next day. The stage is reached where death through negligence or apathy is not far away any more.

The conclusion of the Swiss scientists: varied menus, enough drinking water, and sufficient sleep will help people at great altitudes and/or low temperatures to increase their chances of survival.

The Air Forces of both the United States and the Soviet Union for a while have been studying the possibility of producing a pill that would modify a man's organism so that at great heights he could absorb sufficient oxygen from the air. The pill would have to act quickly enough for an airman to take it when there was a danger of hypoxia, and thus avoid losing consciousness from lack of oxygen. Similarly, other pills for the dangers of great altitudes and severe cold could and perhaps will be developed.

Man can also, of course, get used to long fasts, but records vary depending on conditions. Willi Schmitz of Frankfurt, West Germany, went without solid food for seventy-nine days, losing eighty-seven pounds in weight. That was in the late forties. Quite soon afterward, in the early fifties, his record was beaten by Burmah, an Indian fakir, who ate nothing and drank only water for eighty-one days.

Survival experts are interested not only in how long a man can live without food, but in the minimum of calories he needs to carry out physical activity (or fight), in various climates and under various conditions. They are equally interested in the psychological effects which can be caused by involuntary fasts. One of these, of course, is to concentrate all the attention on food, which becomes the only topic of conversation. "It is scandalous," a member of Shackleton's expedition wrote in his diary. "We all seem to live for food and think of nothing but food. Never before in my life have I taken such an interest in food as I do now, and we are all alike."

In a study of airmen who have made crash landings Richard Howard, a survivor of a party lost in the Arctic for some days, recalls: "Every night, I believe, we felt hungrier than before. We recalled Christmas dinners which had been set before us as children, and talked about the remains we had left on our plates. Suddenly we all raised our hands and vowed we would never again leave anything on our plates."

Later Howard writes: "The thought of food has kept the minds of many survivors occupied, and always gave them something to talk about. Two parties of survivors chose Gandhi as a basis for their calculations on how long a man can endure without food. Men thought or talked of ice cream, steaks, and roast chicken. They talked of colored advertisements in magazines showing food, and wondered whether these could have been genuine. They talked of cooking methods, and planned (illusory) menus for themselves or for a whole company. One party talked endlessly about the merits of every kind of sweet and in the end drew up a list in order of quality of all the makes they could remember. Men dreamed of dishes from all parts of the world, of copious meals containing a lot of potatoes, dumplings and rich gravy. They remembered food they had spurned or left on their plates, and some vowed they would never again grumble about having too much cabbage or carrots. Sometimes survivors made agreements not to talk about food any more, but the next day by tacit consent they had come back to the same subject."

The relatively mild hunger symptoms change abruptly when the condition known as dystrophy sets in. The first signs of this are weakness, fatigue, a drop in blood pressure, often also in the pulse rate. If the fast continues, the body weight decreases, muscles and fat dwindle, and the skin often becomes dehydrated. In the book about Stalingrad quoted previously, Dr. Dibold writes:

"Strange eruptions and discolorations make their appearance, wounds no longer heal, there is catarrh of the mucous membrane, and disorders of the stomach and intestines. There is a weakening of mental activity, the subjects lose all desire to move about, and are like old people. There is a definite reduction in the protein content of the blood; in the wet form we meet with permanent accumulations of water. The majority of these phenomena are to be explained by the body's shortage of protein. But the deficiency of many other substances also plays its part.

"Cases suffering from third degree dystrophy are recognizable at first sight as dangerously ill. Their weakness is acute, and puts their life in danger. They consist of skin and bones. In the wet form . . . swollen, the thoracic and abdominal cavities are filled with considerable quantities of clear watery fluid. The patient suffers from diarrhea; sometimes this diarrhea drains the water from the tissues and body cavities, leaving the body as it were, mummified, this exposes the heart to great danger, and frequently the patient fails to recover.

"The dystrophic body reveals scarcely any reaction to inflammations, infections and purulent accumulations; it does not run a temperature, the white blood cells cease to multiply, the red cells are not renewed. The patients suffer great mental changes. They become listless and self-centered. Psychological changes occur even in the lighter grades of dystrophy.

"Death occurred chiefly through heart failure, produced by even a slight case of pneumonia. Much of this fading away was reminiscent of the death of aged people, and, painful as the psychological break-down may have been to the onlookers, to the patients themselves it brought one great benefit: long before the end came, they were in a stupor, grown indifferent and apathetic. Nature spread the white veil of oblivion over mind and spirit, death came to them as to little children. It stilled the feeble body."

Since Dibold and his colleagues couldn't nurse their fellow prisoners back to health by giving them the right food, they had to make do with very primitive remedies. These men were deficient in gastric acid, for instance, so that they could not completely digest the little food they usually had. An officer who in peacetime was a professor of chemistry, produced sulphuric acid (from "liberated" sulphur), with which the contents of the patients' stomachs could at least be somewhat acidified. In other cases Dibold took some gastric juice with a stomach pump from healthy prisoners, and gave it to the dangerously ill as a medicine. "The patients did not know the origin of this acidulous medicine. In this way we were able to help a few inveterately bad eaters considerably. Once we ourselves found this procedure almost too much for us. One day we visited one of our lame ducks and noted with pleasure how this pale-faced man, who normally ate hardly anything, was devouring a cucumber salad with great gusto. He smiled with satisfaction and said: 'Doctor, it tastes first-rate today. I've given this salad a dressing of my medicine."

Natives in Burma nursed a starving American airman back to health in a similar way. The oldest woman in the village ate a portion of rice every four hours. Then she waited half an hour, brought it up, and stuffed the half-digested and acidified food into the airman's mouth. He rapidly regained his strength.

Survival experts are naturally looking for ways and means of sparing the members of their armed forces the ordeals of involuntary fasts after a crash landing or shipwreck. American women with a craze for slimming have for some time got their doctors to prescribe them a drug which dulls the hunger nerve. It has been suggested that this drug could be included in the survival equipment of air and ground troops. For the hungry members of the forces in an emergency, although of course no substitute for food, it would be an effective means of turning their thoughts from eating to fighting.

Overindulgence as well as hunger is a subject which survival experts find worth studying. A healthy man who is well and regularly fed, can safely eat twice as much as he normally does, if the need arises. (The record is held by the miner Philipp Yazdzik, from Pennsylvania, who periodically "for the amusement of spectators," would devour seventy-seven hamburgers with rolls or thirty-one roast chicken halves, which he washes down with twenty-four glasses of milk and twenty-six bottles of soda water.)

But overindulgence is generally harmful, and often almost fatal, to castaways, etc., who have gone hungry for a long time and greedily devour a lot of food; their stomachs, shrunk from long fasting, cannot tolerate the sudden overloading. After their rescue by natives, Bertram and Klausmann forced themselves to eat often, but only a little at a time, of the chewed kangaroo meat which their rescuers pushed into their mouths. Survival experts warn their trainees against interrupting an "adequate" diet (say of raw fish) with a good (normal) meal, if they are going to have to return to their scanty rations. The dangers are illustrated by Bombard and the meal he took on the steamer *Arakaka*:

"It was the first hot meal I had had for fifty-three days. It consisted of a fried egg, a small piece of liver and some cabbage;

also fresh fruit. In the following days I was to be very sorry I had accepted it . . . In due course, back in Paris again, a famous expert on nutrition told me: 'If we had known you had a meal on the ship you met, we would not have rated your chances very high.' Before my little meal . . . my food had become abnormal. Afterward, losing all appetite for fish, I became undernourished. The human organism gradually accustoms itself to a change and diminution in the normal ration, but after a proper meal the digestive system seems to say: 'There, things are back to normal again, I don't need to make any further special effort,' rather like an athlete who stops in the middle of a race and finds he cannot start again. The stomach becomes prey to a sort of despair. I lost more weight . . . during the twelve days still remaining to land than in the fifty-three days before my meeting with the *Arakaka*."

To find out what men can stand in the way of physical suffering, the doctors in the Cornell Medical Center in New York City have invented a "dolorimeter," which measures the amount of pain suffered by test subjects (taking into account their constitution and many other factors). According to these doctors, the worst pains are those suffered in passing a kidney stone or by women in labor. But castaways far from all medical help have often endured agonies which must be as intense. The American William Willis was attacked on his raft by stomach pains which for several days gave him such torment that he seriously thought of suicide. In his own words: "And then a tiny voice began to whisper that I was myself to blame for what was happening to my body. Take the pain or go over the side. Cut it out with a knife. It has drawn most of your life into its grip. My eyes kept going to the thin-bladed fish-gutting knife stuck above the door of my cabin. You have a knot there tight as steel, and still tightening—you must cut it. Strange how this idea fascinated me. But how could I cut into my body? It would possibly bring relief from the pain, but then I would have a hole in my body. For hours my thoughts dwelt on soldiers on the battlefield shot through the stomach, lying in some gully or in deep grass incapable of movement, waiting in agony to be picked up. Fight it out, Bill—this is nothing—fight it out, man!"

Many pilots who crashed in the war performed self-amputations with a knife, because they found a shattered leg or a crushed foot a hinderance in getting to the nearest settlement. One of the most gruesome descriptions of an emergency operation is given by Bertram in his book *Flug in die Hölle* (*Flight into Hell*). After he and Klausmann had wondered around for days, he was attacked by raging toothache. He decided to have Klausmann perform the necessary extraction.

"We had no upholstered dentist's chair, no clean instruments, no disinfectant, only a rusty pair of pliers. Klausmann must try to get hold of the molar with these and pull it out. . . . He sat on a stone. I lay down in front of him with my head pressed hard into his lap, and dug my hands into the earth. . . . Then he began his work. He tried to grip the rotten tooth, but could only with difficulty separate the pliers far enough to get it round the tooth. He pulled, it slipped off, and broke off a piece of a tooth. For the next two hours the pliers kept slipping off, breaking off one piece of tooth after another, and eventually could no longer get a grip on it. Three or four times I must have fainted, the pain was so savage. . . . We had to try another method to get at the pus.

"We had a safety-pin with us. Klausmann put it into the broken tooth and tried to press it through but wasn't strong enough, so he had to hit it with the pliers. Then the safety-pin went through the tooth; I pulled it out, pus and blood came, we had got through to the seat of the inflammation. The operation was over!"

Today morphine and other pain relievers are part of any adequate emergency equipment; and the trainees in the survival schools not only have a thorough grounding in first aid, but even learn how to perform minor operations.

Survival experts would also like a drug to be developed by which a castaway could "switch off" at will his need for sleep for a certain time, without causing any harmful aftereffects. Castaways (as has been mentioned) are always saying that they couldn't sleep because of the rough sea or the continual pitching of their lifeboat; and in consequence, tormented by lack of sleep over a long period, they were seized by fits of fury and did mad, self-destructive things which would have been inconceivable for them in their normal rested state.

Stopping someone from sleeping, of course, is a well-known third-degree method for extracting confessions, etc. But the record so far for voluntarily keeping awake is held by an American disc jockey, Rick Michaels, who in March 1960 kept going for 243 hours with the aid of coffee, talks with the spectators, and making almost continuous radio announcements. Meanwhile physiologists and psychologists were keeping continuous note of the effects produced by his long "watch":

1 to 65 hours: little change apparent in Michaels. Toward the end of the third day he goes outside several times to cool off in the cold March air, and takes several cold showers.

70 hours: he becomes increasingly nervous; abusive and quarrelsome with his colleagues, wants to give up. They press him to continue. He recovers himself, thanks them, and laughs, saying it was all a joke.

100 hours: gloomy mood becomes triumphant one. He suddenly turns into an unpleasant show-off. Although he has kept awake for under half the 230 hours planned, he acts as if he has already won. "I shall challenge all other disc-jockeys to a competition in keeping awake. I shall beat them, for I am the best."

160 hours: confidence in victory turns into deep depression. He complains of a leaden heaviness in his limbs. Dreams with eyes open, seeing things which aren't there at all: a gray mist on the studio; a blue light leaping like a flame out of the walls and playing round a girl who hands him coffee; smoking ash-trays, which are not smoking. Persecution mania also sets in: he jumps up and dashes out of the room in terror. Yells at someone who follows him: "You're making fun of me. What harm have I ever done you?" He jumps at the man and tries to choke him. Then he lets go and pleads: "No one must know what I'm doing, do you hear? No one, least of all my family." His powers of concentration also give out. He becomes hypersensitive to noises. Uses the wrong knobs and microphones. The telephone, the record-player, even his own voice, almost drive him mad. Then he suddenly forces himself to be extremely polite. Like a volcano before it erupts.

180 hours: "There's a band round my head. Now it's slipping down—over the eyes. I can't see properly any more." Powers of concentration completely lost. He pulls records out of the shelf at random, puts on pieces he has just played and goes through all his motions more or less unconsciously. "I feel as if I were on a cloud," he says at one point. Then he relapses into dull brooding and doesn't know what is going on around him. Gives incoherent answers. Keeps changing the subject and often doesn't know what he has been asked.

220 hours: can only just speak. When he wants to stand up, someone has to support him.

243 hours: falls asleep on his feet and collapses. He is carried onto a bunk without waking. He sleeps fifteen hours continuously, and is then completely recovered and refreshed.

Michaels' experiment, and the observations of others trying to beat his record, led to the realization that after eighty hours at most sleeplessness causes great irritability, and after about a hundred hours makes people unable to concentrate. Many test subjects no longer knew by then what their names were, and couldn't really think straight. In the first sixty hours the body is generally successful in overcoming its weariness through certain not yet isolated substances in gland secretions. After that, apparently, the production of these substances ceases. If they could be isolated and perhaps synthetically reproduced, some physiologists believe it should be possible to keep a man awake in emergencies without the harmful symptoms of long sleeplessness.

The conquest of fear is also of importance for survivors of all sorts, and there is the prospect of a pill being developed which would not only take away fear but give people extra courage, thereby increasing their chances of survival. The U. S. Corps of Chemical Engineers started to develop such a pill in 1959.

Dr. Miller of Yale University carried out experiments in which some rats were first made afraid of a flashlight by giving them a violent electric shock when the light went on; the shock was more intense the nearer the rats were to the lamp. In the second part of the experiment the lamp flashed periodically without the rats getting a shock; but they still beat a retreat at the flash. Then he mixed a certain chemical substance into their food, at which they promptly lost their fear and were quite ready to approach the lamp. The drug had given them extra courage—and it will probably have a similar effect on human volunteers.

But superhuman courage may be needed, and also "superhuman strength." Here are a few examples from the recent past. In 1942 an American freighter was attacked one night by a German submarine. There was a secret agent on board who had locked up his briefcase containing important documents in the safe in the captain's cabin. At the first alarm signal he ran into the cabin to get it out, but the captain, who had the key, was on the bridge. Blindly, without thinking, the agent put his arms round the safe, pulled it out of its strong fitting, propped it on his shoulder, and carried it through the ship onto the bridge. Later it took four sailors to return it to its old place. Then there was the sailor who picked a 200-lb. blind shell off the deck of his aircraft-carrier, and threw it overboard, where it exploded. Yet he was a man of such poor physique that he normally couldn't have lifted a biggish crate.

To turn to civilian examples, there was a seventy-year-old farmer who was in bed when a fire broke out in his three-story house. He escaped to the roof, and when the flames were approaching him, he walked with somnambulistic confidence along a telephone wire nine yards long, to reach a telephone pole, and climbed safely down this to the ground.

On a summer day in 1959 Charles Rogers, aged fifteen, was going to mend his parents' Detroit-made car. He jacked the heavy automobile up and crawled underneath. Suddenly the car slipped forward a bit and jammed him underneath. He shouted for help. His father dashed into the cellar to fetch another jack. But his mother, age thirty-nine, a delicate woman weighing about 125 pounds, acting on impulse, got hold of the bumper bars with both hands and jerked the car up. The boy quickly crawled out, and then she let go. She sustained only a small vertebral crack, which soon healed.

When you ask people how they had the courage and strength to perform these feats of strength and often of heroism, they usually answer to this effect: "I don't know. I acted blindly, without thinking. If I had stopped for a second to think about it, I could never have done it. I'm sure I could never do it again." Such was the case, to take a final and recent example (summer 1964), with British police-girl Margaret Cleland, aged twenty-four, who was awarded the George Medal for snatching a baby from the arms of his father when he threatened to jump sixty feet off the roof. According to a newspaper report, she couldn't stand heights, and said: "I still can't believe it. I am frightened of climbing up a ladder."

Probably every one of us has known a time when in a rage, a great calamity, or great inspiration, it seems possible to "move mountains." It is a heady feeling, and those who indulge it without thinking too much are generally capable, if not of miracles, at least of greatly heightened performance. Physiologists and psychologists have in recent years been trying to analyze the factors which for a few seconds may turn a comparative weakling into a superman. Dr. Hans Seyle, head of the Institute for Experimental Medicine in the University of Montreal, believes that certain hormones are among the most important of these factors. The pituitary gland briefly produces an excess of such hormones in moments of extreme danger, "burning love," and also "blind fury." If the will of the person concerned is concentrated exclusively on reaching the objective set and all inhibitions have fallen away, the hormones are drawn exclusively to the muscles, nerves, and brain cells involved in carrying out the task. For a brief moment—as long as the effect of the "rush of hormones" lasts—"superhuman strength" is produced. Within a few years from now all the factors prerequisite to such feats will have been analyzed and may be produced by pills. A pilot jammed in the wreck of his crashed plane might then be able to free himself after taking a "strength pill."

Another highly sinister possibility is that "crack troops" might have such pills planted under their skin before an action. The pills would have a small aerial, and would not start to take effect until the aerial picked up a signal from the unit's commanding officer. This would mean that the whole unit gave its maximum performance at the same time.

"There is no doubt," Dr. Otto Schmitt, head of the biophysical department of the University of Minnesota, declared in 1961, "that we can alter a person's behavior. We can make him cruel and aggressive, or we can calm him down. We are at present trying to see how we could see our new knowledge for good purposes, such as influencing a man to give a better performance in work."

Pills for influencing emotions might possibly help castaways, for instance, over the worst of all psychological torments—loneliness. How terrible this feeling can get is perhaps best illustrated by quoting the Englishman Sebastian Snow, forty-five, who tried to walk from South to North America in 1973–74. Although, contrary to the situation of the castaway, he was constantly surrounded by people, he hardly took his time to talk to them, because his goal was to cover the longest possible stretch of road in the shortest time possible. After nineteen months and 8,700 miles Snow finally gave up, explaining to several reporters: "It was like traveling in solitary confinement. Often I would wake up in the morning in my tent, not even remembering which country I was in. . . . I felt cocooned from the world. My morale was lowest in the evening after each day's march (his record: 63 miles in 18 hours). When I met a friend I was so groggy that I failed to recognize him. I suffered hallucinations . . . sometimes I imagined I was Charlie Chaplin. I found that objects and landscapes changed their natural colors in a nightmarish way . . . the grass turned red and the sky to rainbow colors. I also felt perpetually threatened. . . . When I fell down and gashed my knee, I lay spread-eagle on the road just waiting for trucks to run over my limbs. . . ."

How much harder then is loneliness for solitary castaways! The countless volunteers who have submitted to every sort of ordeal in the aeronautical laboratories are indeed unanimous that the "isolation test" is the worst of all. At the end of 1962 Whilden P. Breen spent five months in the University of Maryland in a room of ten square yards. Toward the end of the experiment he suffered from "an indescribable weariness," was frantically bored, and felt "incredibly forlorn." He no longer felt like writing, reading, or painting. Eventually he became very hostile and abusive to the people conducting the experiment—which was broken off.

The tests where nothing at all happens for the subject to do or see or listen to, are particularly unnerving. Normally any silence, even the "deathly silence" of an underground cave, has something comforting about it—although even the town-hater may well not be able to stand it for more than a brief time. The complete absence of any acoustic stimuli (often of optical stimuli as well) drives most test subjects to desperation in a very short time; and if the test were carried on to the bitter end, they would presumably go mad. When engineers of the U. S. Army Signal Corps at Fort Monmouth, New Jersey, agreed to be shut up in a pitch-dark, soundproof isolation room, and not allowed to speak or move, the test had to be stopped after only half an hour: everybody's nerves were strained to the limit, and some of them were already suffering from mental disorders.

The record for isolated inactivity was set up in 1962 by two students at the University of Washington and their professor, who held out for weeks in single cells. During the experiment they wore dark glasses, so as not to see anything, and gloves, so that they couldn't feel anything. They were not allowed to sing, talk, or do any physical exercises; but they could walk around and also get their own food, which was in containers of various shapes in a refrigerator. After two weeks they all heard birds twittering and waves roaring—which of course were complete hallucinations. They felt a vast indifference to everything around them, and after the experiment had ended, the professor remained in the state for three days, one of the students for six and the other for eight days.

At the beginning of the last war it was not realized what psychological troubles might be caused a man by even a few hours' isolation; until an increasing number of Air Force men had to be withdrawn from front-line duty because of acute mental disorders. Most of their men so affected, the American authorities discovered with surprise, were rear-gunners ("Tail-end Charlies") in the great Liberator bombers.

The rear-gunner was enclosed in his perspex dome as if in a large bubble. He climbed in before the take-off, and would leave it six to eight hours later, provided the plane returned safely. During the flight he was completely isolated from the rest of the crew. He couldn't see what they were doing, nor hear what they were talking about. He could reach them by the intercom, of course, but such "conversations" had to be confined to a minimum.

After twenty or even ten actions most Tail-end Charlies asked for transfers. The reasons they gave sounded so extraordinary that at first they were taken for shirkers. One man told his officer that after a few hours in his "bubble" he was seeing things which couldn't have been there—people, animals, even vermin. Another declared: "Little green men are always sliding over the roof of my dome and then walking along to the butt of my gun. I always have to wipe them away before I can see through my sights." And a rear-gunner once told me in a New York bar: "If I hadn't been a Tail-end Charlie, I shouldn't be an alcoholic today. After every action I felt so completely indifferent that I always drank myself silly."

Aeronautical specialists today call this indifference the "break-off": it means that the lonely man feels every inner and outer connection between himself and the rest of the world has been broken off. Since the end of the war it has been observed that the occupants of high-altitude balloons are often attacked by it, and so are the pilots of jets when flying alone at great altitudes. "Everything becomes unimportant, seems meaningless," one of them said. "You don't even care any more about your own life." A pilot's break-off feeling only disappears when the earth comes in sight or another plane—so that the subconscious registers: "There's someone else, you aren't really alone."

Castaways stranded on desert islands, etc., have several advantages over the Tail-end Charlies and the subjects of isolation tests: they can move freely, talk, sing, keep occupied; they can see and feel. But they too suffer very soon from their loneliness, and to relieve it begin talking to themselves, though many find that singing is a better antidote. Often they sing all the songs they know until they become hoarse, and then stop abruptly from fear they may be too hoarse to call for help at the crucial moment. Lindemann speaks of "moments of the deepest depression and despair. During my worst moments I found myself singing: songs from my childhood and my student days. If there was a rough sea, I sang soothing songs. I often heard myself repeating for hours the first bars of a song. I had reached the point where the world beyond my horizon had ceased to exist."

William Willis on his raft sang at the top of his voice: "I would burst out singing, roaring some old sea chanty, learned long ago, and long forgotten, now coming out in the wildness of the moment. I would shout defiance to the winds, and elements, my untamed partners playing with me in their strength as I stood with legs straddled on the tossing deck. Singing made all my work easy. . . . Singing was a miracle that worked for me at all times. Would it do the same for others adrift at sea? I didn't know. It was certainly not the musical quality of my voice that soothed me and brought my spirits into harmony."

"The silence was deafening," said one castaway. "I sang all the old hymns I knew, and repeated the Lord's Prayer as often as possible." Then there is the sad little story of a man who tried to dispel his loneliness with an alarm whistle. For hours he blew a single note, over and over again. But in the end this made him so miserable that he burst into tears and stopped!

When there are no human beings to talk to, the animal world soon turns into the best substitute. Lindemann was "grateful to all living creatures in the sea and the air" which he could see from his boat. "They shared my solitude and throughout my voyage were a constant reminder of the 'other' life. They kept me from fully losing myself in dreams, and later they even kept me from the despair which threatened to overwhelm me. . . . Lonely and bored, in the middle of the Atlantic, I talked to the fishes, sometimes in a friendly way, sometimes in anger. My attitude toward them depended on the weather. 'Good morning, my friends, how are you today?' "

A castaway on the Pacific during the war was so often visited by albatrosses that he lived off them for days. Just as he was going to kill another, the idea came to him to make it a sort of pet. He stroked it, and the bird got used to him. For seven days the albatross stayed on his lifeboat, and helped relieve his boredom.

In November 1962 the Frenchman Alfons Vergnes and two friends landed on Cocos Island in the Pacific to look for pirate treasure. His friends went out in their boat in a storm and were drowned, leaving Vergnes on his own. "The worst thing then was having nobody to talk to. I began to talk to myself out loud. I was terrified that this was the beginning of madness." He suffered from hallucinations, and was only kept going by the thought of the ship which was to fetch him after two months. Finally, when he was at the end of his tether, a chicken ran across his path, presumably left behind by earlier inhabitants of the island. He treated it as his companion in misfortune, talked to it and poured out his heart to it.

Augustine Courtauld, a twenty-six-year-old Canadian, was also "relieved" just in time, after five months of loneliness on Greenland's icecap. On December 6, 1930, he had let himself be snowed up in an igloo fitted out as a weather station—he was full of confidence that being alone couldn't worry him much. But after a week or two most of the hours of his working day were filled with wistful or longing daydreams, and he soon cursed the day on which he had decided on his enterprise. After three months his fuel supply was so short that he lay for hours in his cold dark snow hole. The last eight weeks he didn't manage to go outside at all, and he had candles only for a few minutes' light a day. When his friends arrived, he was on the point of running out into the desert of snow without any equipment, hoping to struggle through to the coast on foot, just to see other human beings again.

In 1934 Admiral Richard E. Byrd, at the age of forty-six, decided to spend the winter alone in the Antarctic. His original wish, "to be alone for a while, so as to taste peace, quiet, and solitude and find out what they are really worth," soon gave way to extreme despondency. Although connected with the outside world by radio, he felt forsaken by God and the world after only a few weeks. He was overcome by crying fits and kept reproaching himself bitterly for having treated his family badly. Soon he thought of dying and wrote a farewell letter to his wife. The only thing that kept him from sending out an SOS was the conviction that an expedition to rescue him would have met its death in the extreme cold. In August a patrol at last reached him and ended his ordeal.

Michael Siffre, the young Frenchman who in 1962 stayed in an underground cave (mentioned in the second chapter), could stand only sixty-two days of solitude although he was connected to the surface by telephone with two "guardians."

On July 23, a week after his experiment started, he was already confessing in his log: "I found the time dragging today. The first fit of loneliness."

Wednesday, August 1: For the sake of honesty I would like to mention that I write up this log with great reluctance. Every evening I really have to force myself to do it, because it's extremely hard to remember the various things I've been occupied with all day.

Thursday, August 16: Two days ago I found a small spider as a companion, and since then I have occupied myself with it every day—I am quite moved watching it eat. It is, after all, the only living creature I have to look at. When you are really alone, alone as I am, you can feel friendship even for a spider. . . . The loneliness weighs me down more and more, and the darkness is beginning to disturb my mental balance considerably.

Sunday, August 19: My greatest wish is for life, life, life. . . . When I hear a voice on the telephone, I am overjoyed. Today I phoned for a very long time and it even made me forget the noodles I had on the cooker.

Monday, August 20: For some time I have been simply staying in bed. I feel that what I do is not so important as what I register in my situation in the way of thoughts and emotions. I sing. A bad symptom of distractedness is worrying me. I confused the telephone with the tape-recorder. It's quite incredible, that.

The day which Siffre entered in his log as August 20 was really September 16, the end of his experiment—so he was twenty-seven days out. When his friends climbed into the cave to bring him to the surface, he was a horrifying sight. He had not shaved for two months, his hair was long, his beard untrimmed. Outside his tent there were mountains of empty and half-empty food cans. They kept treading everywhere on squashed and rotten potatoes and tomatoes. There was a dreadful mess. Cans full of jam stood round on the flat rocks. Bags of rice were slit open at random. The ground was covered with currants, spaghetti, and torn food bags. Siffre had apparently lost all sense of order and cleanliness.

Then he lost his nerve too. He began to climb out through a gully leading to the surface. Then, weeping, he called to his friends over and over again: "I'm finished, I've had it, I can't go on, it's too much. . . . It's too much! Please no more, no more!" Sobbing and crying he dragged himself on inch by inch till he was far enough out of the hole for the people standing outside to give him a helping hand. Then he whimpered: "I'm so cold, I'm thirsty." Finally he lost consciousness. When he came to, his body was shaken with convulsions. He was quite unable to take in the excitement all round him, the cameramen and reporters. He was frightened to make the least movement. "Completely disin-tegrated," said the reporters.

In 1972, after years of training, Siffre, then thirty-three years old, tried again. On February 14, he entered a ninety-foot-deep cave near Del Rio, Texas, and stayed in it for 205 days. Again, he lost all sense of time and day—but when he emerged he was in full control of his mental and physical capacities. His first words were: "Now I'd like a drink."

Considering reactions such as Siffre's first experiment, it is un-derstandable that among castaways those left completely on their own have been especially liable to contemplate suicide in their desperation. During the war in the Pacific only two out of a thousand airmen who came down in the water did in fact kill themselves; but this was because they were either more scared of such a step than of their ordeal continuing, or else a new glimmer of hope appeared at what might have been their last moment—which made them wait one more day. Small groups of men showed least tendency to give up hope (and think of suicide), because a close human contact between them had grown up in the first days of their common ordeal. Sometimes they quarreled, which at least left less time for thoughts of suicide, but more often there was a sort of team spirit, which made them help each other, kept up their morale, and allowed hope to survive even in the darkest days.

Every morning, for instance, when the Robertson family, adrift in their small dinghy, woke up, the one person on night watch had to ask: "What's the code word for today?" And the other five an-swered: "Survival!"

Lionel Greenstreet, a member of the Shackleton expedition, reported after his rescue he was convinced that a sort of forced optimism and team spirit had kept them all alive, giving them courage to go on. "We always felt that something would turn up," he recalled. "Even though we knew that after the ship went down we only had an even chance of survival, there was always some immediate goal to be achieved and some progress to be made. But even at the worst, we did not speak our minds, and if anyone ever despaired he certainly did not tell us. Those who seemed depressed were jollied along by the rest."

In larger groups thoughts of suicide may be almost as common as with isolated individuals; for individuals can feel just as lonely in a motley crowd thrown together by fate. There are too many others there for them to make close contact with any. Moreover, they see the same people every day, the same faces, hear the same conversations every day, the same worries, the same jokes. This applies, of course, to the millions of people all over the world who have been, or are, political prisoners or in concentration camps, where the symptoms of suffering from loneliness are the same: the effects of such isolation in the mass can be as bad as with Courtauld, Byrd, and Siffre.

The stages of this collective loneliness in groups have nearly always been the same. People talked to each other at first while waiting for rescue, mostly about their families: their imagination was still vivid enough to work as a substitute for the presence of their dear ones. They thought of their children, their wives, their parents. "But you can't go on thinking of that forever," said a pilot after his rescue. In most cases a vast boredom soon set in. If the isolation continued, many soon started brooding on how their relatives would take the news of their death. One man imagined his fiancée being quite indifferent on hearing the report of his crash, and the thought almost destroyed his sanity.

Time drags interminably, minutes become an age. Castaways are always staring at a watch, which many have called their "best friend." If there was only one man with a watch (in a lifeboat, for instance), he would be plagued by all the others continually asking the time. "Every ten minutes someone wanted to know what time it was, till we eventually thought in all seriousness of throwing the watch overboard. But then we kept it after all. We felt it was more important than all dangers, in fact more important than the injured man we had on board."

Gradually the survivors' nerves are strained to the limits. Whereas a single individual cannot work off these tensions and simply falls into dull brooding, when there are a lot of people together, even the slightest disagreement can be the start for an explosive emotional outburst. The dislike of a companion which a man has always suppressed may suddenly break out into uncontrollable hatred. Castaways who would have got on splendidly with each other in normal circumstances begin insulting each other —Catholics making fun of Protestants and vice versa, Jews abusing Christians, Christians abusing Jews. One man had a harelip, and for months nobody had taken any notice of this; a few days after a crash landing everybody was jeering at him for it. In another case castaways beat up one of their number because he was always whistling the same tune. Many have had fits of mad fury because a shoelace tore or a tent pole broke, because the ticking of a cheap watch disturbed them, or quite simply because the endless monotony "sent them round the bend."

To illustrate the point, here are excerpts of the report of some survivors: in June 1974, four crew members of the yacht *Sospan Fach* (two men, two young women) were rescued off the Middleton Reef in the Tasman Sea (Tasmania), where they had lived for fifty-two days after their Australian yacht had run aground.

"If there is one thing that can be learned from such a disaster," the captain of the rescue party told reporters, "it is this: at sea people feel justified to kill each other whenever they feel like it, and they have done so for centuries."

Indeed, although the survivors did have enough to eat, salvaged from their boat before it sank, they quarreled constantly for the most silly reasons. Anything did seem good enough for a fight. And one of the survivors later confessed: "This lonesome life with so much desperation and hatred confused me. I became afraid what these things could do to me. My greatest fear during those long nights on the reef was that I might kill my companions. Every day I was sharpening my axe (to cut firewood from another wreck) and was weighing it in my hand, thinking: what a beautiful weapon this would be." The other survivors of that episode were constantly afraid of "waking up with a split skull."

It is surprising the crew of the *Sospan Fach* lived that long, because if there is no discipline among a group of castaways, morale sinks abruptly, and with it the chances of survival. Where everyone does as he likes and simply lives aimlessly for the day, energy is squandered, with the same work being done two or three times over, because there has been no planning first. Precious articles of equipment are destroyed through malice or carelessness. On occasions the complete disorganization of an undisciplined crowd may cost lives and even lead to murders being committed.

Probably the most comprehensive research on group behavior in an enclosed environment has been carried out by the U. S. Department for Naval Research. For several years this department has been keeping under observation those members who have to live together in a very confined space. On the Arctic and Antarctic scientific bases too, the naval psychologists have had ample opportunity for observing the effects of isolation on the men stationed there. They were particularly concerned to find out on what psychological principles to select the crews of submarines and aircraft and the members of special services, since these men's "performance" depends on how well each of them can get on with the others and "with himself," in an emergency.

Here are some of the results so far reached. Thanks to their training, all the men realized the occupational hazards. They knew they were dependent on each other, and that if a quarrel broke out between two of them, all the rest would suffer though not directly involved. So everyone tried to control his emotions and tensions. Suppressing their aggression in this way led to headaches, more commonly among officers and scientists than other ranks, who could now and then give vent to their bottled-up anger with a violent oath.

Even worse than the suppressed agression was the complaint called "the big eye": almost all the men stationed in the Polar zones suffered from having to stare into the void all through the dark winter months. The inner tension coupled with a lack of physical activity led to insomnia in many, and a mental lassitude also set in. A lot of the men had brought books and were doing correspondence courses, but even the most intelligent, including the scientists, noticed that the solitude was destroying their powers of concentration. They could only digest the lightest reading matter, and quickly forgot what they had read; almost all lost interest in the courses they had started. They became so completely listless that they tried to relieve their boredom by regular gorging sessions. In their breaks from work, they generally played childish parlor games. Like most survivors of shipwrecks, crashes, etc., they found what Lindemann had experienced in his three-months' solo Atlantic crossing: "I know now that the mind breaks before the body. Although weariness, thirst or hunger may weaken the body, it is the psychological condition and lack of discipline they cause which plunges castaways into panic and leads to irresponsible actions. A castaway must learn self-control as first priority."

To teach this to at least the men in their special services, the Americans in 1953 resorted to a very dubious method: they added "torture courses" to the training in the survival schools. The trainees were to be inured not only to the stresses of a castaway's life but to those of an enemy prison camp. This was after the U. S. General Staff had found to their horror that many of their men taken prisoner by the Communists during the Korean War had become too soft to stand up to brainwashing and to a barbed-wire existence.

The journalist Jost Nolte wrote in the German weekly *die Zeit:* "Most GIs forgot all discipline and all loyalty to their country. Officers who tried to prop up the soldiers' resistance were sometimes even beaten up. The men completely let go, and soon gave up washing or keeping their huts clean. Their wounded and sick were largely left to their own devices. While the Turks in the camp preserved a strict discipline and distributed food and clothing fairly, the Americans sold themselves for coveted positions, increased rations, alcohol, and marihuana. Almost 75 percent took the line of least resistance. They called it 'playing it cool.' Others, like a U.S. general, were so afraid of breaking down and betraying vital secrets under the expected torture of Communist brainwashers, that they preferred to commit suicide." Admittedly, discipline in North Vietnamese POW camps was of an exceptionally high standard.

The events in some POW camps during the Korean War, however, convinced U.S. authorities that these were largely the results of too soft a training and they naturally wanted to avoid any repetition: in case servicemen should become prisoners of the Communists in future, they must realize all that might be in store for them. By their participation in the "torture courses," one of the survival-school trainers explained, "we want to toughen the men and teach them to concentrate on three things while they are behind barbed wire: to preserve their human dignity, keep secrets entrusted to them, and make preparations for escape."

So in some survival schools, conditions of prison-camp existence were copied to become part of each course. At the beginning
of the course a group of trainees were each told some "military
secrets," such as the location of bases. Then, later in the course,
the group was realistically captured. The prisoners had to walk
into a camp barefooted. There they got their food luke-warm,
partly consisting of dry noodles. They spent their nights in the
open in temperatures near freezing point. Anyone who succeeded
in escaping from the barbed-wire enclosure had finished his
course. "Interrogations" started for the rest after thirty-six hours.

As well as the "commissars" some doctors took part in these interrogations, also psychologists from an American university.
They were watching carefully to see how quickly a man could be
"broken," what factors were decisive for his breakdown, and how
these might be overcome by the victims themselves.

When these "training" methods became more widely publicized,
a storm of protest arose, which the U. S. Air Force naturally tried
to allay with soothing words. Colonel Burton E. Mackenzie, then
head of the "torture school" at Stead, answered the protests by
saying: "We never carry through our tests to the bitter end. We
never humiliate our trainees, but instead try to show them through
practical demonstrations what they have to expect if taken prisoner and how they must behave to escape from captivity. We
believe it is our greatest mission to free them from the fear of the
unknown."

Quite apart from the moral justification of the torture schools, it
is very doubtful if they could really achieve the desired hardening
of trainees. What the trainers seemed to forget in their enthusiasm
is that the unknown is often less dreaded than the known: the
trainee's spirit, in fact, is more likely to be broken than hardened
by these humiliations and torments. No torture course can
reproduce reality. It is impossible to make a soldier immune over-
night against big tortures by "small tortures." The Spartans' con-
tempt for death was a product of their education, their whole attitude to life. Resistance to terrible strain both physical and
psychological is not attained, therefore, in a "crash course" behind
barbed wire. Physical training is necessary, yes, but also weeks
and months of meditation, self-mastery or autosuggestion. This is

the only way in which the will to survive can become an element of character, conviction, or creed.

After his first trial voyages in the canoe, Lindemann decided that self-control was the greatest benefit to a castaway; so before his actual Atlantic crossing he devoted several months to training his will. During the actual crossing he was ceaselessly giving himself the suggestion: "I can do it! I can do it!" The longer the voyage lasted, the more his doubts vanished and his optimism increased.

Psychological factors contributing to the survival of groups or individual castaways are now being studied as intensively as what these men ate or drank. For instance, it has been found that the chances of survival were fairly good in all groups where someone in the group (perhaps an officer) took command, drew up a work schedule and told everybody what his job was. Instead of sitting inactive and waiting for rescue, everyone now had a function to fulfill; there was less time left for brooding. Shackleton's expedition, for instance, could never have succeeded without his excellent leadership.

Most people would rather obey than command, rather be led than lead; so they are usually glad when someone else assumes the responsibility, and are quite ready to fall in with his orders. It may be one of the weakest members of a group who suddenly takes charge, driven by some inner power inexplicable even to himself.

To mention once more the ditched Superconstellation and its forty-seven passengers crammed into a single dinghy: a wild confusion was reigning in the boat with everyone yelling, shoving and going berserk. Suddenly a young private first class seized a flashlight, switched it on, shone it in the face of the man next to him and shouted at him to damn-well calm down. The man happened to be a major, but obeyed at once. Then the private shone his flashlight on the next "bundle of nerves," and in this way gradually brought all the people in the boat to their senses. Then he calmly started giving orders, which were obeyed without demur. After the rescue he was himself surprised at his success.

General Twining, after rescue from the Pacific, wrote of one of his fellow castaways: "Sergeant Waggoner understood how to strengthen morale and the will to survive. He was always encouraging the boys and keeping them busy with something. He always had some plan they had to carry out with him."

Then there was Dummer, tacitly accepted as leader by the cadets in that leaky lifeboat from the *Pamir*. He distributed the rations, saw that no one drank too much from the bottle of gin he handed round, and kept telling the others: "Pull yourselves together, boys. They're looking for us. A few hours more and we'll be all right." But they went on sitting about in the boat, apathetic, shivering, frightened, ready to die. Instinctively he realized that castaways must be occupied, must do something which gives them a purpose. He told them to get a plank loose. "This is our only chance of being saved," he said. "We must put up the plank as a mast. Then we'll hang a rag on it, so the planes or ships will surely be able to locate us."

When the mast was finally up, the cadets split up a spare life jacket, which they attached to it for a signal. The life jacket was dark, and probably wouldn't have been seen anyhow; but none of them thought of that. "Right, now we'll rig up a makeshift sail," said Dummer; "then we should get under way a bit." After several hours' work the sail too was fixed to the mast. So he kept them busy whenever they weren't actually sleeping, with no time to brood, and he kept hope alive in them. One of the cadets in the boat swam off when nobody was looking, and was lost; but all the rest were saved. Lifesaving experts attribute this largely to Dummer's courage, leadership, and good sense.

Yamamoto, the Japanese *san-ryu-sha* hiding with eight men in the jungle on the island of Mindoro, kept his men occupied with various activities, including sporting contests (prizes for the winners), and even amateur dramatics! One of the men wrote a play which was performed on an improvised stage. Yamamoto composed music to accompany it, the instruments being flutes (made from bamboo poles) and drums (from hollow tree trunks covered with monkey skins). They also made boards to play games on, and this was done too by airmen who made crash landings in the war.

Some British soldiers tossing on the Mediterranean in a dinghy passed the time with diving exercises. The man who kept his head under water longest was the winner. The contest stopped abruptly when one of them shot up to tell the rest: "Mates—there's a great big mine floating right below us!"

The solitary castaway, of course, has to find different forms of distraction. Vergnes, the Frenchman already mentioned earlier, played a sort of bowls with round stones during his sixty days' solitude on Cocos Island. An American airman on a small tropical island practiced knife-throwing, and when found a month later was so proficient he could have appeared in a circus. Some U. S. Air Force survival kits even contain a small pack of cards, with the rules for several games of solitaire.

Castaways and prisoners have often imagined people to play these games with, and imagination has lightened their lot in many other ways. Courtauld and Byrd in their snow holes pictured flowers, meadows, and green fields around them. Both made plans for the new life they would lead after their rescue.

During the war Christopher Burney (an Englishman) spent 526 days as a political prisoner in a German prison cell. To stop himself vegetating or going mad, he began counting the minutes and hours, the steps he took in his cell, the intervals at which he drank a mouthful of water.

A Hungarian woman teacher spent three years in solitary confinement. The Communist regime hoped to force her to a "confession." But when after all that time she showed no signs of weakening, in fact was more resolute and defiant than ever, they gave it up as a bad job and released her. She knew from the first day that only an iron will power could keep her sane in the small dark cell. At first having neither pencil nor paper, she began writing plays in her mind, and then acting them, taking all the parts: she was author and producer, hero and heroine, minor characters, and audience.

Then she had the idea of escaping from the confinement of her dungeon by "repeating" a journey to the Mediterranean she had once made as a girl. As she walked up and down in her cell, she counted the steps. The steps turned into yards, the yards into miles, and on the first day she reached (in her mind's eye) the old National Gallery in Budapest. She spent the afternoon looking at the pictures there, then found a hotel, had a good meal and retired to bed. After six more weeks of long "marches" she reached

Vienna, then Passau, and then Munich. She never "jumped" several miles, but walked every step to her destination. When the winter came, she had reached Rome, where she began to visit all the churches and museums known to her.

Meanwhile, in her rests from walking she made herself an abacus from straw and bread which she had rolled into pills and dried, and began to work out difficult mathematical problems. With the help of her imagination, she succeeded in enduring the reality. When she was at last released (after the war she went to the United States), she had aged a great deal physically, but her spirit was unbroken.

Often it has been simply some fixed idea which has fortified a missing man's will to survive. Georg Wirth, for instance, one of the *Pamir* cadets, said after his rescue: "For months my eight-year-old sister Micki had asked me to take her to a country fair. I had written to her from Buenos Aires that I *would* take her, as soon as we got back. This small thing suddenly became of terrific importance to me. The whole day I told myself: 'You must keep your promise.' "

Then there was the Australian pilot who had a date with a girl friend which helped him in a similar way to save his life. Although both his legs were badly injured, he made a crash landing, and managed to crawl through the desert on his stomach for four days and nights. On the fifth day he was so exhausted that he thought he was near madness. When a patrol found him, his first words were: "Now I can at least keep that date."

Bertram's will to survive centered on a simple red scarf which his mother had once given him. He clutched it in his hand while he staggered through the bush. Klausmann was soon obsessed by the same idea that this piece of material was their only guarantee for survival. When they had lost it once, although dead tired they both dragged themselves back through the hot jungle till they found it again. Just to touch the sweaty filthy rag seemed to give them new strength.

Admiral Byrd, on the other hand, after his first nervous breakdown in his lonely hut, started thinking over his past life, and became obsessed by the thought of atoning for his former mistakes. Instead of continuing to brood over his bleak situation, he now set up an exact daily routine which would enable him to survive the solitude, and then went purposefully to carry it out. His morbid mood turned into one of confidence.

Many castaways have found comfort and help from prayer. Believers, of course (including Lindemann), would pray to God from the first day of their ordeal, but even some skeptics admit that the attempt to pray fortified them at the last moment and restored their mental balance. Byrd in his snow hole noted that "The human race, then, is not alone in the universe. Though *I* am cut off from human beings, *I* am not alone. For untold ages man has felt an awareness of an intelligence. Belief in it is the one point where all religions agree. It has been called by various names. Many call it God."

Ralph Flores, an American Mormon aged forty-three, attributed his rescue to "matches—and a boundless faith in God." In February 1963 he and his companion, Helen Klaben (a Jewish girl aged twenty-one), were in a small sports plane which crashed in British Columbia; at a temperature of minus 22° F. they chopped up pine trunks for fuel with a hammer and chisel, finished two cans of sardines and a can of fruit salad, then lived for the next fifty days on melted snow.

They read the Bible, and Flores sang hymns. Over forty times search planes flew past very close, without spotting them; but eventually the search was abandoned. Yet Flores went on trusting in God's help. "God won't forsake us," he told the girl. She too finally saw their crash as God's will, and said after the rescue: "His faith has become an example to me, one I shall try to follow throughout my life. I believe we should never have been found if I had not understood why God subjected us to this trial. Ralph and I were both meant to think over our lives. I was not saved until I recognized my sins and promised to atone for past failures."

The rescue came after Flores had the idea—inspired by God, he claimed—of stamping SOS into the snow in letters twenty yards long. A pilot flying over the place spotted them soon afterward and had a search party called out, which safely found the missing pair.

But nothing, neither prayer nor work nor play, fortifies castaways' will to survive so much as the knowledge that a search is being made for them. That is why it is so important to make it un-mistakably clear to survivors that they have been seen and that help is on the way. A message written on a piece of paper and dropped from a plane is worth a hundred times more than a radio message of several minutes. The spoken word vanishes, the paper is something tangible from the world you have left behind.

"We were cut off from the outside world for a fortnight," said a pilot who made a crash landing in Newfoundland with his crew of four. "We were supplied from the air, and were not short of any-thing. But the most precious thing dropped for us was a letter from the wife of one of my men. He had to read it out to us over and over again—although it was a private letter—and it gave us a splendid feeling to be able to touch that piece of paper."

Others fell as avidly on daily papers dropped for them by the rescue plane—not because of the news contained therein, but "because these papers showed there was still a world outside ours, a world in which life had not stood still and into which we could return."

Indeed many missing people who finally returned to this "other world" after weeks or months of solitude, have found that the mental strain they had experienced had been psychologically re-warding. They had become wiser and more mature, and had often gained a healthier attitude toward the material things of life.

It must have been a desert survivor who coined the sentence: "If the desert lets you live you belong to her." The German desert explorer Alphons Gabriel recalled his emotions of desert nights: "In those [lonesome] hours the desert—removed from the hectic hustle of our society, becomes an area of lucid contemplation, where any human being will rid his innermost and his surrounding from all the superficial paraphernalia. Suddenly he will realize a lot of things which up to then he never grasped or experienced. The solitude of the desert does not let you wither but will make you blossom, and perhaps Sven Hedin [the Swedish explorer] meant this when he said: 'Everyone of us needs a piece of desert.' No other landscape is able to give one such an intense feeling of simply being a fleeting guest on earth and a miserable example of transitoriness."

Thor Heyerdahl and his *Kon Tiki* crew had similar feelings

when they drifted on the high sea under a dark sky. "The world was simple," he remembered later. "Whether it was 1947 B.C. or A.D. suddenly became of no significance. We lived, and that we felt with alert intensity. We realized that life had been full of men before the technical age also—indeed fuller and richer in many ways than the life of modern man. Time and evolution somehow ceased to exist; all that was real and all that mattered were the same today as they had always been, and would always be. We were swallowed up in the absolute common measure of history, endless unbroken darkness under a swarm of stars."

Far more prosaic, but none the less guided by a deep emotion, were the words of Sir Francis Chichester after his circumnavigation of the world in his *Gypsy Moth:* "While being alone at sea, it seems to me that I have found the right answer to the 'Why' . . ."

William Willis, shortly before he disappeared at sea during the summer of 1968 on one of his many, lonely ocean crossings at the age of seventy-four, wrote in one of his books: "Living directly on the sea where one had to take what she gave, for better or for worse, I stood alone with Nature. Perhaps this is man's natural condition, one begetting a constant feeling of exhilaration and strength."

Willis also found that: "In solitude the world gradually sinks, as if it had never been. Man is overcome by a feeling that he is floating through space, that he is no longer part of a humdrum materialist existence."

The same feeling must have overcome the French mariner Bernard Moitessier, competitor in a nonstop sailing race around the world, when he—in March 1969—was already close to victory and a $15,000 cash prize. South of Capetown, Moitessier changed his course and, instead of sailing on to Plymouth, England, turned back to Tahiti from where he had just come, leaving prize money, wife, and children behind forever. He flashed a brief message to the harbor master in Capetown, saying "In short, my plan is to continue on my journey, still nonstop, but back to the Pacific Islands. For there I will find a lot of sunshine and more peace than in Europe. Please don't think that I want to set any records. Record is a stupid word. I continue simply because I am happy at sea, and perhaps because I want to save my soul."

When all the confusing stimuli and distractions, the haste and restlessness of our mechanized world fall away from the solitary castaway, he learns at last to sift the wheat from the chaff in everyday life. He begins to understand what life really means, and that he, too, has a place and a function in the world. If he realizes this, he needs neither pills nor torture courses to be what the survival schools call "mentally fit in an emergency." As Coche Inciarte, one of the Andes survivors said: "Up there on the mountain, facing starvation . . . I have learned that life is love, and that life means giving to your neighbor."

Five days to practice contemplation on a lonely raft at sea, on the top of a mountain, or on the edge of the desert can probably do more to increase a man's will to survive than any artificial toughening process. Most of those who have experienced this would afterward say with Byrd: "From my solitude [in the Antarctic] I brought something back which before I had never fully appreciated: a deep feeling for the wonderful and amazing fact of being alive . . . and a much more modest view of the material things of life. A man, I gathered, will not gain wisdom unless he also realizes that he is not superfluous in our world."